Muslim Women in Changing Perspective

Muslim Women in Changing Perspective

TALAT ARA ASHRAFI

Commonwealth

Muslim Women in Changing Perspective

Edition 2027

ISBN 81-7169-172-2

Published by :
COMMONWEALTH PUBLISHERS (P) LTD.
4831/24, Govind Lane,
Ansari Road, Darya Ganj,
New Delhi - 110002
Ph. : 23272541, 23242541
e-mail : commonwealthpublishers2016@gmail.com

Distributed by :
ARJUN PUBLISHING HOUSE
4831/24, Govind Lane,
Ansari Road, Darya Ganj,
New Delhi - 110002
Ph. : 23272541, 23242541
e-mail : arjunbooks2001@gmail.com

Printed at :
Roshan Digital Printers
Delhi

Preface

The Muslim families living in urban regions of the country were exposed not only to the Indian tradition but were also under the influence of religious sanctions, faith oriented rituals and festivities. The Islamic sanction of Purdah was the major hurdle in bringing Muslim women out of the four walls of their houses and thus, education and participation in the outside world were remote possibilities till the third or fourth decade of the present century. After the end of the secohd world war and the achievement of independence much ice has been cut in this regard. Until recently, any systematic attempt was not taken by the scholars for having a sociological insight into the problems of Muslim women living in the urban community of Bihar. The study which is the basis of the present book is a pioneer one in this direction which aims at analysing the existing conditions of the Muslim women living in different areas of Patna. This study reveals that the Muslim women living in Patna have not been alike as they have been brought up in different social, educational and economic background of their families. Hence the condition of educational attainment, rational outlook, adherence to traditions, loyalty to religion and religious sanctions and the level of ambitions and aspirations are not the same everywhere. This fact has been reflected from the analysis of the conditions of Muslim women coming from different strata of Muslim population.

The analysis of various aspects of community life in the urban setting of Patna reveals that Muslim women are experiencing changes at different levels of their activities with varying magnitudes in spite of a number of obstacles and obstructions emerging from the conflicts between tradition and modernity. However, numerous social changes, that are occurring, if they continue, will definitely accelerate the process of modernization among the Muslim women.

The author is highly indebted to Professor (Dr.) S.D.N. Singh, presently the chairman of Bihar State Schools Service Board, Patna for his constant help and guidance. I must also express my thanks to Dr. S. F. Rab, Librarian, A.N.S. Institute of Social Studies, Patna for his valuable suggestions and extending necessary co-operation in this venture. I also wish to thank my husband Dr. Sarfarazuddin Ahmad, Reader in Sociology, Patna University, Patna for his encouragement throughout my career.

TALAT ARA ASHRAFI

Contents

1

Introduction

Indian society is undergoing transformation under the impact of various factors and forces like urbanisation, industrialisation, modern secular education, social legislation, secularisation and democratisation. This process of social transformation is all embracing and covers the totality of life. One significant impact of this process of transformation is the changes taking place in status, role and behaviour pattern of Indian women. The social reformative movements, the spread of education in general and the improvement in the condition of female education are instrumental in bringing about these changes. The Indian women who were confined to domestic affairs and within the four walls of the house in past, have started coming out. They are reading in schools, colleges and universities and receiving technical and non-technical education. They are entering in the white-collar jobs like nursing, teaching, typing, stenography, office secretaryship, administrative services and other bureaucratic jobs. Their participation is also found in social fields and welfare activities, they are contesting elections, participating in the deliberations of state legislatures and Parliament and assuming ministerial berths in the Council of Ministers at state and national levels. These facts are sufficient to show the participation of Indian women in social, political, economic and educational affairs of the country. It is obvious that on one hand the female education and on the other their participation in white-collar jobs and such other prestigious outdoor activities have aroused self-confidence among them and have raised their social position. Such a section of the society is no longer totally dependent on the patriarchs of their families. They are self-earning and self-dependent in many ways and are thus in a position to assert in family matters and decisions. The changes in the attitudes and outlooks of the male members of the community are also helpful in changing the role and status of women. They are being granted a greater degree of social liberty and freedom and they are in many cases no more required to be dictated in all matters. One can find girls and women moving free in public places and cultural centres without being escorted by any male member. In the same way a section of women has developed the courage to travel alone from one place to another. They go to the offices, work with opposite sex and return back to their houses without any assistance or aid from their male guardians. In this way the traditional stigma of 'secluded creature' is no more found in the present-day woman. Women of today are planning their life and performing on their will, in many a cases. It is definitely an index of change in their life pattern, status and role.

But these accounts cannot be said to be cent per cent valid in all cases of the fairer sex. It is true only for a very small percentage of women which has received formal education, lives in an urban environment and belongs to advanced families. In many families dominated by religious orthodoxy and traditional norms the women are not enjoying these liberties even after receiving higher education. In case of poor, uneducated and tradition-dominated families the changes are very slow and not obvious, but even in such families the status quo cannot be claimed to persist in the present age. Some indications of departure from extreme traditionalism are found even in such families.

As regards the changes taking place in the role and status of Indian Muslim women, it may be stated that religiosity is relatively of greater degree among Muslims than among other religious communities. The fundamental sources of religious sanctions and Sharia or the code of conduct in Islam are the Holy Qur'an and Prophet's Traditions. The Muslims throughout the world believe that Islamic sanctions are not the product of human thinking but a divine creation. The Qur'an and Traditions are divine decrees and according to the belief of Muslims the Islamic laws and sanctions are unalterable and nobody except the Divine Authority can change them. Consequently the loyalty to these religious sanctions is of a considerably higher degree among Muslims and they are very cautious of its preservation. The objective evidences to this effect are the organisation of All India Muslim Personal Law Board, the concept of Muslim Personal Law since British days for judicial purposes, the agitations against the judgment of the Supreme Court of India regarding the payment of maintenance allowance by a man to his wife even after divorce, and enactment by the Indian Parliament protecting Islamic laws as well as providing relief to divorcee women Even educated Muslims are particular about observing religious sanctions. Consequently the Indian Muslim women are guided by religious sanctions and the religious orientation is of considerable degree. The degree of social liberty and freedom enjoyed by the women of other religious communities is not found in case of Muslim women. The sanctions of purdah observance have been followed and honoured more particularly in Muslim community. Only Muslim women have been using veil or burqa while going outside. Even today a large number of Muslim women use burqa while going to educational institutions, markets and other public places. But it does not mean that purdah observance or use of burqa is found in cent per cent of the cases. A considerable number of Muslim women are found moving unveiled and without escort at public places. In the past also the Muslim women coming from lower stratum of society and suffering from economic hardships did not observe purdah. But the observance of purdah was very strict in case of upper class and rich Muslim families. But in the present age the situation is appearing to have changed. In many of low-caste Muslim families the women have started observing purdah with the improvement in economic condition, whereas in the upper stratum of Muslim community and particularly in economically well-off families, the women have abandoned purdah in a large number of cases. They are freely moving at different public places. A considerable number of Muslim girls and women are receiving higher education and come to educational institutions without any veil or burqa. Many of them are studying n colleges and Post-Graduate Departments imparting co-education. They sit in the class-room along with boys, talk to them and participate in cultural programmes, sports and games organised by educational institutions. In addition to it, some of them are studying in medical colleges, technical institutions and vocational guidance centres. In this way a trend of change has definitely started among Muslim women and with their participation in outdoor activities, their roles and statuses are also changing. It is also important to point out that educated Muslim women are working as school and college teachers, typists, receptionists, lady secretaries and administrators. Some of them are found engaged in social welfare work and political activities. Consequently they have developed confidence in their self-existence. They are playing effective role in family affairs like marriage, family expenditure and saving, socialisation and education of children and many more related matters. With the improvement in the economic conditions of the lower stratum of society, the Muslim girls and women of this class are also receiving education and participating in different activities not allowed to them in the past. In this way the life and conditions of Muslim women have improved today which has resulted in the enhancement of their status and role. Consequently a process of social transition has set in the Muslim society also.

The present study does not cover the totality of Muslim community in India. This study is concerned only with the women of urban area. The Muslim women living in an urban community are exposed to an environment different from that of rural community. The facilities for better and higher education are mostly available in towns and cities. Consequently the Muslim women living in villages are not provided with the same facilities of education as in case of urban Muslim women. Moreover the employment opportunities in white-collar jobs are mostly available in urban communities. The intensity of exposure to media of mass communcation, urbanisation and industrialisation are much higher in urban areas than in rural areas. Consequently the study of Muslim women in urban context demands a different sociological perspective and the objectives of study are to be specific and urban-based.

The first objective of the present study is to find out how far the attitudes and outlook of the Muslim families are faith-oriented, tradition-oriented and reason-oriented. It will include the analysis of the attitudes of women, patriarchs as well as dependents, educated as well as uneducated, rich as well as poor, upper class as well as lower class, rural-born as well as urban-born. Consequently the differences in the attitude and outlook of the people on the basis of different variables will also be taken into consideration to find out the relevance of the same to attitudes and outlook.

The second objective of the study is to find out the actual behaviour and practice of socio-cultural life among Muslims in urban areas. One may show rationality in his attitude, but he may be traditional or religious in his actual behaviour. Hence it is important to find out if there is gap between theory and practice or attitude and behaviour. This analysis will be helpful in finding out the factors standing in the way of translating attitude into actual practice.

Another objective of the study is to find out the impact of education on Muslim women. As stated earlier, a large number of Muslim girls are also receiving education and they are entering into white-collar jobs and, consequently, they are being exposed to a reason-oriented social climate and it is bound to influence their attitudes, outlook and behaviour. Hence the analysis of the attitudes and behaviour of educated and uneducated women, in a comparative manner, will be helpful in understanding the role of modern education in bringing about change and generating a process of rationalisation.

Urbanism and modernisation are other important factors of social change in the present age. One objective of the present study is to find out the impact of urbanism or urbanisation and modernisation on Muslim women, on their attitude and behaviour.

Purdah system and purdah observance have been of basic importance among Muslims in the past. Purdah was favoured not only at attitudinal level but was also observed in actual practice. In traditional society it was more rigid and strict than the actual sanction of religion. But in the present age purdah observance and attitude towards purdah are changing. The objective of the present study is, therefore, to find out what changes are taking place in this field, and to what extent the Muslim women are faith-oriented, tradition-oriented or reason-oriented in the outlook and behaviour. It will also include the analysis of direction of change in the conceptual contexts of rationalisation, modernisation and re-Islamisation.

The institution of marriage and family are primary social institutions. Islamic sanctions prescribe definite norms and procedures for them. But in actual practice only Islamic sanctions are not observed, rather traditional and customary sanctions are also in operation. In certain aspects even religious sanctions are ignored for the sake of customary observances. Moreover the impact of Hindu culture on Muslim society has also been of vital significance. Hence the objective of the present study also includes the changes taking place in these institutions, showing the changes in the role and status of Muslim women.

Another objective of the present study is to find out the changes taking place in the attitudes of Muslim women towards their own role and statuses and their position in family life. Are they satisfied with their present position or do they want an improvement? As there are differences of views and attitudes among women due to variation in age, educational background, caste, economic position and self-employment, etc , it is of sociological importance to probe the extent and degree of their own evaluation of the Muslim women in an urban setting.

And with these objectives in mind we have planned our research design and studied the Muslim women of Patna.

For a systematic analysis of any social problem, a social

researcher is required to formulate a working hypothesis or research design. This hypothesis is a tentative generalisation, the validity of which remains to be tested. On the basis of cursory knowledge of the problem, the social investigator singles out, by trial and error method, the factors that throw light on the problem. He also establishes causal relationship between various sets of facts on the basis of his imagination. This supposition or the penetrating hunt is known as a working hypothesis. This hypothesis serves as the basis for conducting social investigation, because it states what we are looking for. Moreover a hypothesis 'looks forward' and gives the direction of research. The investigator needs the help of a hypothesis in outlining the areas of enquiry and in deciding or formulating research tool and the appropriate data to be collected. In this way hypothesis serves as a significant tool in conducting scientific social survey.

As stated earlier the problem under study is "Muslim Women in Urban Setting", the investigator was to formulate a hypothesis on the basis of his own experiences, knowledge and the literature available on the problem concerned. Some of the studies conducted by different scholars throw light on the changing role and status of Indian women in which are also included Muslim women. In the same way some of the studies are concerned with Indian Muslim community, urban as well as rural, and these studies also help in understanding the changes taking place in the life style, role, status and position of Muslim women in their families as well as in society. Moreover the novels, short stories and other pieces of literature in Urdu language also help in understanding the changing trends in Muslim society in general and in Muslim women in particular. The personal observance of the events and occurrences taking place in society, observation of Muslim women and girls in public places, cultural centres and other such experiences are also valuable bases in imagining and guessing about the present role and status of women, the changes therein, and the changes taking place in their attitudes and outlook. These sources helped the present investigator in formulating a hypothesis. Following hypotheses were sought to be tested:

1. The Muslim women in urban setting are different from their counterparts in rural social setting due to differences in their social orientation, patterns of socialisation and exposure to indoor and outdoor social environment.

2. The Muslim women in urban social setting are experiencing a continuous change in their attitudes, behaviours and approaches, towards marriage and family, etc. This change marks a departure from traditional standpoint to rational standpoint and thus a process of rationalisation has started.

3. The Muslim women in urban community are not fully liberated from traditionalism. The grip of traditionalism has grown weaker in many aspects of life, but still in other aspects like sex and family planning traditional and customary sanctions are highly valued by them. In this way they are in the phase of tradition-rationality-continuum.

4. The facility of education in general and for females in particular is greater in urban community and hence in urban community a higher percentage of Muslim girls is receiving education. Due to improvement in their educational level in urban Muslim community, the Muslim women are developing rational outlook.

5. Under the impact of urbanism, greater degree of exposure to the media of mass communication and education, the Muslim women are experiencing a change in their role and status. They are no more under the complete authoritarian dictatorship of the patriarch, rather they are also enjoying some liberty in family as well as in social life and are playing effective role in family decisions.

6. The Islamic sanction of purdah observance is not challenged at the ideological level but in actual practice purdah observance is diminishing and in

some of educated high class Muslim families it has been completely abandoned. But non-observance or observance of purdah is not uniform among all urban Muslim women, rather variations are found on the basis of different variables like age, economic condition, educational background of the family and attitude of the husband (in case of married women) or father (in case of unmarried girls) towards purdah observance.

Muslims form the second largest religious community and the first major minority of the state of Bihar. They are spread over the entire length and breadth of the state. For a better understanding of the life and conditions of Muslims we need cross-section of the Muslim population. Patna being the capital city of Bihar for thousands of years till today, it has been the centre of attraction of people of different origins and different socio-cultural backgrounds. Muslims of different origins and different socio-cultural backgrounds came and settled here at different stages of time. They lived here as ruler as well as ruled or commoners, rich and poor, illiterate and educated, rural as well as urban, as traders, businessmen, industrialists, agriculturists, artisans, public servants, etc., making the population a heterogeneous community having different shades of socio-cultural behaviour and attitude. This quality is seldom found in any other city of Bihar. Hence the city of Patna has been choosen as the universe for the present study.

After determining the universe, the next task before the investigator was to select a representative sample, because it was neither feasible nor fruitful to cover all the units in the population within the given time and limited money and energy factors and make a deep and detailed sociological research into the problem. For this purpose, therefore, it was decided to draw a representative sample from the universe comprising of women living in different mohallas of the Patna municipal area. Patna is a big city where about 8 lac people reside, and about one-fifth of it is comprised of Muslim population and half of which must be Muslim women.

Muslims are located in all the mohallahs of the town in lesser or greater number. Similarly the nature of Muslim population differs from area to area in respect of their economic, educational and cultural backgrounds. For an objective and impartial study of the life and conditions of Muslim women it was planned to give representation to women belonging to different ages, different areas and different socio-cultural backgrounds. In this background and the limitation of time, energy and money, a sample of 300 Muslim women was drawn from the universe for making a sociological enquiry into the problem under study.

For this purpose 'family' was selected as unit. However, firstly, 300 families representing the aforementioned criteria was choosen. Then from each family one married woman was selected for collecting relevant information. Thus a heterogeneous sample of Muslim women was taken into consideration for a better representation of the cross-section of Muslim women and hence for a deep and detailed study of their life and conditions, status and role in the changing milieu.

Now, for drawing the sample, appropriate sampling method was to be considered. Most commonly known sampling method is known as random sampling method in which different techniques are applied according to the suitability of researcher, nature of research and universe. One of the most important pre-requisites of the use of this technique is that the researcher should have complete and up-to date list of the universe. Apparently this criterion may look simple but in practice this is very difficult to find a latest position of universe. Secondly random technique may be applied only by trained and experienced persons and for some specific type of research. For the present researcher too it was neither easy to prepare such a list of vast population in limited time, money and energy, nor necessary to have such a list in view of the present research. So the researcher depended on other method known as 'convenient sampling'. This was decided after critical analysis and comparative understanding of different sampling methods. It means that the selection of families and then of the respondents as the units of sample was done on the basis of purpose and convenience of the investigator. In all the cases the researcher was fully conscious about the sample being representative of the whole universe. For this purpose, first, the whole city was divided into three broad areas—i.e., Patna city (the eastern part of the city settled during ancient and medieval period and still the seat of Hindu and Muslim culture), Bankipore (the town settled during British regime and located in the middle region) and the New Patna (the southern and western parts of the city settled mainly after independence of the country). All these three main parts of the city depict three different socio-cultural backgrounds of the inhabitants. With this background in mind, the investigator selected 100 respondents from each of the three parts. For this purpose families and hence the respondents belonging to different mohallas, castes, income groups, educational levels and occupational backgrounds were selected after great objective considerations and research conveniences.

The table presented below gives full light on the characteristics of the sample.

Age category	*No. of Re:pondents*	*Percentage*
Up to 25 yrs.	75	25.0
26-35 yrs.	90	30.0
36-45 yrs.	82	27.4
46 and above	53	17.6
Total	300	100.0

Marital status	*Number*	*Percentage*
Married	282	94.0
Divorced	3	1.0
Widowed	13	4.4
Polygynous	2	0.6
Total	300	100.0

Caste category	*Number*	*Percentage*
Saiyid	55	18.4
Shaikh	60	20.0
Pathan	49	16.4
Mallick	36	12.0
Ansari	55	18.3
Rayeen	15	5.0
Chiq (Qassab)	20	6.6
Kalal	10	3.3
Total	300	100.0

Educational level	*Number*	*Percentage*
Illiterate	58	19.4
Up to Middle	95	31.6
Up to Matriculation	84	28.0
Up to Graduation	45	15.0
Post-Graduate	18	6.0
Total	300	100 0

Occupational category	*Number*	*Percentage*
No work	19	6.4
Housewife	202	67.3
Indoor earning	34	11.3
Outdoor earning	45	15 0
Total	300	100 0

Family type	*Number*	*Percentage*
Joint	53	17.6
Nuclear	105	35.0
Extended	142	47.4
Total	300	100.0

Family income (per month)	*Number*	*Percentage*
Up to Rs. 500	30	10 0
501-1000	55	18.4
1001-1500	92	30.6
1501-2000	90	30.0
2001+	33	11.0
Total	300	100.0

The majority of the women in the sample belong to the age-group of 26-35 years and overwhelming majority belongs to 26-45 age-group. All of them are married. 94% of them have their husbands alive, while others are either divorcee, or widowed or polygamous. Respondents belong to eight different caste categories of which two-thirds are from Ashraf or high caste families. Only about 19.3% are illiterate and 31.6% semi-literate (maximum up to middle standard) and the rest half either educated or highly educated. The overwhelming majority of the women were housewives while about 23 per cent were engaged in indoor or outdoor economic activities to supplement the family income or ultilize their education and training. Out of all these 300 respondents 47.3% lived in nuclear extended families, 35 per cent in nuclear and only 17.6 per cent in joint families. The respondents belonged to the income category of Rs. 1001-2000 or the middle income group. Only 11 per cent were members of upper class families while 28.3 per cent were from lower class families.

The respondents were assured that individual responses would be kept confidential. Each of the respondents was questioned about the various topics mentioned below, though not necessarily in the order presented.

(*i*) *Personal Information about the Respondents* : The respondents were asked to furnish facts regarding their age, marital status, caste or birathari, sect, level of education. their own occupation and the occupation of their husbands and fathers, monthly family income, duration of stay in Patna, type of family from which they come and the type of family of procreation, etc.

(*ii*) *Marriage and Family Life* : Age at marriage of the respondents, ideal age for marriage of a girl, age difference between husband and wife, selected characteristics for a marriage partner, decisions regarding marriage, self-evaluation of married life marital happiness, mahr (dower), nafaqa (maintenance), decision making process in the family, inheritance, polygyny and divorce and widow re-marriage.

(*iii*) *Educational Aspect* : Attitude towards education, type of education received, attitude towards secular and co-education system, general and technical education, purpose of education, utilisation of education, educational programmes for the new generation, etc.

(*iv*) *Purdah System* : Prevalence of purdah, type of purdah observed, relevance of purdah to the present-day life, attitude towards purdah, causing of diminishing purdah observance.

(*v*) *Family Planning* : Knowledge about family planning methods, attitude towards family planning, need and importance, method used, number of children desired, number of children born, etc.

The researcher being herself a woman and married, there was no gap between the investigator and the respondents and she could talk to the women respondents freely after assuring them of the secrecy of the personal information. Hence there was no difficulty in gethering even subjective and exclusively personal information from the respondents.

For conducting the research it was essential to decide about the tool or tools of data collection from the field. There are many tools which are frequently used in sociogical research. But all of them could not be used for every type of research because they differ in nature and utility. After a careful comparative analysis of different tools it was decided to use mainly interview method aided sometimes with observation and content analysis in order to understand things more closely and objectively. Interview, as we know, is the conversational method of data collection in face-to-face conversation. In this case the investigator as well as the respondents sit together, talk to each other in a pre-planned and formal manner on some issue at hand and the responses given by the respondents recorded during or after the question-answer process ends. This is why it is defined as a meeting of persons, face to face, on some points or as a process of social interaction. In other words in case of using interviewing technique the investigator personally goes to the field, establishes rapport with the respondents, talks to them directly, convinces them about the purpose and secrecy of the information and then enters into formal interviewing process for collecting relevant information minutely and systematically on the points related to problem under study. This very nature of the tool reveals that every section of society, literate or illiterate, can be studied equally and information about the past as well as the present can be known through this method. Both obvious and hidden information can be gathered through interviewing technique. Information about attitude, opinion as well as reactions of the people may be studied well through this method.

Apart from the technical qualities of this technique and its suitability to the objectives of research and nature of the universe, some subjective factors were also responsible in selecting and using it. The main subjective reason is that there was not much pressure to finish the field work hurriedly as the researcher lives and works in the same town where this study has been done. The fact that she is born, brought up, educated and serving as a lecturer in Patna itself, she knows the field well, can contact the respondents easily, and she can converse with them in the language of respondents conveniently which facilitated collection of data from the field easily. The data gathered from interviewing technique was also cross-checked and added, if needed, by visiting the respondents at home or working places, where accessible, and observing their life style and behaviour pattern, etc. personally. Thus observation was also used as a supplementary tool of data collection.

After finalising the tool for data collection, the next task before the investigator was to choose the type of interviewing technique to be used in the field situation. Out of the two main types of interviewing technique, known as 'structured' and 'non-structured' interview, the former was found to be suitable. The structured interview is based on an interview schedule which consists of fully framed questions concerning the issues under study and arranged systematically in logical continuum. Through the help of this list the investigator is able to ask questions and collect the information in a planned and systematic manner. He has not to depend on his memory and hence the probability of missing any important item or forgetting any response is absolutely nil. Its next equally important advantage is found in the coding, classification, tabulation and analysis of data. Thus it makes the work systematic and easy both.

Now the actual interview schedule was to be constructed. For this purpose the investigator framed the relevant questions in view of the different aspects of the problems to be studied and the objectices to be achieved. Then the questions were arranged mainly in two parts in a systematic and logical continuum. In the first part of the schedule questions related to preliminary information regarding respondents and in the second, items concerning general information about different aspects of the problems under study were arranged in such a way that a logical coherence between them is found. Thus an interview schedule is constructed. It is important to mention here that the researcher, in view of the convenience of communication and response, used the Urdu version of schedule because it is the mother tongue of the Muslims and all women know this language better than any other language.

After formulating the interview schedule its reliability was checked. For assessing its reliability a pre-test or inspection in the field situation of the schedule is a must from scientific point of view. So a pilot study on a sub-sample of twenty respondents was made. During the course of pilot study some shortcomings were found which were removed and thus the schedule was okayed for its final implementation in data collection.

After the finalisation of schedule, actual interview with the respondents was started. The interviewer contacted the units of the sample in a planned manner. She felt that data collection through this method was not so easy and smooth as it looked to be, because during actual interview it was felt that in most of the cases it was difficult to convince the female respondents, especially of lowly educated category, about the objective of the research and the value of such study. Most of them are suspicious to find a stranger interested to know about her personal life, attitude and opinion. In some cases the women were interviewed after the approval of the husband or other elder male member of her family. Even if those who were convinced, were not willing to give frank views and correct and complete information on many issues. There were many respondents who had to be visited many a time for the interview to be started and completed. Sometimes even after fixing the appointment the respondents were either absent or were unwilling to give up their leisure hour or posed very much busy. In this way the field experience revealed that interviewing to females and specially illiterate or semi-literates is a tough job. It requires a lot of patience, tact, pursuance and presence of mind as well as experience of the work of dealing women in general, otherwise sometimes unpleasant situations and frustrations were not ruled out. Generally when the rapport was established, the respondents were very cordial and co-operative. On the whole the researcher got a lot of insight from the field situation.

The actual field study relating to this research was conducted during the years 1985 and 1986. The use of Urdu version of interview schedule helped greatly in collecting data correctly and smoothly. Actually this solved the twin vital problems of research—the problem of communication and the problem of response—and made the tool more smooth, effective and reliable.

After completing the field work the entire collected data were to be systematically arranged and presented in tabular form for their proper analysis and interpretation of facts. The items and the responses were coded and then classified logically. Thereafter they were presented in tabular form for a systematic analysis. The tables have been discussed in the concerned chapters which depict the real life and conditions of the Muslim women of Patna. But the findings cannot be limited to the women of Patna, rather whole of Bihar and to a greater extent on the Muslim women of Northern India.

2

Social Setting

The present study was conducted in Patna, the capital city of Bihar where a good number of Muslims are living from long past. This chapter presents a brief account of the salient features of the area and the people under study. The location of the city, its evolution and phenomenal growth, socio-economic and politico-cultural conditions have a profound bearing on the problem under study.

Patna is bounded geographically by the river Ganga in the north, flood plain of river Punpun in the south, flood plain of the Sone in the west and the confluence of the river Punpun with the Ganga near Fatwah in the east. The city of Patna is located between latitudes 25°34′ and 25°38′ north and longitudes 85°5′ and 85°16′ east.[1] It is one of the most important and ancient historic cities of India located along the river Ganga. The river Sone meets the Ganga about 20 miles west of Patna. The Sarju joins a little above that. The river Punpun joins the Ganga seven miles below Patna, running parallel to the parent river for a considerable distance above its confluence. Within the state of Bihar Patna occupies a central place between the two major physical units, viz., the Gangetic plain and the Chhotanagpur Plateau. Patna is at an

1. Survey of India, Topographical Sheet No. 73G/2.

elevation of 185 feet above the sea level. It extends to a distance of about 12 miles in length stretching on the southern level of the river Ganga and 4 miles broad and covers an area of 27.29 sq. miles.[2] The shape of the city is like a sword, with the handle in the west and the point in the east.

This is a linear city which has grown on either side of the main road (Ashok Raj Path) running east to west on the ridge of the natural level of the river Ganga. While the river always formed a natural barrier for expansion towards the north, any possible southward expansion is greatly restricted because of the danger of floods by the river Punpun. This has now, however, been controlled by building a parallel embankment and three ring bundhs to protect the city from the flood havocs of the Punpun and Sone.

Patna is not a planned town in the modern sense of the term. Hence one can find the mingling of the new and the old. The haphazard, narrow turning and twisting roads and lanes create traffic bottlenecks, especially in the commercial belts.

The city can be divided into three distinct zones according to their functions and physical characteristics. The *eastern zone*, known as Patna city, is the old city. The ancient capital is full of old buildings built among narrow lanes with insanitary conditions. This zone is thickly populated and is the biggest centre of wholesale central trade. Contiguous to this zone and towards its west is the *middle zone*, or the Bankipur area, extending roughly between Pather-ki-Masjid in the east and the Patna-Gaya road (New Buddha Marga) in the west. This zone is really the business and commercial core of the city, and also has the bulk of institutional, cultural and district administration buildings. It is the most overcrowded and congested part of the city. The *western zone*, which is the new capital area, differs significantly from the other two zones in its newer buildings and well-laid ring and radial road patterns, highlighted by a 200-ft. wide avenue with the Secretariat and Raj Bhavan forming its terminal feature. Apart from governmental buildings, a considerable amount of

2. Calculated from Municipal Reports

private development has also taken place in this zone in both the north and south wings.

At present Patna is expanding towards south and west. The middle income group housing is fast developing towards south (Kankerbagh) increasing the width of the city. The upper class residences are developing towards north, south and west of the city.

Thus Patna, being the capital of Bihar, is a city having some regional importance. It is the administrative focus of the entire state as it is the headquarter of the District, Divisional and State administration. It is the headquarter of local administration, judiciary and Legislature, and is marked by educational, medical and professional services and trade and commerce.

The city is connected with other parts of the State by different means of transportation. It is an important railway junction of the Eastern Railway. The main broad gauge railway line of the Eastern Railway, connecting Howrah and Delhi, etc., runs parallel to the Ganga along the southern margin of the city. The Patna-Gaya line connects this city with the Grand Cord Line of the Eastern Railway, and via the South-Eastern Railway to the industrially rich regions of the Chhotanagpur Plateau. The North-Eastern Railway plied steamers between Mahendru Ghat (Patna) and Pahleza Ghat (Hajipur) till the recent past, before the construction and opening of the Ganga Setu bridge over the Ganga river connecting Patna to Hajipur. There was also private ferry service for passengers from Bans Ghat and for goods from L.C.T. Ghat to Pahleza Ghat besides country boats serving a number of smaller ghats along the river bank of the city. These services have, however, now been discontinued due to construction of Ganga Setu, the giant road bridge over Ganga near Gaighat touching Hajipur in the north.

The city is also airlinked with Delhi, Calcutta, Kathmandu, Ranchi and now with Hyderabad by the Indian Airlines. Local plane service to other cities of Bihar is also being implemented soon.

These transport and communication facilities have enhanced the mobility and migration potentiality of the people of Bihar, consequently bringing about changes in their socio-economic life.

Evolution and Growth of Patna

Ancient Period: Patna is one of the oldest cities of the world. According to historical records it was settled some 2,000 years ago, but even before that it was famous throughout northern India as the capital of Magadh. It is said that the early history of Magadh is a great part of the history of India.[3]

Various legends exist regarding the origin of the name of the city. The most popular ascribes it to Prince Putraka, who created it with a stroke of his magic staff and named it in honour of his wife, the princess Patali. The city was also known with the Sanskrit names Kusumpura or Pushpapur, which mean 'the city of flowers'.[4] It is also said that originally Patliputra was a village known as Pataligram or Pataliputra and later on it came to be known as Srinagar.[5] However this term appears to have been derived from 'Patali' or trumpet flower (*bigonta suaveolens*) The Greek (Magasthenes) called it 'Palibothra' and the Chinese 'Pa-lin-fou'.[6] In 1704 it was called Azimabad after its Governor Prince Azim-us-Shan.[7] The first authentic reference to Patliputra of which data can be fixed, are in Emperor Ashoka's Girnar Rock Edict No. V and his Sarnath Pillar Edict.

It was during the second urban revolution in the 6th century B.C. that Patliputra found expression as an agglomeration of settlements on the bank of Ganga in Eastern India, largely based on agricultural economy. Kosambi and Karimi[8]

3. Kumar, N., Bihar District Gazetteer, Patna, 1970, p. ii.
4. Ghosh, M, "Patliputra", the Patna Law Press, 1919, pp. 1-2.
5. Kumar, N., op. cit., p. 1.
6. Ghosh, M, op. cit., pp. 2-3.
7. Imperial Gazetteer of India. op. cit., p. 68.
8. (a) Kosambi, D.D, The Culture and Civilization of Ancient India in the Historical Outline, Vikas Publication, New Delhi, 1970, p. 90;
   (b) Karimi, S.M., "Origin and Evolution of Towns in Ancient Bihar", Journal of the Bihar Research Society, Vol. LIX, 1-4 p. 78.

have noted that the urban centres in the 6th century B.C., notably Patliputra, Champa and Vaishali had grown. The city of Patliputra or Kusumpura was founded by King Udavana, grandson of King Ajatsatru. During the reign of Ajatsatru (499 B.C.), Rajgriha was the capital of Magadh. In order to contain the growing might of the Lichchivis of Vaishali, he constructed a fort at Patliputra. King Udayana transferred his capital from Rajgriha to Patliputra. It was then not only the capital of Magadh but in fact of whole India. In the 5th and 6th centuries B.C., Magadh (present Patna, Nalanda, Nawada, Aurangabad and Gaya districts) was a very powerful kingdom.

Kautilya, a statesman and founder of political-economy, compiled his treatise 'Arthshastra' at about 300 B.C. at Patna. Aryabhatt (5th century A.D.) propounded here his scientific theories in the fields of Astronomy and Algebra.[9] Ashoka sent from here an emissary to the King of Singhal (Ceylon) through his daughter Sanghmitra and his son Mahendra. The cultural conquest of the contemporary world by Ashoka through the philosophy of Buddhism is of universal significance. The fostering of Arts and Science under Samudragupta alongside his conquests is no less remarkble, indeed his regime was regarded as the 'golden period' of India.

The Buddhist accounts also mention the strategic significance of Patliputra saying that its riparian location served the Janapada as a stranglehold to check upon the ravages of the Vajian or the people of Viji who used to plunder either bank of the Ganga.[10] Patliputra, in those days, developed into a military camp. The strategic significance of Rajgriha, the earlier capital of Magadh in the pre-Mauryan period, declined sharply because it was extremely difficult to take military actions against the Lichchivis across the Ganga and a military camp was thus founded at Patliputra at the confluence of the Ganga and Sone, and soon it became an ideal base for strategic operations. Earlier Patliputra functioned as a frontier

9. Kumar, N., op. cit., p. ii.
10. Hunter, W.W., 'A Statistical Account of Bengal', Vol. XI, Concept Pub. Co., Delhi (Repr.), 1976, p. 67.

capital because of its location close to an active frontier. Being located on the confluence point, it commanded the river traffic over Ganga, the Sadamia, the Sone and the Sarju, and developed in course of time as a great trade emporium for the entire region. It was during the pre-Mauryan period that Champa and Patliputra were ports from which boats sailed to Ceylon and Svarnabhumi (the Java Sumatra area) and were connected with Varanasi, Kausambi, Sravasti and Tamralipali.[11]

Patliputra witnessed a conscious development during the Mauryan rule. It had a population of about 4,00,000, was 9.2 miles long and 1.7 miles broad.[12]

It was during the reign of Ashoka the Great that Patliputra rose to its prominence as an unparallel imperial city. The architecture of Patliputra was a change during the Mauryan period (322-185 B.C.) when magnificent monuments executed in stone appeared in the city.

In 1896, Col. Waddell discovered a quasi-ionic capital and broken fragments of gigantic pillars at Kumhrar in South Patna.[13] In his accounts and findings he has tried to locate the ancient village of Pataligram, Mauryan Palace and other chief monuments. The death of Ashoka and the fall of Mauryan empire as a result of Brahmanical revolution carried the glory and prosperity of Pataligram into obscurity. But it continued to remain a traditional centre for Buddhist culture.

Because of its strategic location and with rich fertile lands Patliputra again rose to prominence and became the capital city during the reign of Samudragupta (335 A.D. to 375 A.D.). However, the city was again reduced to ruins by the Huns as reported by Huen Tsang.

11. Diwaker, R.R., 'Bihar Through the Ages', (ed), Orient Longmans, Bombay, 1959, p. 181.
12. Alankar, S.V., 'Patliputra ki Katha', Hindustan Academy, Allahabad, 1949, p. 210.
13. Waddell, L.A., 'Report on the Excavations at Patliputra', Calcutta, 1903.

Medieval Period

Patliputra went into oblivion for about 1000 years after the mid-7th century A.D., when the centre of political activities shifted to Kannauj. However, it regained some of its glories when in 1641 A.D. Sher Shah built a fort on the bank of Ganga in eastern Patna, of which 'Paschim Darwaza' and 'Purab Darwaza' are the two significant remnants even to this day.[14] At this time there developed a large market settlement outside the Purab Darwaza, which later on developed into an important market centre and the area around Marufganj grew into significance as the principal market of Patna dealing with a large trade in agricultural products. The city became an important administrative-cum-commercial centre during Sher Shah's rule.

Patna ceased to perform the function of an imperial capital after the death of Sher Shah. Though it lost its political significance as an important city, it became a flourishing trade centre. In 1580, Portuguese settlments developed along the river but they could not survive long because the Dutch established their control gradually over some portions of Bankipur in 1610. It was not until 1704 that Patna again became an imperial seat during the reign of Azim-us-Shan, the grandson of Aurangzeb, who named it Azimabad. The accounts of Manucci, Taveniers and Bowrey etc., reveal that Patna in the middle of 17th century developed into a great centre of trade and commerce of international repute and it was one of the largest towns of India.[15]

Modern Period

With the establishment of East India Company in 1757 Patna came under British rule only after the Company soldiers

14. Master Plan of Patna—Text and Photographs, Vol. I, Patna Improvement Trust, Patna, 1962, p. 45.

15. Dayal, P. and Thakur, B, "Commercial Ribbons in Patna: Spatial Growth and Functional Structure, National Geog. Journal of Ind. Vol. XXIII, Parts 3 & 4, 1976, p. 168.

plundered the Muslim garrison of Nawab Mir Qasim. During British era Patna functioned as a secondary capital, when Calcutta and Delhi became the national capitals. On the creation of the new provinces of Bihar and Orissa in 1911-12, Patna became the provincial capital and a new capital city was laid down towards the west of Patna Gaya road. Thereafter, several new buildings—Raj Bhavan, the Secretariat, the Legislative Council and Assembly, the High Court and the residences of Ministers, Judges and other high officials developed gradually. The establishment of the Patna University in 1919 provided a cultural significance to the provincial capital. Thus it was during the British period that Patna expanded rapidly with an increase in large-scale building activities, mainly in the western part of the city both in public and private sectors.

Post-Independence Era

Patna continues to be the capital of the state of Bihar. Today it is about 15 miles long and 2 miles wide. The existence of the river Ganga has checked its northward expansion, but a southward and westward expansion is rapidly taking place.

Language

The vernacular current over the whole district is the dialect known as Magahi. It is mainly spoken in the rural areas roughly corresponding to the present districts of Patna, Jehanabad, Gaya, Nalanda, Nawada, Aurangabad, northern Hazaribagh, north-eastern portion of Palamu and southern and western portions of Monghyr. Actually the spoken language of the Patnaites is neither Magahi nor Hindi or Urdu, but an intermixture of all the three languages. The mother tongue of the Muslims is Urdu which they use in everyday life. Alongwith Urdu, Muslims are also taught Persian and Arabic. Teaching of Urdu and Persian is provided in more or less all the schools and colleges. While teaching of Arabic is confined mainly to the homes and Madrasas and in a few other educational institutions.

Religious Beliefs, Festivals, Shrines and Customs

Monotheism is the basic principle of Islam. So a Muslim has no God but Allah, and has his Rasul, the Prophet Mohammad. Thus the Muslims worship only God, the Almighty, the Omnipotent, Omnipresent. But saint and Pir worship has become a common feature among Muslims. A Pir's tomb often becomes a place of pilgrimage. In Patna and around it there are several tombs of Muslim saints where 'urs' ceremony is held. The devout Muslims keep awake for the whole night and after the recital of *milad* and *chadar* by which the tomb of the Pir is covered, is changed. The urs congregation is held by the Hanafite sect while the Wahhabis do not favour such sort of worship.

Festivals form part of the life of the people. Their importance in social life has been recognised both by the Central and the State Governments which allow a number of holidays in their offices and workshops to enable their employees to celebrate them. They have religious origin and are observed with fast, offering of prayers, mournings and sometimes rejoicing it. The important festivals observed by Muslims of this area are: Muharram, Fatiha-Dwazdahum, Shab-e-Baraat, Idul Fitr and Id-uz-Zoha.

Muharram is the first month of Islamic (Arabian) Calendar. This month, or occasion, is observed in the memory of the martyrdom of Imam Hussain, the son of Hazrat Ali and the grandson of Prophet Hazrat Mohammad. He died fighting at Karbala against the illegitimate and corrupt ruler Yazid, the son of usurper Moaviah of the Caliphate of Islam. Imam Hussain and his companions, young and old, sacrificed their lives for saving Islam from the alteration and adulteration of Moavites. This festival is observed by Muslims in general and Shias in particular. As the festival is in the memory of the tragic events of Karbala, it is a mourning festival. There are different ways of mourning the martyrdom of Imam Hussain. Shias hold Majalis (mourning congregations) where the tragic events are commemorised, *marsia*, *souz* and *nauha* are recited and devotional respects are paid to the Martyr or Karbala. Generally the Shiite women wear black dresses and avoid to wear red, pink and yellow garments on this occasion, because these colours are believed to be the index of joy. Moreover, they abstain from using cosmetics and participating in entertaining programmes, whether in theatre, cinema, radio or T.V. The married women do not wear bangles and do not apply sendur (vermilion). The Shias particularly observe this festival with great sanctity and pathos. The 40th day after the Muharram is known as 'Chehlum', when the last rites of the deceased are performed and the poor fed and given gifts.

However, the illiterate Sunni Muslims observe Muharram through taking out Tazia (i.e., replica of the funeral shrouds or tomb of Imam Hussain) and akhara in which musical bands of different types are used. This type of commemoration of the event of Karbala is, however, not approved by the literate Shia and Sunni Muslims and they try to convince the illiterate masses of the Muslim community to derive some decent and legitimate method of commemorating the Martyrdom of Imam Hussain. But these people pay very little attention to it.

The Fatiha-Dwazdahum commemorates the birth anniversary of Prophet Mohammad when life and works of Prophet are highlighted.

Shab-e-Baraat is observed on the night of the fourteenth day of the month of Sha'ban, the eighth month of Hijrah Calendar. On this occasion the Muslim devotees read Qur'an, visit the tombs of their ancestors and relatives to split candle and pray for the peace of their souls. Thereafter, the youngsters and children play with Atishbazi and rejoice the occasion while the elders gather in mosques and offer namaz and recite Qur'an throughout the night and express thankfulness to Allah for the mercy showed by him by releasing all the souls for one night to meet whoever they like. This night is also said to be 'Shab-e-Qadar', as it is the night when the twelfth and the last apostle of Prophet Mohammad was born in the year 256 A.H. Shias hold 'mahfil-e-milad' of Imam Mahdi at this night.

Ramazan is one of the most important festivals of Islam. It is not only the month of fastings, but a token period of complete dedication of Allah, a severe refresher course of discipline, a psychological boon of self-reliance, self-restraint and self-remodelling on the pious lines of Islam. There are three aspects of Ramazan—i.e., educative, reformative and biological. During this month all adult men and women practise fasting continuously for one month. The word 'Ramazan', in Arabic, means 'the summer season'; and it is this month in which Qur'an, the supermost bounties of Allah was bestowed upon the Prophet of Islam. Humanity was conferred upon this Divine Light in this pious month of Ramazan, to which Allah has said to be 'His month' and that is why recitation of Qur'an is one of the most cherished worships of Allah. This month is declared as the 'Month of Peace and Harmony', the 'month of cleanliness—both objective and subjective, spiritual and pathological' and the 'month of devotion and dedication to Allah'. It has thus three aspects—spiritual, social and biological. Continuous thirty days' fastings create self-confidence against adversaries, tolerance against social evils and self-restraint against improprieties. One who has habituated himself of fastings with all its pre-requisites, he can withstand any type of adversary and hazards of life without much perplexity with his mind working properly and reacting sanefully. In the same way these fastings overhaul the digestive system and tones up absorptive power providing a high rate of utilisation of essential ingredients of food by the system.

Idul-Fitr is celebrated in the first day of the tenth month of Hijra Calendar in token of thankfulness to Allah who endowed us with courage and strength to perform fastings during His month, e.g., Ramazan. On this occasion they wear new garments, sprinkle scants and gather in Id-gah to perform Namaz of Idul-Fitr in huge congregation. On the day of Idul-Fitr every Muslim has to pay Fitrah (zakat), @ three kilograms in Shia fiqh and 1.6 kilograms in Sunni fiqh, per head. This zakat is meant especially for the poor and destitute, orphans and widows. It must reach the poor before performance of Nemaz of Id, so that they also may join the affluents in congregational Nemaz of Id.

Id-uz-Zoha or Baqr-Id or Id-e-Qurban is celebrated on the tenth (till twelfth) day of the last month of Hijrah calendar—Zilhijjah. It is in the memory of the Zibh-e-Azim, i.e., sacrifice of the only son Ismail by the father Hazrat Ibrahim Khalilullah in the path of Allah, catching the peak of sacrificial devotion by a servant and Prophet of God. This festival remembers us that anything, however, near and dear, can and must be sacrificed for Allah and His Divine Path (Islam). This sunnah of Hazrat Ibrahim has been included in the Sh'air-e-Hajj as an important ingredient of Hajj ritual. Hajj is also performed during these three days of Zilhijjah, when Muslim devotees of the entire world assemble in Mecca and perform Hajj in one fashion and at one place and time. This memorises homogeneity, equality and brotherhood of faithfuls of the entire world in disregard of all man-created differences of caste and creed, region and religion. Islam discards and abhors such differences among the servants of God. Hajj preaches us devotion to God, International Brotherhood among the Faithfuls and abhorrence to the Devil and his followers.

The dargahs and tombs of Pirs or saints are places of pilgrimage to which people, mainly women, resort for blessings, to seek cure of diseases or ward off evil spirits. At Biharsharif there are the Dargahs of Mallick Ibrahim Baya and Hazrat Makhdoom Shah Sharfuddin, the tomb of the latter being held in special veneration by the Mohammadans, who assemble there at the anniversary of the death of the saint on 5th Shawal. At Jethuli near Bankaghat the dargahs of Shahabuddin Jagiant and Shah Adam Sufi are also places of pilgrimage and a fair is held there on the 21st Zi-Q'ad. In Patna proper there are the shrines of four Pirs called Mansur, Maru, Zafar and Mahdi and also the shrine of Shah Arzani, which attract large gatherings of both males and females. An 'urs' is also held at Phulwarishariff every year on the day of Fateha-Dwazdahum

A large number of Muslims, men and women, from far and wide assemble there to celebrate the Urs.

Some of the important Muslim customs followed in and around Patna are as follows:

Birth—Muslim women during pregnancy observe, like Hindus, a number of restrictions. After the birth of a child the father or any male member of the family recites *azaan* into the ears of the child. For the first forty days the mother abstains from the regular prayers. Every Muslim circumcises his male children before they reach the age of seven or eight years, while many of them circumcise the child on the sixth day of his birth. They also perform 'Bismillah' or Maktab ceremony of the child at the age of five reciting three verses of the Holy Qur'an. This ceremony is supposed to mark the beginning of educational career of the child as a pious and holy day. On this occasion sweets are distributed to friends and relatives. *Aquiqa* is the fourth important ritual of Islam, in which the first hair on the head of the child is removed, an animal is given in sacrifice for the child and silver equal in weight to the removed hair is given in alms. The meat of the animal given in sacrifice of Aquiqa is forbidden for father, mother, grandmother, grandfather and others having direct blood relation with the child. Aquiqa is necessary for both male and female child and it must be performed before the child attains puberty. Many of the Muslim families perform aquiqa of the child on the sixth day of its birth.

Marriage—The marriage customs of the Muslims are simple. Two male witnesses bear the testimony to the celebration of the marriage after taking consent of the bride. After her consent they declare her intention to the public and then the sermon of Khutba-e-Nikah is recited. The bride's father or *wali* gives away the bride in marriage to the bridegroom. On the eve of the departure of the bride to the house of bridegroom, the *jalwa* ceremony is performed, when the couple is made to see each other's face in a mirror and to read the Qur'an together. It is *sunnat* for the guardian of the bridegroom to give a feast to his fellow at his place on this occasion, which is known as *Walima*.

Death—Into the ears of dying man verses of Qur'an and Kalma-e-Shahadat are recited in low voice. The dead body covered with white cloth (Coffin) is placed in a janaza and is carried by men to the mosque for namaz-e-jenaza and then to the graveyard for burial and prayers. On the fourth day 'Qul' ceremony is performed or a 'Majlis' is held at the house or in mosque or Imambara where recitation of Qur'an and pray for the peace of the departed soul is done. On the tenth, twentieth and fortieth day similar rites are performed for the peace of the departed soul. On all such occasions alms and feasts are also arranged for the poor.

3

Patterns of Studies

In order to ascertain the status and role of women in Muslim society, we have dealt with their life and conditions at different stages of time. This has been studied in historical perspective, which reveals that the status and position of women have not remained the same through the ages. It means that the process of change in the life of Muslim women has been continued throughout the time and space. Constant fluctuation with respect to the power and position have been taking place from the time Muslim society came into existence and flourished far and wide. With the spread of cultural area as well as the cultural contact the Muslim society experienced varied changes. This shows that the community has never remained unchanged rather the wind of change, which has always blown, has affected the community to a lesser or greater degree. Thus it is a fallacy to assume that the Muslim society is traditional or conservative in nature as opined by many a social scientists. This has been proved with the help of historical evidences and factual data in the previous chapter. Such a wrong notion exists mainly due to the fact that till recently no scientific study of comprehensive nature has been undertaken in India or elsewhere which can depict the actual form and content of present day Muslim society.

Imtiaz Ahmad[1] has rightly remarked that while we know something about the structural and organisational characteristics of specific Muslim groups, there is little sociological information on the social framework within which Muslim groups operate. In the same way S. Musi Raza[2] has also felt about the dearth of sociological literature based on primary data on the Muslims of India, especially of Bihar. He says that the studies conducted so far on Indian Muslims by different historians and scholars of other branches of knowledge have either been partial in scope or historical and non-sociological in approach. These facts speak about the dearth of sociological literature on Indian Muslims both in quality as well as in quantity. Similarly Indu Menon[3] also observes that no systematic effort has been made so far to find out the factors behind the low status of Muslim women. She further notes that the theme of social status of Muslim women has been comparatively a neglected field of study in Indian sociology. Brijbhushan[4] had also become conscious of the need for a book on Muslim women in India. This led her to study various aspects of the life of Muslim women.

So far as the sociological studies concerning the Indian women in general is concerned, Beteille[5] opines, "There is no dearth of discussion on what may be called the women's question in India. But in absence of systematic studies, this discussion often leads to opposite conclusion, and indeed, it often starts from opposite assumptions about the position of women in society." He further argues, "There are equally sharp differences of opinion about the changes, taking place

1. Ahmad, Imtiaz, 'Caste and Social Stratification among the Muslims' (Ed.), Manohar Book Service, Delhi, 1973, p. vii.
2. Raza, S. Musi, 'Changing Patterns of Muslim Community in Bihar', unpublished Ph. D. Thesis, Patna University, 1976, p. 2.
3. Menon, Indu, 'Status of Muslim Women in India', Uppal Publishing House, New Delhi, 1981, p. viiz.
4. Brijbhushan, J., 'Muslim Women', Vikas Publishing House Pvt. Ltd., New Delhi, 1980, p. vii.
5. Beteille, Andre, 'The Position of Women in Indian Society', in 'Indian Women' (ed), Devaki Jain, p. 61.

in the position of women in India. Some regard these changes as profound and pervasive. . . . Others maintain that the position of women has changed very little and that Indian society continues by and large to be a male-dominated society."

Singh[6] states that specially after the International Women Year, 1975 studies on different aspects of women have started. The Committee on the Status of Women in India aimed at putting together a basic statistical and social profile of women on a national level brought to light a myriad of problems and disturbing trends which had previously been obscured. Sociological research on women had previously focussed almost exclusively on role conflicts of middle class working women. After 1975 there was a push to broaden the base of knowledge of low income rural and urban women. Economists, historians, demographers, lawyers and political scientists have joined the sociologists to contribute a broad base of expertise and knowledge about the status and need of women. Similarly research on women is no longer seen as simply a theoretical in nature, but is becoming increasingly policy oriented as the need is recognised for public action.[7]

The Committee on the Status of Women in India itself accepts the paucity of research in this field and claims its study as the first investigation of its kind dealing with the status of women in India. Haniff[8] remarks, "Even though there has been a great rise in the study of women in India, the Muslim woman has been grossly neglected in this process." She further points out, "This only mirrors the monolithic Hindu approach of the Indian social scientists and male orientation of those who write about Muslims in India."

6. Singh, Andrea M., 'The Study of Women in South Asia: Some Current Methodological and Research Issues', in 'Women in Contemporary India and South Asia' (ed.), Alfred de Souza, Manohar, New Delhi, 1980, pp. 61-62.
7. Report of the Committee on the Status of Women in India, Deptt. of Social Welfare, Govt. of India, New Delhi, 1975, p. vii.
8. Haniff, Niesha Z., 'Muslim Women and Minority Mentality', in Modernization and Social Change among Muslims in India' (ed.), Imtiaz Ahmad, Manohar Pub., New Delhi, 1983, p. 201.

Since the recent past, the Indian sociologists have started paying attention to this so far neglected area of sociological study. They have conducted a few studies on Indian Muslims from sociological point of view. Though most of these few studies are concerned with the Muslim community in general, yet these throw light on the conditions, roles and statuses of Indian Muslim women and the changes taking place therein, because women constitute an important part of society and are equally important in understanding social structure and community life. Hence in the following pages a brief description of some of these studies is being presented to understand the changes taking place in the role and status of Indian Muslim women.

A comparative analysis of the role and status of women in different religious communities has been presented by Kidwai[9] on the basis of a content analysis of religious scriptures, historical accounts and other relevant materials. He has also analysed the actual position of women in different communities and of the women of same religious community in different countries. As regards the analysis of the condition, role and status of Muslim women, the author has examined their position in various Muslim countries. Giving a comparative account, he has drawn a conclusion and has observed that the position of Muslim women has gradually fallen with the passing of time in different countries. It is because of gradual decline in the importance of observing true religious sanctions in actual social life and a gradual departure from religious to traditional and customary standpoint. The traditional and customary sanctions of different countries have not been alike and hence the condition of Muslim women is not universally uniform, but a trend of decline in their status is found everywhere. But the author does not conclude with a pessimistic note and has shown optimism for the future.

Status of Muslim women in North India by Shibani

9. Kidwai, Shaikh M.H., Women, Seema Publications, Delhi, 1976, p. 201.

Roy[10] is based on the data collected during 1970-72. The work mainly centres around the two cities of Delhi and Lucknow believed to having Islamic background. In total 300 families of Sayyad, Shaikh, Mughal and Pathans were investigated. They all belonged to the middle income group. Both Sunni and Shia Muslims, most dominant religious groups, were investigated.

For collection of data an interview guide was used, while observation and participant observation techniques were also employed.

The chief aim of the work is to bring into light the extent and quality of changes which have occurred in the Muslim families within three generations and its effects on the status of the women. The placement of women in the society shifts along with the shift in the basic attitudes of the people and in the Indian context even the Muslims, in spite of their rigorous and effective pattern of conduct, have felt the wave of change in their home front. How far these outside factors have penetrated and affected the family life and role pattern of the women are some of the questions posed by the author. The author has critically examined the status of contemporary Muslim women in the context of their mothers' and grandmothers' status.

The whole work is divided into seven chapters. The first chapter deals with the theoretical framework used, methodology, a brief survey of literature and also describes certain socio-historical movements responsible for the change in the community. The second chapter is on purdah where typology, function and effect of purdah have been described. In the third chapter effect of education on the changing status of women has been shown. The fourth chapter critically evaluates marriage as an institution and its significance for the women. In the fifth chapter the role of women in economic sphere has been discussed. In the sixth chapter the impact of religion on the status of women has been described. Lastly, an attempt has been made to show how the women placed as

10. Roy, Shibani 'Status of Muslim Women in India', B.R. Publishing Corporation, Delhi, 1979.

they are in the social set up make multi-directional efforts to better their status.

After studying and analysing the facts gathered the author concludes that with the change in social climate the attitude of Muslim men changed and they wanted the women to participate in more areas of social life prohibited to them so far. Regarding purdah, she says that the Muslim women of today are in purdah but not the same kind of purdah as practised before by the grandmothers. Education has rapidly spread among Muslim women of the present generation, yet it has not succeeded in drastically altering the Islamic pattern of life in so far as it concerns the general life style of women. She concludes that as long as the women were ignorant about the importance of 'mahr' money, they were invariably duped by men. The educated Muslim women realise that mahr money is one of the strongest defences against the easy divorce. Unfortunately, the women cannot avail of this because the youngmen of today are very cautious and in spite of the possibility of social criticism they insist on keeping this amount of mahr well within their financial means. But the basic level of women's participation in family finances is comparatively higher than that of the males due to traditional reasons. This high status of women is due to the change in their wider intellectual climate, the young husbands have started taking their wives into confidence, mainly because the present day women are mentally at par with their menfolk. Thus in any case the basic level of women's participation in family finances is comparatively higher than that of the males due to traditional reasons. This high status of the women with respect to family finances is further elevated with the increase in their education and employment. She argues that the Muslim women are more religious than men. The religious activities are conducted at home and form one of the most popular means of keeping up social relations. The present day educated women do not necessarily follow the rituals blindly, but try to understand the Holy Book. Education is making them more religiously conscious but at the same time reducing their blind faith in ritualistic beliefs.

This study can be cited as an example in the sociological literature so far as the study on Muslim women is concerned. It has covered more or less all important aspects of women's life which are helpful in understanding Muslim women closely.

Jamila Brijbhushan,[11] the author of the present book under review, is a journalist by profession. She published this book in the year 1980 on the basis of the data collected through interviews with women in and around Delhi, representing all religions of the country and belonging to all levels of society. The main objective of this study was to dispel the existing misconception about the position of women in Islam and to present a realistic picture of their status today.

The author has discussed all aspects of Muslim Personal Law like marriage, polygamy, divorce, inheritance, adoption along with their educational condition, purdah, and the adoption of family planning measures. To examine the rights given to the Muslim women in Islam and their application in the present-day society she undertook the present study.

The author observes that most of the Muslims who came to India took local women for wives who converted to Islam. Again, the individual and mass level conversion also continued. The social customs continued to be practised in the age-old way having, most often, nothing to do with those prescribed by Islam, some of the converts also honour the Hindu taboo of beef eating. Thus there has been a mingling of Hindus and Muslims in a way that the general public has been quite unaware of. Muslim society consists of Ashraf and Ajlaf or Atraf. The process of Ashrafisation has been given added impetus by the process of Islamisation.

Regarding purdah, she observed that since independence the number of women leaving purdah has been increasing every year. In many families the non-purdah observing women exist happily side by side with the purdah nashins.

11. Brijbhushan, Jamila, 'Muslim Women in Purdah and Out of It', Vikas Publishing House Pvt. Ltd., New Delhi, 1980.

None of the women considered purdah as being special hardship in their lives, rather according to some it offers security.

She found economic changes have brought changes in marriage preference. Rising costs and changing values have considerably reduced expenditure resulting in the curbing of rituals and, therefore, bringing marriage more in line with the original intention of Divine law-maker.

On the basis of data collected through interviews the author further says that the phenomenon of polygyny is disappearing fast from Muslim society, while among Hindus its rate is high. This system is very much disliked by the women.

During her study she came across women favouring and disfavouring divorce. Majority of them expressed that it is beneficial for men and harmful for women. So most of them wanted it to be abolished.

According to her findings the women are overwhelmingly in favour of family planning and birth control. They said that the whole matter of family planning would be greatly simplified and much more readily accepted if some foolproof device was invented for the use of women.

The author gathers that usually the daughters or sisters do not get their normal share of property due to bad intentions. Most of the women do not want to fight for their proper share as they thought it would entail many problems.

Regarding the problem of adoption among Muslims, the author found contradictory views for and against it. It is mainly because neither Islam has emphasised in favour of it nor the Tradition has explicitly shown any support. The author favours the inclusion of the right of adoption in the Muslim Personal Law.

Jamila opines, various factors are responsible for the low response of education among Muslims like, the lack of curiosity, lack of means to acquire education, lack of interest on the part of parents and guardians in the education of their children and the lack of conviction that education can provide a better future for every one. Wherever there are educational facilities and interest for it, parents send their sons and daughters to the educational institutions. She concludes that Muslims are lagging far behind in educational pursuit.

An impartial review of the present study reveals that the author has touched all important aspects of women's life in Muslim society. But it lacks field data in a scientific sociological style. Hence a descriptive anthropological type simple study does not help in understanding the women's life objectively.

Indu Menon[12] conducted a study on the Muslims of Kerala in the year 1974 to ascertain the stutus of Muslim women there. For this purpose 450 women and 150 men were selected on the basis of simple random method from four districts of Kerala, namely, Malappurem, Calicut, Palghat and Cannanore. The respondents represented both rural and urban settings of the four districts and were having comparatively higher educational background.

Data was collected mainly through interview schedules, separately meant for male and female respondents. Besides personal data of respondents the schedules contained questions relating to status indicators and attitudes and practices in this area.

The objective of the study, according to the author, was to find out whether education plays any significant role in raising the social status of Muslim women. If it contributes significantly, then it was to probe the specific areas in which improvement in their status was visualised or apparent. If education does not help in improving the status of Muslim women, in that case it was planned to identify the factors and forces responsible for inhibiting status improvement in spite of education.

The whole study is divided into nine chapters dealing with the theoretical framework, methodology and research setting, educational background of the respondents, marriage and family, economic and occupational background, political and social background, attitude and behaviour of men respondents and lastly the summary of findings.

12. Menon, Indu M., 'Status of Muslim Women in India', Uppal Publishing House. New Delhi. 1981.

Data showed that in every major institutional sphere education has contributed to raise the status of Muslim women i.e., those who are highly educated have more status and vice versa. But it was found that the factors which hinder the availment of education among women are still active and are able to keep the position of women low in society. She observed two main reasons for the low level of education the lack of meaningful role for educated women in the community and the practice of seclusion.

The author finds that the institution of marriage and family are also obstacles to the improvement of the status of Muslim women. The traditional roles of wife and mother and the customs and practices centring around marriage, which still continue in Muslim society, compel women to be entirely dependent upon men as well as it hinders the educational pursuit of women.

She observes in the economic and occupational spheres the position of Muslim women continues to be subordinate to men. Though entitled to the enjoyment and disposal of her personal property in her own way, seclusion at home makes her utterly dependent on the husband in the matter of use and disposal of their property. Since Muslim women are not expected to perform any occupation outside home, education which is necessary for this is not considered to be very essential for them and as such Muslim society under-emphasises women's education.

The study reveals that Muslim women do not think that politics is a legitimate field of activity for them. Majority of them do not approve of Muslim women's active participation in politics. Likewise only a negligible part of the respondents were members of any club or association.

However, the author finds that in spite of the traditionally ascribed subordinate position to Muslim women, education has been able to contribute significantly to raising the social status of women. The higher the education of the respondents, the more modern was their attitude and behaviour and the higher was their status in the society. Other factors like income, age, place of residence, etc. were not significantly related to this attitude and practice.

Though the author has beautifully tried to examine the important aspects determining the understanding of status of Muslim women, only one variable, namely, education, has been taken into consideration. This is an important variable, no doubt, but it cannot sufficiently show deep and detailed picture of the women's life in Muslim society.

A pioneer work in the field of sociological literature related to Muslim community has been presented by S. Musi Raza[13] in the year 1976. His study on 'Changing Patterns of Muslim Community' is a deep and detailed study of the urban Muslim life of Bihar with special reference to Patna.

In his study the author has taken many aspects of Muslims' life into consideration, e.g., marriage and family, purdah system, economic life and occupational patterns, patterns of education, social stratification, entertainments, habits, dress patterns and ornaments, attitude, values and observances related to religion, etc. All these aspects have been examined in three time sequences—traditional, medieval and modern. In the first stage help from Quran, Tradition and Sunnah, etc. has been taken for the understanding of Islamic sanctions and traditions concerning Muslim socio-cultural life. In the next stage the existence of these aspects has been watched with a view to see the changes in these aspects and finally facts and figures from field sources have been procured to assess the existing conditions of life. Thus in order to examine the changing patterns in Muslim community the author has taken both male and female into consideration.

In this way the study under review is comprehensive one in nature and scientific in approach. This is the only study of its time conducted on urban setting in a very systematic manner.

The study conducted by Sarfarazuddin[14] in the year 1983

13. Raza, S. Musi, 'Changing Patterns of Muslim Community in Bihar', unpublished Ph. D. Thesis, Patna University, 1976.
14. Sarfarazuddin, 'Social Structure of a Muslim Village in Bihar', unpublished Ph.D. Thesis, Patna University, 1983.

is also worth mentioning while discussing the Muslim society and culture in India in the field of sociology. The author did a pioneer sociological research in the rural setting on the basis of primary data. While dealing with the situation help from secondary sources has also been taken into consideration.

The author has studied various aspects of Muslim society like social stratification, marriage, family and kinship, education, purdah, economic relations, political relations, cultural relations and the institution of waqf, etc. Thus all aspects have been covered in the present study. All these structural aspects and the changes taking place in these components have been dealt with in detail. Problems relating to women's life and conditions are the intrinsic part of the study. The data have been analysed in changed perspective.

Thus the study presents a deep and detailed picture of the socio-cultural life of Muslim community living basically in rural Bihar. In short the study is helpful for the present work.

A renowned scholar of international repute, Murtaza Mutahhari,[15] wrote a book in the year 1981 entitled 'The Rights of Women in Islam'.

The author has rightfully examined various aspects concerning Muslim women's rights and duties. Important aspects covered in the book are marriage, social independence, modernity, family rights, dower and maintenance, inheritance, divorce, polygyny, etc. All these problems have been examined in the light of Islamic sanctions and the rule of nature. In other words, the author has tried to show that the status and role of Muslim women prescribed in Islam is justified and natural. For this purpose he has taken the help of secondary sources, especially of Quran, Tradition and various interpretations of it.

The book is helpful in understanding the life and condition of women in Islam.

15. Mutahhari, Murtaza, 'The Rights of Women in Islam', World Organization of Islamic Services, Tehran, 1981.

Ellickson[16] conducted a study in the village Shaheenpur (pseudonym) in Comilla district of Bangla Desh (the erstwhile East Pakistan) in the year 1968-69. She studied different aspects of the Muslim social and cultural life in the village, especially an enactment and effectiveness of the Pakistan Muslim Family Laws Ordinance 1961, regulating marriage, divorce and inheritance.

The author finds that the villagers were not in favour of the enactment of these national laws because they thought it to be imposed by the outsiders and not in accordance with the Islamic Shariah, as held by the villagers' Imams or as per dictates of village customs. Thus the villagers had greater faith in local customs as well as in the sayings of Imams. Nevertheless, on the other hand, a few started using it for their own gains. Their aims were not to overturn the village social structure but to gain a momentary advantage.

The author, while dealing with the deservance of purdah system, found that the rural women maintained strict purdah whenever they went outside their homes. He found that a few rich Muslim ladies who own burqa always use it whenever they go outside. Majority of the rural Muslim women does not attend public gathering or public places and if circumstances compelled them they used rickshaw covered from all sides to avoid public gaze.

The author also found a dispute settlement of a mediation council which acts as the primary organ of social control in the village. Villagers generally do not take their affairs and problems outside the local arena or to have outside agencies come in to interfere in the village matter.

The study under review is micro in nature. It has covered only few aspects of Muslim life and only one aspect of Muslim women. Thus it is very short and simple study—better to call it an insufficient study.

16 Ellickson, Jean, Islamic Institutions in Bangla Desh, in T.N. Madan's 'Muslim Communities of South Asia', Vikas Publishing House, Pvt. Ltd , New Delhi, 1976.

Shahida[17] conducted a micro-level study about the role and status of women in contemporary Muslim societies in the year 1975. This paper divides into four parts. Part one attempts to identify historical factors which made the modernising process in the Muslim community lack both in unity and cohesion. It further examines the effect it had on Muslim women and on the community's pre-partition development. The second part examines whether modernisation stimulated the desire in the Muslim community for economic progress and modernisation and analyses the implications of it on the role and status of Muslim women. Part three is an analysis and assessment of the extent to which Muslim women are limited by the community's adherence to the Shariah. It probes the direction and resolution of their desire to change. The fourth part sums up and considers the prospects and possible direction of further changes.

It may be concluded, on the basis of facts mentioned in this article, that the author has limited the scope of study. All aspects of women's life have not been taken into consideration for the better understanding of their actual position and role in social life.

Based on micro-sociological study, Haniff[18] has tried to understand the Muslim women's attitude and behaviours towards various problems they are facing in the day-to-day life. The article examines the minority mentality stereotype often ascribed to Muslims in India and its presence among Muslim women. A study of poor working Muslim women in the Delhi area was conducted to gauge these women's self-perception. In this process their ideas on many issues were discussed including their feelings as Muslims and about the Muslim community in free India in general. The author found that these women were relatively free of the minority complex,

17. Lateef, Shahida, 'Modernization in India and the Status of Muslim Women', in Imtiaz Ahmad (ed.), 'Modernization and Social Change among Muslims in India', Manohar Publications, New Delhi, 1983.

18. Haniff, Niesha Z., 'Muslim Women and Minority Mentality', in Imtiaz Ahmad (ed.), 'Modernization and Social Change among Muslims in India, op. cit.

were secular in outlook and were somewhat modern in their approach to their roles as working women.

Though the study is based on factual data, it cannot be called a study sufficient for the understanding of women's position in the Muslim society. It is because it has taken very few variables relevant for the understanding of power, privileges, status and position of the Muslim women in the present-day society.

The studies quoted above throw light on various aspects of the life of Muslim women. Though many books and articles have come up to deal with Muslims in India and elsewhere, very few can be called to be a representative study of the Muslim women in the present-day context. Firstly, because most of it are of descriptive nature and historical account. Secondly, because most of them are micro-sociological studies limited in time and space. Thus there is dearth of a comprehensive sociological study based on field data and covering the various aspects of women's life in general and the Muslim women's in particular based on field data. Most of the authors have chosen one or the other aspect in dealing with the problems of Muslim women according to their conveniences. With the differences in material and non-material conditions of the people of different areas, a difference in life conditions and social status is bound to occur. Hence in such a situation a planned and systematic sociological study of comprehensive nature is needed in order to assess the real life conditions and power and privileges of the Muslim women in the society.

4

Marriage and Family

The concept of family, in Islam, is primordial. The first human existence on the Earth, Adam and Eve, was husband and wife. It means that there is no pre-family stage in human life and the institution of family has been existing since the very emergence of man's advent on Earth. Islam rejects any stage of sexual communism or sexual promiscuity as advocated by Western philosophers and social scientists. Islam also does not accept the evolutionary theory of institutionalisation of human life patterns, and it suggests that the first Prophet of Allah brought a code of conduct with him from heaven.

Marriage, in Islam, is essentially a civil contract made in the Name of Allah. The pre-requisites of marriage according to the Islamic sanctions are—(1) consent of the partners, (2) fixation and acceptance of the 'Mahr' (dower) by the bridegroom, and (3) Nikah, i.e., declaration of the terms of marital contract (in Arabic language) by the representative of bride and acceptance of the same by the representative of the bridegroom in the presence of at least two just witnesses. Marriage, according to Muslim Law, is a simple ceremony void of all sorts of pomp and show. This contract is made in the Name of Allah, and hence it is taken as a pious treaty.

Kufv

The first and the most important problem in respect of marriage is the problem of 'kufv'. The Muslim society, under the impact of age-old imperialistic rule, has been divided into various sects and castes whereas Islam hates casteism and sectarianism and it stands for global brotherhood of Muslims. 'Kufv' is an Arabic word which means 'homogeneity of belief and conduct'. But in the Islamic Fiqh (jurisprudence), this word is used in relation to marital ties. According to Islamic juries the word 'Kufv' means equality of 'Hasab and Nasab', and 'hasab' means belief and conduct whereas 'nasab' means lineage. Thus kufv, according to Islamic fiqh, means equality in belief and nobility of conduct and lineage: Two persons having similar (or the same) religious belief and bearing good conduct and clean lineage. This cleanliness of lineage does never mean stratification on the basis of caste, region or economic status—there is no such stratification in Islam. From the following verses, on the subject, the real meaning of 'kufv' will be apparent:

(1)	...wala tankihul mushrikate hatta yo'minna.... (Al-Baqarah: 221)	...and never establish marital ties with infidel women till they become believers....
(2)	...fa-in alimtomuhunna mo'minatin fala tarjioo-hunna ilal kuffare; laahunna hillullahum wala hum yahilloona lahunna.... (Mumtahinah: 10)	...and if you find them believers then never return them to non-believers; because neither these women are lawful for them nor they (non-believers) are lawful for these believing women....
(3)	Al-khahisato lil-khabisina wal-khabisoon lil-khabisate (Noor: 26)	The wicked women are for wicked men and wicked men for wicked women.

(4)	Az-Zani-la yankiho illa zaniyatan au mushrikatan, waz-Zaniyato la yankihoha illa Zanin au mushrekun; wa-hurrima alal Mo'menina. (Noor: 3)	The adulterer, never marry him but with an adulteress or infideless; and the adulteress, never marry her but with an adulterer or infidel.
(5)	Wat-Taiyibato lit-Taiyebeena wat-Taiyiboona lit-Taiyibate (Noor)	And the clean ladies are for clean males and clean males for clean ladies.

It is evident from the above verses of Qur'an that Islam allows marital ties between homogeneous beliefs and conducts, and it has forbidden the believers to establish marital ties with non-believers and bad characters. Cleanliness of belief and conduct is, thus, the basic criteria for marital ties of a Muslim man or woman. The meaning of 'hasab' and 'nasab' should be seen through these verses of Qur'an. Any other meaning of Hasab and Nasab, based on caste, region and economic status, is quite un-Islamic. Islam stands for global brotherhood among the believers regardless of caste, class or lineage. Islam advocates marital relations between persons of clean belief and conduct. The practice of the Holy Prophet of Islam corroborates the above version in toto. Everybody knows that the Prophet of Islam accepted women of different groups and himself married his own cousin sister Zainab to his Negro slave Janab Zaid. This practice was followed by his successor Caliphs and Ashab-e-Kiram. Hence the 'kufv' of a believer lady must be a believer of good character; and, similarly, the 'kufv' of a believer man must be a believer lady of good character. There is no restriction of high and low caste, high and low status or high or low level of economy. These restriction are un-Islamic and irrational bottlenecks created by imperialists.

Nikah

Nikah is the first and the basic ceremony, without which marriage cannot be said to be religiously legitimate and lawful. According to the Muslim Law, 'Nikah' is a contract of union between two strangers of opposite sexes which legalises their sexual intercourse and mutual co-existence and imposes certain duties on and confers certain rights upon the two partners. Nikah is a formal declaration of the terms (in set Arabic language) of the wedlock in the presence of at least two witnesses. Shustery observes, "The chief function of marriage, according to Muslim Law, is the ceremony of Nikah, an Arabic word which means conjunction and understanding in the sense of contract. It is a simple ceremony, for which the consent of the man and the woman to marry each other is necessary." The Prophet of Islam said, "An-nikaho Sunnati", i.e., the contract of marriage is my tradition. He further said, "One who is inclined towards my tradition, he is from me; and inclination towards my tradition is inclination towards God." This tradition shows the importance of conjugal life and familyhood in Islam, as against the Vedic and Biblical celibacy. This means that Islam does not approve of secluded life, rather it likes a social life. Islam presents a practical life in consonance with the human nature. It has ordained for constant remembrance of Allah through service to parents, children, family, society and humanity.

The Qur'an says: "And marry those among you who are single (virgin or widowed or divorced), those who are pious among you, male or female slaves; and if they are poor, Allah will of His bounty enrich them. Allah is All-bounteous, Knowing."[1]

Contrary to Christianity and Hinduism, Islam allowed divorced women to re-marry.

Marriage is the most important problem of women's life. It confronts a woman with the serious problems of adjustment, status, independence and inheritance besides the problems of rearing children and regulating family life. The traditional man being generally in ruling position, dictates his own way and will and she has either to mould herself according to the dictates of her spouse, or to groan under unfavourable

1. Qur'an, Al-Noor, verse 32.

situations, or to decide a separation. Then, what to do after separation and how to control her natural pull? Islam has solved all these questions.

She is independent in selecting her spouse.

Qur'an stopped woman being treated as a property and being inherited by a son from his father. Marriages of this incestuous nature were common among Ante-Islamic Arabs and Jews:

> "And marry not women whom your fathers married, except what has already passed; this surely is indecent and hateful, and it is an evil way."[2]

A woman is independent in choosing her spouse.

The Prophet says:

> "No widow should be married without consulting her; and no virgin be married without her assent, and her assent is her silence." (Bukhari & Muslim)

Even after the marriage ceremony if she declared that she did not assent to it, the marriage is dissolved.

A similar case came before the Prophet of Islam when a young girl, in a state of fear, stood before him and said:

> "O Prophet of Allah! my father..." said she.
>
> "What is the matter? What your father did?", asked the Prophet.
>
> "He has a niece, and he gave me in his wedlock without consulting me", she said.
>
> "Now when he (your father) has done so, you also should concur with him and should live as a wife with your cousin", advised the Prophet.
>
> "But, O Prophet of Allah! I do not ike my cousin and I do not like to accept him as my husband", said she.

2. Qur'an: Al-Nisa, verse 29

"If thou don't liketh him, the matter finishes here; and thou art free in thine choice, go and select to whomever thou liketh to be thine husband", said the Prophet.

"By chance I love him most, and have no love for anyone other than him nor I wish to become wife of anybody other than him. But because my father has done it without my assent, I came to your Holiness so that I may put the problem before your Holiness and inform all the women folk that, henceforth, no father has the right to give her daughter in the wedlock of anybody according to his own sweet will", said she.

"This tradition has been recorded by Shaheed II in 'Masalik' and by the writer of Jawahir in his book 'Jawahirul Kalaam'. During the days of ignorance, both Arabs and non-Arabs supposed themselves to be the attorney in respect of their daughters, sisters and even of their mothers; and in the matter of selection of spouse they did not allow any right to them. Generally the father, or in his absence the uncle, had the right to decide the matter.

"This right was exercised to the extent that the father used to give even the would-be daughter in the wedlock of somebody and when she was born, the would-be husband had the right to take her to his house and keep her as his wife."[3]

From the above historical report, a few points of significant importance emerge:

(i) That a woman can question the authority of her father in the matter of selection of her spouse.

(ii) If a father gives his daughter in the wedlock of somebody without taking her consent, the daughter can reject the wedlock.

3. Mutahhari, Murtada, "The Rights of Women in Islam", quoted in Rahe Islam, monthly, Jamadius Sani, 1406 H.

(iii) A good daughter should honour the marital contract made by her father in good faith even if he missed taking consent from her.

One of the unique points with regard to marital ties is the exemplary liberalism of Islam which has allowed a Muslim to marry a woman of other religions that have "Books", like Judaism and Christianity. The Jews never recognized a mixed marriage. To them Gentiles are hardly human. At one time, under Christian law, if any Christian married a Jewess both were to be killed. But Islam allows a Muslim man to marry of all religions which have been given Divine Books. The relevant verse reads as follows:

> "This day are ye allowed to eat such things as are good, and food of those to whom scriptures are given is allowed as lawful unto you and your food is allowed as lawful unto them; and ye are also allowed modest women, that are believers, and modest women of those who have received the scripture before you, when ye shall have assigned them their dower, to live chastely, neither fornicating, nor taking them for concubines."[4]

Other features of this verse are: (1) Muslims are allowed to eat lawful (Halaal) things of the people having Divine Books, and vice versa; (2) they are also allowed to marry non-Muslim women of those who have been given 'Books', if they are Believers; and (3) Islam has not discriminated between a Muslim and a non-Muslim wife in regard to 'respect' and other familial rights. Had it been so, the Qur'an would not have made a mention of the 'believing women' with those of non-Muslim women.

But one must not confuse that there is any contrast between the verse under consideration and those laying norms for 'kufv' mentioned earlier. Idolators and infidels of either sex belonging to even those who have been endowed with Divine Book are certainly out of 'kufv' of a Muslim male and

4. Qur'an, Sura v, Ayat 5.

female. In the present verse, too, there is a paramount condition "if they are believers", preceding to the clause permitting marital ties with modest women of those who have previously been given a Book, which excludes all those women who believe in 'Trinity' or ascribe shape, sex, etc. to God. Belief in Unity of God is the prime condition, which, according to Qur'an, makes a woman admissible to the wedlock of a Muslim man, or vice-versa. According to Qur'an all Prophets of God professed and preached Unity of God. Any deviation from the belief of Unity found in the Holy Books is due to alterations in the Book by the people. The word 'believer' in Qur'an stands for 'belief in Wahdat' (Unity). At best a Christian or a Jew may not believe in the Prophethood of Mohammad, but he/she must believe in Unity of God for being admissible for a Muslim (male or female). The present permission is, therefore, confined to such non-Muslims who are not idolators or infidels and believe in their original Book and their own Prophet.

The criteria for selection of spouse, as per Qur'an, are chaste and belief—the other qualities having been left to the choice of proposer or couple. Qur'an advises to select a mohsina' (chaste lady) as wife. Beauty, disposition and physical soundness find place in various relevant Tradition of the Prophet, which one must care for. This is a wise safeguard against conjugal bitterness and disturbance in the family peace.

Mahr (Dower)

Nikah is conditioned by Mahr (dower) and maintenance. While Mahr is payable at the time of Nikah, maintenance is a recurring burden. If Mahr is not paid at the time of Nikah, it will remain as debt on the husband and is recoverable from him or his property or his heirs any time during or after his death. In other words, it is a 'debt-on-call' payable on demand by the wife. Likewise maintenance is also an unquestionable right of wife, recoverable from him at all times through legal process. The wife may even refuse to take her abode with her husband if he has not paid *mahr* at the time of *nikah*.

If anybody thinks that *mahr* is not a debt his *nikah* is void.

Mahr is a tool against exploitation of the fairer sex and a security against adversity. It is also a check against sudden divorce. If somebody divorces his wife she may realise the *mahr*, through legal process. In case the husband or the wife dies before payment of *mahr* it can be realised by the legal heir of the wife from the property or heir of the husband. A suit for ejectment against a widow in possession of her husband's estate for unsatisfied *mahr* will not be allowed.

There being no maximum limit fixed for dower, the woman is at liberty to demand any exorbitant amount; but, at the same time, it is negotiable before *nikah* and the amount agreed upon by both the parties is called *mahr*.

But, according to tradition, the lady whose *mahr* is exorbitant or higher than the paying capacity of the husband, has been placed in the category of 'hated ladies'.

The object of marriage, as given by Qur'an is "Purity, not passion."[5]

Islam's main theme in ordering for marital ties is to maintain a marked distance between man and animal, so far passion is concerned. The other object is to provide an orderly mode of procreation in order to maintain human generation. An orderly manner is called 'a pure manner' and a disorderly manner an impure manner. It is the manner which makes a thing pure or impure, legal or illegal; otherwise everything on this earth is created for man. While Islam has given due consideration to this human weakness (passion), it has not succumbed to it nor it plans to surrender before debauchery. It has dealt unlawful union of men and women with an iron hand, inasmuch as the crime of adultery in Islam carried the punishment of life; whereas under the materialistic laws it simply carries price in terms of a few coins: Such a harsh punishment for adultery of the degree of sensitivity of Islam to the purity of manner, or character. For the protection of chaste women from being scandalized, the punishment suggested by Islam for slanderers is: "And those who asperse chaste women, and then bring not four

5. Qur'an, Al-Nisa, 24. Qur'an, Sura xxiv: 4.

witnesses, scourge them with eighty strips (lashes), and believe not their testimony for ever; and these, they are wicked doers". It is incumbent upon the slanderer to produce four eye-witnesses to prove the case; and if he fails, he must be lashed with eighty strips and debarred from appearing as witness before any court of law for ever.

Jahez (Dowry)

Marriage is such an important religio-social duty of parent that exchange of gifts has taken the shape of institutionalised custom in India for many centuries. Traditionally, rich and royal families not only gave the bride as a gift at the time of marriage but also accompanied her with small gifts in cash, and or ornaments. These gifts were not called dowry in those days as they were presented after the marriage and as a symbol of affection and love. As long as dowry was voluntary, it was not a financial obstacle to marriage. Since the medieval period, however, dowry demands have increased significantly in parts of the country. By the late nineteenth century, the custom of dowry payment had slowly spread to other castes and subsequently became a prestige issue. Unfortunately, after independence and especially with the economic fall after vesting of zamindari in the State, dowry demands have creeped into the Muslim society. The dowry system has not only become an obstacle in the way of marriage but also an avenue for some affluent families to display and enhance their social status and economic worth. Before vesting of zamindari this system was not known to Muslim society, as it did not find any place in Islamic Shariah or Sunnah. Now Muslims are not lagging behind their Hindu counterparts in demanding and offering dowries in heavy cash, kind and landed propery. In a country where more than 80 per cent of the people live below subsistence level, dowry is undoubtedly a social curse. The Prophet of Islam married his daughter to Hazrat Ali and gave her a mattress of palm-leaves, a sheet of camel leather and a bed sheet of Yemen, besides an earthen *lota* and *chakki*. These were all which the Prophet of Islam gave in Jahez to his daughter, Shahzadi

Fatma. At that time the Prophet was the ruler of Arab. The dowry given by him to his daughter shows that the Prophet wantonly kept the level of Jahez so low that even the poorest of his followers may not feel bothered or exploited at the time of marriage of his daughter, and it may not become a source of exploitation by the groom side. Had the Prophet of Islam thought any iota of status in mind his Ashab might have heaped dowries worth millions of Dinars for the daughter of the Prophet. But Rasool-e-Karim stood as model for the entire Islamic world and it was unbecoming of him to set a devastating example. Thus those who claim to be the follower of Mohammad, should not claim dowry. Claim of dowry from the bride's party is a sort of exploitation, and Islam stands against all sorts of exploitation. So far marriage is concerned, Islam has given women an edge over their husband insofar as it has obliged bridegroom to pay 'mahr' (dower) and maintain the wife and her children in a decent way. The Barat feast is also not obligatory on the part of bride's guardians. On the contrary the groom has to give a feast to community members and relatives when he brings his wife to his house. It is quite rational. Bride's father gives a fruit of his life permanently under the sway of the groom and he, on behalf of his daughter, is rightful in charging the value which he does never do; rather, on the contrary, the groom side demands heavy cash, landed property and other perishables as dowry. It is quite unjust and shameful demand, and in case of a poor bride it is a cruel demand. This custom has taken such a shape where Government of India had to intervene to check this evil through a social legislation in the shape of Anti-Dowry Act.

Polygyny

The most vehemently opposed Islamic institution, after purdah, is polygyny—wrongly termed as polygamy. What is allowed in Islam is polygyny, which means 'a form of marriage in which one man may be united with two or more recognized wives at one time' (Dictionary of Sociology by Fairchild, Henry Pratt & Others, Adams & Co., Littlefield) whereas 'polygamy' means 'a form of marriage in which a person of either sex is united to more than one spouse: includes polyandry as well as polygyny, with which it is often incorrectly confused'. Bible is silent on this point, though it names several prophets having more than one wife. For instance, Solomon had seven hundred wives and three hundred concubines, David had ninety-nine wives, Abraham three wives and Moses had four; whereas Jacob (alias Israil) too had four wives. Still the Jews and Christians question the legitimacy of polygamy, and say that it is denegrading for women and hence irrational. They know very well that, in fact, polygamy or polygyny is not compulsory in Islam, nor it is an encouraged institution rather it is a device against the danger of adultery.

Schopenhauer frankly admits, "We all live, at any rate for a time, and most of us always, in polygamy. And so, since every man needs many women, there is nothing fairer than to allow him, nay, to make it incumbent upon him, to provide for many women. This will reduce woman to her true and natural position as a subordinate being, and the *lady*—that monster of European civilization and Teutonic Christian stupidity—will disappear from the world, leaving only *women*, but no more unhappy women, of whom Europe is now full."[6] He further asserts, "There is no use arguing about polygamy; it must be taken as *de facto* existing everywhere, and the only question is as to how it shall be regulated."

M.H. Kidwai has further reported that a certain German military officer had recommended the introduction of the Turkish system of polygamy in Germany to save the country for the future from a falling birth-rate. He aroused the wrath of Christian priests. However, the question was going to be discussed in the German Reichstag.

M.H. Kidwai has quoted Mr. Higgins to say: "Because Muhammad, following the example of this legislator of the oldest ceremonial religion west of Euphrates, and, as all Christians maintain, of the world—Moses—allowed his people,

6. Schopenhauer, quoted in "Woman Under Different Social & Religious Laws" by M.H. Kidwai, Seema Pub., New Delhi, p. 109.

the descendants of Ishmael, the son of the father of the faithful, a plurality of wives, he has been constantly abused by Christians, to use their own words, 'for pandering to the base passion of his followers.' But why the allowance of a plurality of wives should be visited with such a very harsh censure, I do not know. Surely the example of Solomon, and David—the man after God's own heart, which He had found to fulfil His law—might plead for a little mercy, more especially as Jesus nowhere expressly forbids in any of the twenty gospels which were written by some or other of the multitude of the sects of his followers to record his commands."

M.H. Kidwai further notes: "Thomasius in his learned treatise *De Concubineta* proves that in all ages among all nations polygamy was permitted. Not only all over the East but in the West also polygamy was permitted."[7]

John Davenport says: "Muhammad did but legalize a practice not only honoured but even blessed of God Himself, under the old dispensation, and declared to be lawful and honourable under the new one; and consequently he must be exonerated from the charge of having sanctioned polygamy, and thereby encouraged licentiousness."[8]

The great English orator, Edmund Burke, also admitted, "The Muhammadan Law is binding upon all, from the crowned head to the meanest subject; it is a law interwoven with an enlightened jurisprudence that ever existed in the world."[9]

From the above quotations one thing which is amply clear is that the opposition by the Church to the institution of polygamy is not because it is against the Biblic injunction, but because they have maintained celibacy and monogamy which they want to prove superior, whereas the fact remains that—(1) the Bible is silent on the point of polygamy, (2) it has not made celibacy compulsory rather it has advised to marry if one cannot control his sexual trait, and (3) the Bible

7. Kidwai, M.H., "Woman under Different Social & Religious Laws", Seema Pub., p. 110.
8. Ibid., p. 111.
9. Ibid., p. 111.

has itself granted women a position 'subordinate to man'.[10] In face of these bare facts their propaganda against the Islamic legalisation of polygamy is nothing but a religious bigotry and a political stunt to subdue the cogency of Islamic laws.

Divorce

Divorce is a corollary to the marriage laws. Perhaps it is a special institution for man. Nature has not gifted animals or birds with such sensitiveness as would prompt them to change their spouse as to human beings. The natural instincts of harmony and fidelity among animals and birds discard the chances of any change. Man being a free thinker and having a temperament of his own, can differ from each other. It is not very rare that tastes and temperaments of a husband and wife differ so radically as to upset the whole social life and happiness. Women, on the other hand, suffer from some weaknesses—of being temptative, hesitative, greedy towards worldly riches and comforts, short-temperamental and revengeful; while men are generally regardful for their prestige, for high social values, for decency of action and manners. No doubt, women also have been gifted with valuable instincts of self-suffering, self-abnegation, love and affection for nears and dears with a remarkable sense of adjustability; whereas men are lustful, selfish and proud. These differences give rise to unpleasant situations when, at times, it becomes unbearable and uncontrollable necessitating a separation in order to secure peace and harmony in rest of the family. It is in this context that divorce is permissible (*mubah*), though a painful permission. It is also a measure against exploitation of either sexes.

Almost all religions except Hinduism have allowed man to divorce his wife. But no religion except Islam has allowed a woman to get rid of her tyrant and indecent husband.

But one thing is quite certain that there was nothing more abhorrent to the Lord and his Last Messenger than

10. Bible, Corintians: 11: 8-9.

divorce. The Prophet's words, "Abghazul halal elallah at-Talaq" (the most abhorrent thing before God is divorce), jeopardises the whole family set up—especially the life of children.

The provision of divorce in Islam is not meant to provide an easy means to lustfulness and sexual infidelity. There are conditions for it:

(i) Immorality,
(ii) Bad disposition and ill-temper,
(iii) Disclosure of husband's secrecies, and
(iv) Denial of sexual conjugation,
on the part of women make her liable to be divorced; and
(i) Non-maintenance,
(ii) Misbehaviour,
(iii) Tyranny and debauchery,
(iv) Desertion of wife for more than a year,
(v) Impotency of a husband, and
(vi) Change of religion,
make a husband liable to be divorced by wife.

There is no question of marriage between an infidel man and a Mo'mina woman or an infidel woman and a Mo'min man. In case, however, if any one of the spouses changes his/her belief from Monotheism to idolatry or infidelity the *nikah* itself stands dissolved and all familial rights forfeited and there is no need to formal divorce.

The main difference between the divorce laws of Christianity and Islam lies in this, that while Christianity recognises only one condition of divorce i.e., infidelity and makes divorce a matter of public proceeding, Islam insists on conciliation and arbitration and allows divorce only on conditions of unchaste and misbehaviour. "In Christian Russia, which is more Christian than any other Christian country, there are now allowed thirty-five reasons for giving divorce. In America divorce has become a plaything. In England itself an agitation has been raised to make divorce possible under other conditions, and not to restrict it to infidelity alone."[11] The Western society being much more free today than sometimes past, the curse of divorce has jeopardised the entire social system and family of Christendom. In England, despite its stringent laws with regard to divorce, there are thousands and thousands of such couples whose life is an unbearable misery; there are hundreds of thousands who have been condemned to live a bachelor's life separately from each other. A woman separated from her husband has to forego her children. In India, of 100,000,000 Muslim population, not one in a hundred thousand takes recourse to divorce. The same is the case in Afghanistan and Turkey, though the Arabs in Hejaz and Egypt do sometimes misuse the restricted permission of divorce In Muslim countries in general divorce is considered to be the most contemptible in society. Saudi Arabia, which follows basically the Hambali doctrine, has however now recognised the principle of Talaq. A decision of the Judicial Council of Saudi Arabia (1347 AH) lays down that if the judges find that any rule of Hambali doctrine may in its application to any particular case cause hardship and be opposed to public interest, they may apply an interpretation prevailing in the other schools of law (i.e., Hanafite, Shafiite, and Malikite laws).[12] Jordan, Syria and Egypt follow the Ottoman Family Rules of 1920 with minor improvements.

The problem of divorce is not even a mentionable cause of panic in Muslim societies of the world, and even then the Christian world has been making hue and cry against this Islamic institution despite the fact that they are the worst sufferers because of its permissibility in Christianity, and the unbridled freedom and modernity. Counteracting the evil propaganda of the West the world renowned Theologian Mohammad Qutb of Egypt remarks, "As to the suggestion that divorce should take place only if the court is convinced that the fault lies with the wife and if the husband should

11. Kidwai, M.H., Ibid.
12. Faridi, F.R. & Siddiqui, M.N., "Muslim Personal Law", Markazi Maktaba Islami, Delhi-6. p. 151.

prove that to live with her is a nuisance, we wonder what honour to these people want to bring to women by making her live in the house where she is despised and where the husband ever reminds her that he no longer loves her ? Should she even then stay on in his house in order to defraud him ? Surely the law cannot sanction such a conduct. . . ."[13]

Widowhood

Widows have the same status as any other woman, whether virgin or divorced, in the sight of God. Islam does not look down upon the widows and prevents them from leading a happy and prosperous conjugal life. It not only permits but even encourages widow remarriage.

Widows have the right to inherit property from their parents as well as from their husbands. If she is issueless, she is entitled to get one-fourth of her husband's property both in cash and kind. If there are children she is entitled only for one-eighth. If the widow is the only surviving heir of the deceased she is entitled to the whole of the property of her husband. As an authority she has full right to manage her property. If she remarries, she enjoys the full right of a wife with the second husband. Thus widow is the master of her own property, either inherited from her parents, or from her husband or acquired or saved by herself.

A widow is expected to observe 'Iddat' for four months and ten days after the death of her husband. During this period she should not remarry and should remain, if possible, in the house of her husband. The main aim of Iddat is to confirm whether she is pregnant through her deceased husband or not. If she is pregnant this period is extended up to the delivery of the baby. Iddat, thus, provides a clarification against any doubt about the paternity of a child she is about to bear.

Alongwith this she will have the opportunity to observe the attitude and behaviour of her in-laws and supporters for

13. Qutb, Mohammad, "Islam—The Misunderstood Religion", Centre of Islamic Studies. Qum, Iran, p. 118.

finding out the extent to which she is liked by them during this period. This will enable her to plan the future course of action of her life in the changed situation. Now she has to perform the multiple role of mother as well as a father in looking after the well-being of children if she has a new born child. She has to take great care in the preservation of the property of her children till they are mature. She has to act as a trustee of the property inherited by her children. Even if she re-marries, responsibilities towards her previous children remain the same.

Religiously a widow is as good as any other modest woman. She can freely exercise her rights personally either in law or by religious observances. Widowhood, according to Islam, does not cast any ominous shade over her destiny. In this sense she is as pure and dignified as any married or unmarried woman.

"Marry your children, as well as the virtuous among your slaves, whether male or female; if they are poor, God will turn them into rich by His generosity, and God has an extensive knowledge of everything." (Para 18, Surah 24, Verse 32). This verse of the Holy Qur'an has very explicitly conveyed the message that every one should essentially marry, no matter whether virgin or widow. It has made obligatory on the parents, masters as well as male and female to encourage marriage. One should not hesitate to do so due to poverty, for God has taken the responsibility of providing the livelihood or making them rich. The philosophy behind it is that restraining anybody, male or female, master or slave, virgin or widow or divorced, from satisfaction of his/her sexual/natural urge in one's own interest is against the Will of God. It is the duty of the persons concerned and the society to see that no widow is restrained from remarrying if she wants. If she is issueless she must be encouraged according to the principles of Islam to remarry and lead a happy conjugal life.

What Qur'an ordained later, Prophet Mohammad did it by marrying a widow Khadija. Till the lifetime of Prophet there was no chack on widow remarriage. No inhibition of widow remarriage was found because such marriages were considered as desirable as a fresh marriage. The same ideas continued in practice among the relatives as well as his companions. The importance of marriage from religious point of view also becomes very clear when Prophet Mohammad himself says, "Wedding is my tradition, and he who refuses it refuses my tradition and is not from me." These injunctions apply to both the virgins as well as the widows. Thus the Prophet describes it as a virtuous deed.

The Islamic sanction of widow remarriage remained unchallenged throughout the Muslim world at every stage but in actual practice very few cases of remarriage have been found in the Muslim society. Everywhere, specially in the Indian sub-continent, a divorced lady is looked down upon by her in-laws as well as by the society. Nobody is readily willing to marry a widow, excepting in exceptional cases. In the traditional Muslim society they were treated as a symbol of misfortune. They were not welcome at all occasions. They also avoid taking active part on ceremonial occasions. For instance, among the Bohras a widowed mother would not break the coconut on the occasion of her son's birthday. This is an impact of Hindu culture, and it has lowered the status of women in the society.

Maintenance (*Nafqah*)

Nafqah or maintenance is one of the terms agreed upon by husband at the time of *nikah*. As per Qur'an a person becomes liable for 'nafqah' or maintenance on account of three causes, namely:

(i) From being a wife,
(ii) From being a relative, and
(iii) From being a slave or servant.

The general rule in this regard is, that only such person is entitled to maintenance (i) who has no property of his own, (ii) who is related within prohibited degrees to the person from whom he claims is in 'easy circumstances'. Exception to these general rules is as follows :

(i) it does not apply when the claimant is wife,

(ii) it does not apply when the claimants are minor sons, unmarried daughters, parents and grand-parents.

It means that wife and minor children, parents and grandparents have the right to maintenance even if they are in easy circumstances, i.e., even if they could maintain themselves on their own. Even a divorced wife, if she is expected or wants to nurse her children (up to 7 years in case of a daughter and up to 10 years in case of a son), is entitled to maintenance at her place of living. In its legal sense maintenance signifies and includes three things: (i) food, (ii) clothing, and (iii) lodging, according to the status and worth of the man.

According to the Islamic Shariah and the Muslim Personal Law, a Mohammadan is under an obligation to maintain the following persons:

(1) His descendants
(2) His ascendants
(3) His collaterals
(4) His wife.

1. *Descendants*—(a) Father's liability. The father's liability to maintain his children is absolute and is not affected by his indigence so long as he can earn. He is bound to maintain them, even if they are in their mother's custody. A father is liable to provide maintenance to the following:

(i) Minor children of either sex.
(ii) Unmarried daughter.
(iii) Married daughter, if she is poor (restricted right).
(iv) Adult son, if he is necessitous (indigent).

(b) Mother's liability. When the father has no means and is indigent, the mother is liable to maintain her children, but she is entitled to recover the expenses from the father, when circumstances permit.

(c) Grandparent's liability. If both father and mother fail to maintain their children, it is the duty of the grandfather or grandmother to maintain their children.

(d) Father-in-law's liability. There is no obligation on father-in-law to maintain the widow of his son.

2. *Ascendants*—(a) Childran's liability. As the parents are under an obligation to maintain their children, so are the children liable to provide maintenance to their parents. Every child, whether male or female, adult or minor, who has sufficient property, is responsible to supply maintenance to his parents. Under Sunni Law, whether the parents are capable of earning or not, makes no difference but under Shia Law, the children are relieved of their duty, if the parents are capable of earning.

(b) Grand-children's liability. If there are (i) no children or (ii) the children are indigent, it is the liability of the grand-children to provide maintenance to their grandparents.

3. *Collaterals*—A Mohammadan is under an obligation to maintain his collaterals (distant relations) only in the following cases:

(i) When he himself is in 'easy circumstances', and
(ii) The relation claiming to be maintained has no other means of maintenance.

4. *Wife*—(a) 'During subsistence of marriage'. The husband is bound to maintain his wife. Her right of maintenance in this case is absolute. Her right remains unprejudiced even if she has property or income of her own. The husband is bound to maintain if she fulfils the following conditions:

(i) She has attained puberty, i.e., an age at which she can render to the husband his conjugal rights.

(ii) She places and offers to place herself in his power so as to allow free access to herself at all lawful time and obeys all his lawful commands.

(b) She is not entitled to maintenance under the following circumstances:

(i) If she abandons the conjugal domicile without any valid cause.

(ii) If she refuses access to her husband.

(iii) If she is disobedient to his reasonable Commands.

(iv) If she refuses to live with her husband without any lawful excuse.

(v) If she has been imprisoned.

(vi) If she has eloped with somebody.

(vii) If she is a minor on which account marriage cannot be consummated.

(viii) If she deserts her husband voluntarily and does not perform her marital duties.

(ix) If she makes an agreement of desertion on the second marriage of her husband.

Separate maintenance can be claimed by the wife when the husband has turned her out, or the treatment or misunderstanding between them is such that it is irremediable and her return to the husband's house is likely to give rise to fresh troubles and disputes. A wife, but no other relative, is entitled to claim arrears of maintenance from her husband.

Scale of Maintenance—According to Hanafite Law, the social position of both the husband and wife must be considered in determining the scale of maintenance; in Shafe-i Law the position of husband alone and in Shia Law legitimate requirements equal to her status in society in the same city is the yardstick of maintenance.

Rights and Duties of a Wife

Besides *Mahr* and *Maintenance*, a wife owes four fundamental rights from her husband—(1) respect, (2) polity, (3) amusement, and (4) not to be deserted for four consecutive months at a stretch. In such matters the believers have been directed to follow the *sunnah* (traditions) of the Holy Prophet, whose words and manners, as per Qur'an, are the practical picture of the Commandments of God. Here a few *hadiths* are being noted in this context:

> "That is the best of Muslims whose disposition is best; and best of you are they who behave best to their wives."
>
> "Women are twin-halves of men."
>
> "The world and all things in it are valuable; but the most valuable thing in the world is a virtuous wife."
>
> "When a woman observes the five times of prayer, and fasts in the month of Ramazan, and is chaste, and is not disobedient to her husband, then tell her to enter Paradise by whichever door she likes."
>
> "God enjoins upon you to treat women well, for they are your mothers, daughters and aunts."
>
> "The rights of women are sacred. See that women are maintained in the rights granted to them."
>
> "A virtuous wife is a man's best treasure."
>
> "To give one's wife the money she requires is more important than to give alms."
>
> "Suppose a man spends one dinar in religious war, another in rescuing a slave, a third in charity, and gives the fourth to his wife, the giving of this last surpasses in merit all the others put together."
>
> "When husband and wife eat their meals together, God sends His blessing upon them and the angels pray for them."
>
> "He who bears the ill-humour of his wife patiently will earn as much merit as Job did by the patient endurance of his trials."
>
> "He who deserts his wife and children is like a runaway slave, till he returns to them, none of his fasts or prayers will be accepted by God."
>
> "You husbands have rights, and you wives have also rights. Husbands, love your wives and cherish

them. You have taken them as your wives under the security of God. Treat them well."

As against this, husbands owe from their wives five fundamental rights—e.g., (i) right to obedience, (ii) right to respect, (iii) right to safeguarding his children and property, (iv) right to maintenance of secrecy, and (v) not to be hostile to sexual satisfaction of the husband.

As man is not the subject of this work, quotations about the right of husbands is cut short here. The above-mentioned duties of wives form the right of husbands.

The Family and the Role and Status of a Woman

The very basic concept of 'nikah' (marriage) is aimed at formation of family as a social unit of the society. An Islamic family includes husband, wives, children, parents and other dependents. In Islam a family means *wijibun nafaqah*, *i.e.*, whose provision is compulsory for the sane and earning head of the family. As soon as a daughter is married, or a son starts earning, or a wife is, or takes, divorce she/he is excluded from the meaning of *wajibun nafaqah* whereas parents, whether earning or non-earning, remain as such.

Woman as a wife is a uniting force between the husband and children and as a mother a condition for salvation, whereas as a daughter she is 'Rahmat' (a blessing). The basic role of a woman (wife) is to procreate, to upbring and to discipline the offsprings. The next role of a wife is to guard her chastity, to protect the earnings and properties of her husband (in which she is also a coparcener) and to be incharge of her family affairs. She is never a servant of her husband and she can even deny to feed her children, and if she denies the husband has no right to compel her to feed his children. If she is ill-treated, or deserted for more than a year, or not maintained, or not paid 'mahr' on call, she can apply for a divorce before a *Qazi* (a religious Judge) and is entitled to get divorce along with 'mahr' and the cost of lapsed maintenance. Her role in family is no less important than that of her husband—rather, according to Qur'anic injunction, she occupies a position superior to her husband so far her right over children is concerned. According to a *hadith* if a mother calls her son/daughter engaged in *Namaz* (prayer) it is incumbent upon him/her to make voice so that she may know that he/she is engaged in *namaz*, if she again calls him/her the same or louder voice should be made, and if she calls a third time it becomes obligatory on son/daughter to break *namaz* and to rush to her and obey her order. But such provision in not available for one's father. In the matter of salvation of children both father and mother stand equal, the mother having an edge over the father inasmuch as her name comes first and then of the father. Rights of parents do not absolve even after their death. The offspring cannot speak loud or raise brows, or say 'fie' even when hurt or shocked at their hands. They cannot change their belief from infidelity to Monotheism but after taking their mother's permission. But after once believing in Monotheism parents' right to interfere in following the 'wajibaat' (essential) of Islam ceases.

Education is 'wajib' (compulsory) equally for male and female with the only condition of 'hijab' (purdah) and safety of chastity. Neither parents, nor anybody else is allowed to prohibit his son/daughter from the pursuit of knowledge.

In case of inheritance, a woman gets half the share of her brother in her father's property and one-eighth in her husband's properties if she has born children and one-fourth if she has no children, besides *mahr* and maintenance.

In all other social and political matters a woman has rights equal to that of a man. The husband cannot check her from meeting her parents or other near relatives but where her chastity or life would be in danger. In case of immoral practices both husband and wife are equally entitled to take divorce, but both at pecuniary loss. The rights of women in Islam are sacred.

A woman is entitled to stipulation at the time of marriage and that is binding upon the husband. It must be fulfilled and adhered to otherwise she would have the right to get the marriage dissolved. In the fixation of *mahr* the woman has a high-hand and she is at liberty to lay her own terms and amount of *mahr*. She can bargain on her terms.

Jihad and maintenance of family are not the obligations of a woman. Her *Jihad* is to be loyal to her husband. She is free to adhere to her original faith or to change over to her husband's faith—nobody can compel her to follow his suit. She is allowed to vote. If the husband misbehaves her, she can sue in the court of law for damages.

Though maintenance of family is not obligatory for women, they are allowed to take up jobs suited to them in times of need.

On divorce, the husband is not entitled to take away the custody of his children until nine years in case of daughter and seven years in case of a son, when the obligation of marriage/tutelage comes over the head of father. For this period she is entitled to maintenance of children.

Women's right to property is exclusive of all family obligations, whereas men's right to property carries the burden of the entire family. During pre-marriage period her upkeep and livelihood is the responsibility of her father, during marital tenure of her husband and after husband of her children. Woman is fully entitled to procure, to hold and to exploit her wealth to her benefit according to her sweet will. She has a right to pre-emption in respect of her 'mahr' and maintenance.

The legal position of a woman is thus quite secured, and her social position as wife dignified and as mother exalted to the highest rung, in Islam.

The family laws of Islam are interwoven with mutual rights and obligations in order to ensure the best cohesion between its members to keep its shape intact and ensure peace and harmony, love and dignity of each individual. The family or social laws of Islam do not allow any one 'complete freedom'—be it male or female, husband or wife. There is nothing like Western freedom in Islam. Every right carries some obligations, and everyone has to pay for the sincerity, love and affection of the other in the same coin. The prestige and dignity of man, whether male or female, young or old, is completely secured in Islam. Nobody is allowed to cast aspersion or use derogatory words or act in an ugly manner against any one, without earning a sin and being liable to punishment before the law. Nobody can deny or usurp the social or material right of other. Nobody can deny his familial obligations.

The data collected from the field on various aspects of married family life of women are being presented here in tabular form along with their analysis and interpretation in the light of classified data.

The first question asked from the respondents was—"Please state (a) Your and your husband's age at marriage, (b) The prevalent age of marriage of girls and boys, and (c) The ideal age of marriage for girls and boys. Their responses are given in Table 1.

It is evident from the table that the majority (55.0%) of the respondents were married in the age-group of 16-20 years whereas the majority of 64.0% of the husbands were married in the age-group of 21-25 years. According to the present biological advice the proper age at marriage for girls is 20 and above and that of boys 25 and above. In this light the ages of marriage of respondents and their spouses appear to be early, as majority of the women respondents were married at ages below 20 and their husbands at ages below 25 years. 21.6% of the respondents were married in the age-group of 21-25 years and 19.0% in the age below 15 years whereas only 4.3% of the respondents were married at 26 and above. Thus it can be said that the second majority of the respondents were married at the correct and advised age for marriage of girls and an insignificant percentage (4.3%) of respondents were married at an age of 26 or above, which may be because of their engagement in academic pursuit. On the basis of these data it may also be interpreted that a sizeable percentage of 19 were married in early age of 15 or even below that. The same picture is evident in case of their husbands. 10.6% of the husbands are reported to be married in the age-group of 16-20 years and 25.3% in the age of 26 years or above. Thus, in their case, it can be said that a significant percentage of husbands were married early; but, at the same time, 25.3% of them were married at an age advised by biologists. It may,

Table 1

Age at Marriage

(Percentage in brackets)

Age at marriage (yrs)	*Respondent's and her husband's age*		*Prevalent age of marriage*		*Ideal age of marriage*	
	Respondents	*Husband*	*Girl*	*Boy*	*Girl*	*Boy*
Up to 15	57(19.0)	—	—	—	—	—
16-20	165(55.0)	32(10.6)	221(73.6)	—	131(43.6)	—
21-25	65(21.6)	192(64.0)	79(26.4)	97(32.4)	169(56.4)	222(74)
26+	13(4.4)	76(25.4)	—	203(67.6)	—	78(26.0)
Total	300(100)	300(100)	300(100)	300(100)	300(100)	300(100)

therefore, be interpreted that the process of rationalisation has set in the Muslim society; but it cannot be said that they are not completely out of the traditional clutches of society.

So far the prevalent age of marriage in the Muslim society is concerned, 73.6% of the girls are reported to be married, in the present age, in the age-group of 16-20 years and 26.3% in the age-group of 21-25 years. This figure suggests a little improvement in the situation in case of women and a marked improvement in case of boys, in whose case 67.6% are reported to have been married in the age-group of 26 and above and only 32.3% in the age-group of 21-25 years.

With regard to the ideal age of marriage, the majority of 56.3% of the respondents are in favour of 21-25 years of age for girls and 74.0% of them suggest the same age for boys as the ideal age of marriage. In the opinion of 43.6% of the respondents the ideal age for girls is 16-20 years and 26.0% of them suggest the age of 26 and above as the ideal age of marriage for boys. While the majority view with regard to girls is rational, it is irrational in case of boys. Only 26.0% of the women respondents have given the rational age (of 26 years and above) as the ideal age for marriage of boys and 56.3% have given rational age of 21-25 years for girls. These figures also suggest that the process of rationalisation of attitude as well as practice has well set in the Muslim society. But, at the same, they cannot be said to be fairly out of the clutches of traditionalism.

The next question asked from the women respondents was, "What, in your opinion, is the most important reason for a change in the marriage age in present day society ?" This question was asked to identify the factors and forces instrumental in changing the attitude of the Muslim society with regard to age of marriage.

It appears from Table 2 that the most important reason given by the respondents for change in marriage age is the poor economy of the community (51.0%). 20% of the respondents have said that education is instrumental in rationalising the attitude of the Muslims in respect of age of marriage, 15.0% of them have reported that it is non-

Table 2

Reasons of Change in Marriage Age

(Percentage in brackets)

Educational Level	*Reasons*					*Total*
	Marriage law	*Poor economy*	*Education*	*N.A of good partner*	*Western influence*	
Illiterate	4(6.8)	36(62.0)	7(12.0)	7(12.0)	4(6.8)	58
Middle	6(6.3)	60(63.1)	10(10.5)	15(15.7)	4(4.2)	95
Matric	4(4.7)	31(36.9)	30(35.7)	14(16.6)	5(5.9)	84
Graduate	5(11.1)	18(40.0)	11(24.4)	7(15.5)	4(8.8)	45
Post-Graduate	3(16.6)	8(44.4)	[illegible](22.2)	2(11.1)	1(5.5)	18
Total	22(7.3)	153(51.0)	62(20.6)	45(15.0)	18(6.0)	300

availability of suitable match which lingers marriage, especially of girls; whereas insignificant percentages of 7.3 and 6.0 of the respondents have admitted the fear of law or the western influence to be instrumental in changing marriage age. Thus it may be interpreted that poverty and spread of secular education are the two main causes of change, or upgradation, of the marriage age.

On literacy basis we find no consistency in the pattern of response in favour of any of the reasons mentioned by the women respondents, hence literacy does not appear to be relevant in this respect.

From Table 3A it is evident that the most important qualities favoured by the highest and the second highest percentages of respondents is 'employment of the boy' and his academic achievements, the third quality being lineage or caste, fourth economic status and then soundness of his physique and character. It means that the approach of the women respondents in the matter of selection of spouse is realistic and wise, and at the same time materialistic one. These Muslim women have given the least importance to the qualities of character, outlook and physical soundness which are more dependable and durable and they have relied in economic factors, and for the very purpose to educational factor, which cannot be relied upon with surety. Thus it can be interpreted that the Muslim women are seized of the impact of materialism and their religious wisdom is dooming down with the advancement of material world. On age basis, however, there does not appear any significant relevance of age to the response patterns; and, hence, it can be interpreted that age variable is not relevant in this respect.

So far Table 3B (education basis) is concerned we see almost similar response and nothing new has emerged excepting that the two former qualities of employment of the boy and education achievement have been favoured by a greater majority of respondents and the other four qualities by a smaller percentage. In this table also we do not find any significant consistency of educational level to the response pattern.

Table 3A

What qualities would you appreciate in selecting a spouse for a girl of your family? (Age Basis)

(Percentage in brackets)

Age-Group	*Qualities*						*Total*
	Education	*Employment*	*Economic status*	*Lineage*	*Physique*	*Character and outlook*	
Up to 25	13(17.3)	18(24.0)	14(18 6)	11(14.6)	10(13.3)	9(12.0)	75
26-35 yrs.	20(22.2)	30(33.3)	13(14.4)	10(11.1)	10(11.1)	7(7.7)	90
36-45 yrs.	23(28.0)	31(37.8)	8(9.7)	9(10.9)	7(8.5)	4(4.8)	82
46+	10(18.8)	16(30.1)	3(5.6)	12(22.6)	3(5.6)	9(16.9)	53
Total	66(22.0)	95(26.3)	38(12.6)	42(14.0)	30(10.0)	29(9.6)	300

Table 3B

What qualities would you appreciate in selecting a spouse for a girl of your family? (Education Basis)

(Percentage in brackets)

Education level of respondents	Qualities					
	Education	Employment	Economic status	Lineage	Good physique	Character and outlook
Illiterate	4(6.8)	29(50.0)	11(18.9)	10(17.2)	1(1.7)	3(5.1)
Literate	11(11.5)	55(57.8)	12(12.6)	10(10.5)	3(3.1)	4(4.2)
Matric	20(23.8)	40(47.6)	8(9.5)	8(9.5)	2(4.4)	2(4.4)
Graduate	18(40.0)	15(33.3)	3(6.6)	5(11.1)	2(4.4)	2(4.4)
Post-Graduate	10(55.5)	4(22.2)	1(5.5)	—	3(16 6)	—
Total	63(21.0)	143(47.6)	35(11.6)	33(11.0)	11(3.6)	15(5.0)

Table 4A

Would you like to give freedom to your daughter in selecting her spouse? (Education Basis)

(Percentage in brackets)

Educational level	*Extent of freedom*				
	Not at all	*To some extent*	*To a greater extent*	*Depends on circumstances*	*Total*
Illiterate	33(56.8)	7(12.0)	—	18(31.0)	58
Literate	57(60.0)	15(15.7)	—	23(24.2)	95
Matric	10(11.9)	32(38.0)	2(2.3)	40(47.6)	84
Graduate	4(8.8)	11(24.4)	8(17.7)	22(48.8)	45
Post-Graduate	—	5(27.7)	3(16.6)	10(55.5)	18
Total	104(34.6)	70(23.3)	13(4.3)	113(37.6)	300

Table 4B

(Income Basis)

Up to 500	17(56.6)	2(6.6)	—	11(36.6)	30
501-1000	19(34.5)	1(9.0)	—	31(50.3)	55
1001-1500	22(23.9)	17(18.4)	5(5.4)	48(52.1)	92
1501-2000	14(15.5)	29(32.2)	7(7.7)	40(44.4)	90
2001 +	3(9.0)	11(33.3)	4(12.1)	15 (45.4)	33
Total	75(25.0)	64(21.3)	16(5.3)	145(48.3)	300

From Tables 4A and 4B it is evident that the highest percentages of response (37.6% and 48.3%) have gone in favour of 'depends on circumstances'. It means that majorities of respondents in case of the two variables have kept their opinion reserved in the matter of giving freedom of choosing spouse by their daughters. It depends on situation where they can or cannot allow the bride to choose their spouse directly or indirectly or not at all. Despite this reservation, this much is clear that they are not against giving a free hand to the girl in the matter of choosing her spouse—and this is a great departure, in case of Muslim women, from their traditional rigidity in such matters. It shows that the attitude of Muslim women has undergone a drastic change and now they are ready to allow their girls or daughter to exercise their free will in the matter of selecting their spouses if and to the extent the situation allows them to do so.

Neither education nor income of the respondents appear to be relevant to their responses with the rise or fall in their levels of education or income.

It is evident from Table 5 that in case of 32.6% of the respondents the patriarchs consult them occasionally in family affairs, 31.3% of the respondents report that their patriarchs consult them frequently, 18.3% of them have said that the patriarchs consult them in each and every matter relating to family affairs whereas in case of 17.6% of them the patriarchs never consult the respondents. In the light of this pattern of response it may be interpreted that the patriarchs of 18.3% of the respondents have realised the importance of their housewives and have given them equal status and due position in family and 31.3% of the patriarchs have shown a good degree of rationalism by consulting their female counterparts frequently, whereas 32.6% of them give little importance to their female members of the family and 17.6% of the patriarchs are still rigid in their traditional attitude that 'women have wisdom of very low degree and hence they should not be consulted in important matters or in any matter'. Thus about 50% of the patriarchs have conceived or have admitted the wisdom and importance of women, 32.6% are in mid-way

Table 5

Do the patriarchs consult you in making decisions in family affairs?

(ercentage in brackets)

Educational level	*Frequency of consultation*				
	Never	*Occasionally*	*Frequently*	*Always*	*Total*
Illiterate	18(31.0)	25,43.1)	11(18.9)	4(6.8)	58
Literate	27(28.4)	43(45.2)	18(18.9)	7(7.3)	95
Matriculate	8(9.5)	22(26.1)	34(40.4)	20(23.8)	84
Graduate	—	5(11.1)	24(53.3)	16(35.5)	45
Post-Graduate	—	3(16.6)	7(38.8)	8(44.4)	18
Total	53(17.6)	98(32 6)	94(31.3)	55(18.3)	300

wheras 17.6% are hundred per cent tradition-oriented and conservative in their attitude and outlook, which is un-Islamic. Islam has trusted in their better-halves and has given to women a status equal to men. It is another thing that women being mostly engaged in household affairs, they might not be well-versed with the affairs of the outside world as the menfolk of the world are ignorant of females' domain; and, in view of this reality the male members might not consult their female partners on many occasions. But both being life-partners of each other, such discussions and conversations cannot be ruled out and carry no stigma if they do so.

The next question asked from the respondents was "What is the significance of Mahr?" The respondents were provided four response categories of (1) security for the wife, (2) religious decree, (3) price of wife's self, and (4) a help to bride's guardian. The responses obtained from them are given in Table 6.

It is evident from the table that 39.3% of the respondemts take *mahr* as a safeguard or security against divorce, sudden demise of the husband or any other such mishap, 31.6% treat it as a divine bounty conferred upon by religious sanction, 17.0% treat it as the price for their self-surrender to the husband or a stranger and 12.0% think it to be a sort of help to their guardians. In reality, *mahr* is a safeguard like an insurance against a mishap or divorce or death of the husband, which the majority of the respondents have accepted. It may, therefore, be interpreted that the majority of the respondents realise the importance of *mahr* as an insurance of life for chaste housewives. On education basis, however, the table does not show any significant variation in the response pattern with the rise or fall in the level of education. Hence education cannot be said to have any relevance with the response pattern.

Another question asked from the respondents was, "Do you favour dowry system? If no, please suggest its solution." The problem of dowry is the most-talked of and the burning issue of the present age and both people and government are equally anxious to get rid of this social evil and for that

Table 6

What is the significance of mahr in your opiuion?

(Percentage in brackets)

	Significance of m hr				
Educational level	*Security for wife*	*Religious decree*	*Price of wife's self*	*A help to bride's guardian*	*Total*
Illiterate	22(37 9)	16(27.5)	9(15.5)	11(18.9)	58
Literate	35(36.8)	30(31.5)	17(17.8)	13(13.6)	95
Matriculate	35(41.6)	22(26.1)	18(21.4)	9(10.7)	84
Graduate	16(35.5)	20(44.4)	6(13.3)	3(6.6)	18
Post-Graduate	10(55.5)	7(38.8)	1(5.5)	—	18
Total	118(39.3)	95(31.6)	51(17.0)	36(12.0)	300

government of India has passed an Act known as 'Anti-Dowry Act'. Every now and then we find incidences of dowry-murders in the newspapers. Women being the main target of this evil, are supposed to think over the problem and conclud-ed some ways and means of eradication of this evil. With this fact in view, this question was put to the Muslim woman respondents to know their reaction with regard to dowry system as well as their suggestions for its eradication. The responses obtained from them are given below in Tables 7 and 8—this question having been split up in two parts—(1) reflecting the attitude of Muslim women regarding dowry system and (2) suggestions.

Table 7

Do you favour Dowry System?

(Percentage in brackets)

Educational level	*Yes*	*No*	*Total*
Illiterate	10(17.2)	48(82.7)	58
Literate	13(13.6)	82(86.3)	95
Matriculate	6(7.1)	78(92.8)	94
Graduate	4(8.8)	41(91.1)	45
Post-Graduate	—	18(100.0)	18
Total	33(11.0)	267(89.0)	300

It is obvious from the table that 89.0% of the women respondents are against the dowry system and they do not approve of it. Still it is surprising that despite well-known evils of this curse 11.0% the Muslim women under study have supported this system, which speaks of the fact that the seed of the crime lies in the society itself; and, therefore, the remedy also should come from within the society. These people, though in minority, like this system to continue and support it. These people may be those who are well-to-do and/or who have ambitions for getting or catching big fries for their daughters as spouse with the help of heavy offers. On literacy basis there does not appear to be any significant relevance, but this much is evident that with the rise in literacy level the response against the system has risen which means that literate and educated people do not support this evil.

During conversation it was revealed that many poor families are also in support of dowry system, because without offering dowry or fulfilling the demands of the groom it is very difficult, if not impossible, to get even an ordinary match for poor girls. The respondents complained that dowry system is the creation of the affluent and they are raising the rate of offers day by day making a hell for the poor stratum of the society, whether Muslim or non-Muslim. They also revealed that there is a competition among the rich and higly-placed category of the Muslim community to catch better and better match for their daughters, may what he demand. It was also disclosed during conversation that among those who favour or like dowry system to continue are those poor or rich people who have only sons or sons in higher number than daughters.

It is apparent from the table that the respondents were provided four categories of response in order to know their reaction to rational approaches to the problem. The response categories were—(1) the youth should be educated against it, (2) the supporters of dowry should be boycotted, (3) the guilty should be publicly punished, and (4) the guilty should be legally punished. The table shows that the majority (58.0%) of the respondents have favoured legal action against the persons taking or demanding dowry. 30.0% of the respondents have favoured punishment of the culprits in public gatherings, 10.0% of them have supported social boycott of such persons and an insignificant percentage of 2.0% has suggested education of youth against this evil. This response pattern suggests that people under study have put in greater reliance in the legal process, but, perhaps, they do not know the helplessness of law for want of proper evidences. Unless there is proper will and enough courage among the people to help the law, such type of offences cannot be brought on paper. The law is, no doubt, ready to help the people provided they generate courage to fight against this evil. Public prosecution of the guilty people may also be provided for in law if people make

Table 8

If no, please suggest its solution

(Percentage in brackets)

	Suggestions				
Educational level of respondents	*The youth should be educated against it*	*The supporters of dowry should be boycotted*	*The guilty should be publicly punished*	*The guilty should be legally punished*	*Total*
Illiterate	2(3.4)	5(8.6)	20(34.4)	31(53.4)	58
Literate	—	5(5.2)	28(29.4)	62(65.2)	95
Matriculate	2(2.3)	12(14.2)	20(23.8)	50(59.5)	84
Graduate	1(2.2)	6(13.3)	17(37.7)	21(46.6)	45
Post-Graduate	1(5.5)	2(11.1)	5(27.7)	10(55.4)	18
Total	6(2.0)	30(10.0)	90(30.0)	174(58.0)	300

such demand and the process is helpful in bringing the culprit to book. A very small support for social boycott among the women respondents suggests that they do not, perhaps, find the social environment congenial to such action. It was, no doubt, a good and effective suggestion but it could not fetch equally higher favour from the respondents. And it is this situation which makes law helpless. Unless people are wilfully ready to eradicate this, or any such, evil no amount of legislation can bear fruit. Education of youth was also a good suggestion, which also failed to fetch proper support. People should know that dowry system is not only a social evil but a social crime giving birth to many greater crimes and, hence, it must be nipped in the bud. Government is making its every possible effort to help the people, but for that public opinion must come forward in support of the law and the executive. A resolve on the part of people shall surely eradicate this evil.

On literacy basis there does not appear any consistency in response patterns, and hence literacy variable cannot be said to be relevant to the response pattern.

The next question put before the respondents was, "What would you do if your husband stops your maintenance and is not ready to pay the same honourably?" Every Muslim woman knows that *mahr* and maintenance are the two basic rights of women, because it is contracted on the very occasion of marriage. But many of them might not be aware that these constitute to be their legal right and they are at liberty to realise the same from their husband through legal process. Some may not have the courage to go to court, for social reasons, and fight the case. Some may be afraid of the lengthy process of law and the heavy expenses and botherations in the contest. Keeping these factors in view, the respondents were asked this question. The respondents were also provided four response categories mentioned in Table 9.

It is evident from the table that the majority of 41.3% of the respondents have preferred to press their husband to pay maintenance, whereas 35.6% have stated that they will

Table 9

What would you do if your husband stops your maintenance and is not ready to pay the same honourably ?

(Percentage in brackets)

Educational level	*Actions suggested*				*Total*
	I shall press him socially	*I shall take divorce*	*I shall take up a job*	*I shall contest in law court*	
Illiterate	26(44.8)	[illegible](10.3)	18(31.0)	8(13.7)	58
Literate	46(48.4)	4(4.2)	30(31.5)	1 (15.7)	95
Matric	36(42.8)	4(4.7)	29(34.5)	15(17.[illegible])	84
Graduate	12(26.6)	3(6.6)	21(46.6)	9(20.0)	45
Post-Graduate	4(22.2)	1(5.[illegible])	9(50.0)	4(22.2)	18
Total	124(41.3)	18(6.0)	107(35.6)	51(17.[illegible])	300

take up some earning job to mitigate their miseries than to quarrel with the husband. 17.0% of the respondents have shown courage to realise maintenance through legal proces in the court of law and 6.0% of them have said that they would take divorce and shall lead a free life. This minority of the respondents preferring to take divorce may be those who have means of livelihood at their maternal place or have saving balance to support themselves after taking divorce. These response patterns show that majority of the respondents believe in the effectiveness of the social pressure in realising the maintenance or are shy of adopting daring measures and utilising their right to seek justice through the legal process. This is obviously because they are still tradition dominated and have not developed enough courage to face their arrogant husbands in the law courts. The second majority of the respondents proposes to take up job and earn money for their maintenance. Their approach seems to be fairly rational, but sneaks of want of courage and propriety.

The table further shows that 13.7% of illiterates, 15.7% of literates, 17.8% of matriculates, 20.0% of graduates and 22.2% of post-graduates are ready to ventilate their grievance and seek justice from the law courts. At the same time 31.0% of illiterates, 31.5% of literates, 34.5% of matriculates, 46.6% of graduates and 50.0% of post-graduates have said that they would take up some job. These response patterns show a consistent rise in the percentages of response with the rise in literacy level. Hence it may be interpreted that literacy is relevant to the response patterns in both the latter cases signifying rational approach for acquiring their right.

The next question put to the respondents was, "Do you favour re-marriage of the following?" The types of widow's case placed before the respondents were—(1) childless young widows, (2) widow having children, (3) a middle-aged widow having no support, and (4) none should marry. The case of old widows was not placed before them because they might not require re-marriage for sexual reasons, and they have earning children to support her even if the husband dies. Middle-aged and young ladies may be in need of a male both for sexual reason and for maintenance of self and children. It is

Table 10

Do you favour re-marriage of the following?

(Percentage in brackets)

	Type of widow				
Educational level	*A childless young widow*	*A widow having children*	*A middle-aged widow having no support*	*No widow should marry*	*Total*
Illiterate	35(60.3)	8(13.7)	7(12.0)	8(13.7)	58
Literate	39(41.0)	40(42.0)	5(5.2)	11(11.5)	95
Matriculate	27(32.1)	41(48.8)	11(13.0)	5(5.9)	84
Graduate	17(37.7)	22(48.8)	6(13.3)	—	45
Post-Graduate	6(33.3)	10(55.5)	2(11.1)	—	18
Total	124(41.3)	121(40.3)	31(10.3)	21(8.0)	300

a well-known fact that Islam allows widow re-marriage and, unlike Hindus, widow re-marriage is not a taboo in Muslim society.

The table shows that the first (41.3%) and second (40.3%) majorities of the respondents have favoured re-marriage of childless young widows and widows having children and very small percentages of 10.3 and 8.0 have favoured re-marriage of middle-aged widows having no support and 'no widow should marry'. While the case of the third category of middle-aged supportless ladies is not so serious to necessarily justify their re-marriage, the fourth category of responses is traditional or irrational; and hence these two cases have fetched little or the least support from the respondents. The response patterns show that the approach of majority (81.6%) of the respondents is quite logical and rational, while 8.0% of the respondents appear to be tradition-dominated.

It is further evident from the table that in case of the former two categories of widows, i.e., childless young widows and widows having children, the responses have either consistently fallen with the rise in literacy level or have consistently risen with the rise in literacy level (in second case). This consistency in response patterns in the first two cases is the relevance of literacy level to the response patterns. Hence it may be interpreted that literacy is relevant, in the case of first two categories of cases, to the response patterns.

The next question put to the respondents was, "Why, in your opinion, a male prefers to become polygymous?" The causes generally attributed to polygamy or polygyny are—(1) Man's excessive sexual urge, (2) female's desertion of rude behaviour, or (3) permanent illness of the wife, or (4) issuelessness. In view of these facts the respondents were provided with six response categories of (1) no issue, (2) negligence towards husband, (3) refusal to sexual intercourse, (4) disobedience of wife, (5) her quarrelsome nature, (6) bad character of wife, and (7) any other. The responses obtained from them are given in Table 11.

Table 11

Why in your opinion a male prefers to become polygynous?

Educational level	*No issue*	*Negligence towards husband*	*Refusal to sexual intercourse*	*Disobedience*	*Quarrelsome nature*	*Bad character of wife*	*Any other*
Illiterate =58	11 18.9	7 12.0	10 17.2	7 12.0	5 8.6	8 13.7	10 17.2
Literate =95	18 18.9	13 13. 6	12 12.6	7 7.3	22 23.1	8 8.4	15 15.7
Matric =84	9 10.7	7 8.3	10 11.9	14 16.6	15 17.8	9 10.7	20 23.8
Graduate =45	7 15.5	3 6.6	5 11.1	7 15.5	5 11.1	7 15.5	11 24.4
Post-Graduate =18	3 16.6	4 22.2	2 11.1	2 11.1	—	—	7 38.8
Total =300	46 15.3	34 11.3	39 13.0	37 12.3	47 15.6	32 10.6	63 21.0

Decimal figures are percentages.

The above table indicates that the respondents' majority of 21.0% has responded in favour of reason other than the six specified reasons. It may be some chronic disease or disablement of the wife which might restrain the husband from all comforts of life and compel him to have an alternative in the shape of another wife. Generally Indian males, especially Muslims, do not like to have another wife except in very distressing circumstances. The next majority of 15.6% has given the reason of 'quarrelsomeness of the wife'to be the next important reason for polygyny. 15.3% of the women respondents have declared issuelessness of the wife to be the reason of polygyny, whereas 12.3% of them have suggested disobedience of wife and 11.3% have suggested negligence towards husband to be the reasons of polygyny. Thus disablement, quarrelsome nature and issueless and refusal to sex union of the wife appear to be the most important reasons, in the opinion of respondents, of polygyny. The other reasons like negligence of husband and disobedience of the wife appear to be of lesser importance. Indian temperament is generally a tolerant one and males of Indian origin are much more submissive, tolerant and accommodative than their counterparts in other countries and they ignore petty matters in order to keep family coherence and peace intact. It is only in very exceptional and distressing cases where divorce or polygyny are decided.

The table further shows that except in case of refusal to sex union, in no case consistency of response is found with change in education level of the respondents. It may, therefore, be interpreted that literacy and education are not much significant in this regard.

Summary

The data analysed in the present chapter reveal that in the past 19.0 per cent of Muslim women were married below 15 years of age and men between 21-25 years of age, which is rational in case of males and early age in case of girls as per the yardstick fixed in the present days. The tables also show that the marriage age of both men and women has risen inasmuch as 67.6 per cent of the boys were married after

26 years of age and no girl was married below 15 years. Majority of the girls are reported to be married between 16-20 years which is quite rational. Thus the tables show no gap between ideology and practice, because the ideal age suggested by the respondents as well as their practice in the present age both are quite in consonance with the norms fixed by government. The shift in the age of marriage has been attributed to poor economy, mass education and non-availability of suitable match. According to the respondents, education, employment and economic status are the most important qualities which one should seek in a proposed groom for one's girl. The traditional norms of lineage, physique and character and outlook of the boy have been meagrely favoured by the respondents. Hence it can be said that the attitude and normative behaviour of the Muslim society has started shifting from traditionalism to rationality. A drastic change in the attitude is also witnessed with regard to freedom to girls in the matter of selecting their spouse. The women under study are ready to allow their young girls to select their spouse either directly, or indirectly according to the demand of the situation; whereas, in traditional Muslim society virgins were not allowed even to raise voice or to talk to a stranger or express their opinion in the matter of settlement of their marriage. This indicates a marked shift in the attitude and outlook of the present-day Muslim society from traditionalism to modernity. A marked change in the attitude of Muslim patriarchs has also been reflected from the response in respect of consultation in matters of family affairs. The patriarchs, in majority of the cases, are reported to be consulting their female members of the family either occasionally (38.6%) or frequently (31.3%) or invariably (18.3%); whereas in the traditional Muslim society women were rarely consulted in any affair of life by the patriarch. In the past *mahr* was just a symbolic term, but now, according to the statement of respondents, the Muslim women have realised the importance of it as an effective security against mishaps and divorce by husbands has been accepted by majority of the respondents. Dowry system has been rejected by 89 per cent of the Muslim women and majority of them (58.0%) have suggested drastic

legal action against those who demand or take dowry. But the responses reveal that still there are women (11%) who support dowry system and through the informal chat it was disclosed that these supporters of dowry system come from both rich and poor families. It was also reported by the respondents that this system has become so rampant in the society that if a poor does not afford to meet the demands of the groom side his daughter cannot be married. The women respondents also complained that the rich people have started a competition in offering dowries for catching better and better match for their girls and this trend has made a hell for the poor. Majority of the women respondents are in favour of widow remarriage, especially of childless young widows and widows having children. Remarriage of middle-aged widows has been favoured by a very small percentage of 10.3, whereas 8.0 per cent of the respondents completely reject the idea of widow-remarriage. Consciousness with regard to maintenance being the right of women has aroused and a sizeable section (17.0%) of Muslim women are ready to realise this right from their arrogant husband through legal measures and 35.6% of them have developed a courage to take earning jobs in order to mitigate their miseries in case their husbands desert them and refuse to pay maintenance to them. This is a marked shift in the attitude of Muslim women, because in the traditional Muslim society no woman could think to take a job outside the home or to go to court. Chronic disease, permanent disablement, refusal to sexual intercourse and quarrelsome nature of the wife has been said to be the main reasons of a husband preferring polygyny. The table reflects that the Indian males in general and the Muslim males in particular are submissive and tolerant with regard to their family life and they do not decide to have another wife except in very exceptional and distressing circumstances where there is no way out. Thus, in totality of the case, we find the Muslim society coming out from traditionalism and stepping towards rationalism and in many aspects towards modernism. Thus it can be interpreted that the urban Muslim society is passing through a transitional phase and tradition-modernity-continuum has set in.

5

Education

Education has been the primary concern of all civilizations and revolutions. At all times in the history of Man he has been bestowed with divine Teachers and Reformers, whom we know as 'prophets' or messengers of God. The first Man on this Earth was a prophet, whom God specialised with 'Ilm' (knowledge).[1] In order to enlighten the human race and reform their manners God had have sent 124,000 divine teachers and reformers to this earth giving His mission the final shape at the hands of Muhammad (PUH). It is the divine apostles through whom God has been giving impetus to the fatigued wheels of human destiny from time to time.

According to Qur'an it was 'Ilm' of Adam which falsified the claim of Angels with regard to the governance of the earth.[2] Hence man is born leader of the universe with special instincts of '*Ilm*' and '*Wisdom*', and he must protect these precious blessings of God. And it is this goal to achieve which education has been made compulsory for both men and women: "Talab al Ilmo farizatun 'ala kulle mo'minun wa mo'minatun" (i.e., acquisition of knowledge is compulsory for every believer and believeress).

1. Reyaz-a-Nazira, Vol. II, p. 218.
2. Qur'an, Sura 2, vv.

God laid the foundations of this Universe on '*Ilm*' (knowledge) and '*hikmah*' (science) and He encouraged us, at 756 occasions in Qur'an to meditate into the Creation; and this was a necessary corollary to His blessing of 'wisdom. 'Meditation into the creation of God' has been said to be the 'best worship'. Babul Ilm Hazrat Ali says: "*Laisal ibadata kasratis Sawm was Salat, innamul ibadat at-tafakkure fi Son'ati-Allahe'Azz wa Jalle*" [Verily abundance of *namaz* and *roza* is not the only devotion (to God), rather meditation into the creation of Allah, the Greatest and the Most Magnificent, is the real worship]. Again fortified it Al-Imam as-Sadique: "Inna-at-tafakkure Sa'atin khairum min qeyam-il-Laile" (i.e., an hour of meditation into the words and creations of God is better than standing the whole night in prayers).[3] All these and other such efforts are destined to the glory of Man. How can one say that religion is opium ?

Meditation into a thing brings man nearer to reality and removes doubts, widens one's experience and knowledge and gives way to new discoveries, encourages man to explore new avenues of life and comfort, and best of all it gives a staunch faith in God, thus providing him peace both corporally and spiritually. It removes poverty of thinking and living and makes man conscious of freedom and stability. Meditation makes man able to resolve the knotty problems of life and disciplines his manners. Call for meditation into the Creation of God is in itself a call for peace and progress. Meditation makes man optimistic, brave and believing in action, and this is the symbol of Life.

Meditation into the creations of God has widened the field and scope of knowledge and activity of man. It is the persistent meditation of Aristotle, Socrate and others which acknowledged the Roman civilization throughout the world. It is the meditation of Aryabhatta, Brahmagupta (A.D. 628), Bhaskara (A.D. 12th century) and others which introduced the Indian civilization to the Arabs; and it is the meditation of Jabir bin Hayyan, Bu Ali Senna, Tusi, Al-Kashi and many

3. Mahdi, S.M., "Meditation Worship and Its Importance", an essay published in 'Iqra' Daily of Calcutta, 4th May, 1984.

others which introduced the Islamic civilization to Europe, Russia and America. And it is the meditation of the Western scientists which has unfolded the secrets of celestial world. It is meditation which will one day bring us nearest to the Most Glorious Truth—Allah.

While the modern world lays great emphasis on the scientific and objective goals, i.e., acquiring power over the nature, the Islam suggests a more vicious scope of education. The Prophet of Islam says: "Al-Ilmo Ilmane—Ilm-ul-Abdan wal Ilm-ul-Adyan", i.e., knowledge is for two sorts—corporal knowledge and spiritual knowledge. This definition of knowledge includes both physical and spiritual universes within the meaning of 'Ilm', thereby expanding the field of education. While the object of physical knowledge is to cater to the worldly needs and requirement of man, the spiritual knowledge aims at character building. Human being in its creation is a synthesis of matter and spirit, and, hence, his requirements are also two-dimensional—first material requirements of food, cloth, shelter and comfort; and second spiritual requirements of respect, peace and harmony, justice and fairplay. Hence mere material well-being is not enough for the all-round progress of human race. Commendable technical advancement has, no doubt, contributed to a large number of faculties of material knowledge but at the same time it has retarded the pace of advance in thought, wisdom, religion, government and morality. Morality has doomed down and man has either been left to a jungle of bewilderment or has gone mad in the lust for power and self-comfort. Kindness, love and pain for the grieving human population has become the legend of past. 'Self-above-all' and 'the-might-is-right' has become the motto of the so-called civilized and most advanced countries of the world, creating an unhappy world.

Dr. Alexis Carrel writes: "The applications of scientific discoveries have transformed the material and mental worlds. These transformations exert on us a profound influence. Their unfortunate effect comes from the fact that they have been made without consideration for our nature. Our ignorance of ourselves has given to mechanics, physics and chemistry the power to modify at random the ancestral forms of life. Man should be the measure of all. On the contrary, he is a stranger in the world that he has created. He has been incapable of organising this world for himself, because he did not possess a practical knowledge of his own nature. Thus, the enormous advance gained by the sciences of inanimate matter over those of living things is one of the greatest catastrophes ever suffered by humanity. The environment born of our intelligence and our inventions is adjusted neither to our stature nor to our shape. We are unhappy. We degenerate morally and mentally. The groups and the nations in which industrial civilization has attained its highest development are precisely those which are becoming weaker, and whose return to barbarism is the most rapid."[4]

Pondering on the morality of his own policy-makers, the renowned American sociologist and philosopher, Will Durant writes, "Has a government such power in economic and ethical matters to preserve all the heritage of knowledge and morals and art stored up over generations and woven into the warp and woof of a nation's culture ? Can it increase that heritage and hand it on to posterity? Can a government, with all the modern machinery at its disposal, bring the treasures of science to those depressed classes who still think of scientific utterances as blasphemy and witchcraft ? Why is it that such small men govern America's biggest cities ? Why is our administration conducted in such a way as to make one weep over the lack of noble policies and true patriotism ? Why do corruption and deception enter into our elections and make havoc of public property ? Why has government's basic task dwindled today to an attempt merely to prevent crime ? Why do governments not seek to understand the causes of war and the conditions of peace ? Churches and families ought to undertake the imposition of civilization on such governments."[5]

One can imagine the agony of the western philosophers, who fie upon the wisdom of their own policy-makers and administrators. Why such an abhorrence ? What is wrong behind all these ? Dr. Alexis diagnoses the cause—the system

4. Carrel, Dr. Alexis, "Man, the Unknown", pp. 27-28.
5. Will Durant, "Pleasures of Philosophy", pp. 326-27.

lacks consideration of the human nature itself, and advises the cure—'Man should be the measure of all.' America and many other developed nations have besottedly turned a deaf ear to the calls of reason of their own thinkers and philosophers.

Commenting on the remarks of the above writers, S.M.R. Musavi Lari exhorts: "Western society can only continue to tolerate moral confusion and its ways of destruction because of its limited powers to take reform into its own hands. But the continuation of this state of affairs already tolls a warning bell. Peril lies close at hand, for civilization stays stable only so long as there is a balance between ends and means, between authority and aspiration. When this equilibrium breaks down, such violence ensues that no goodness can stop it. It rushes headlong to an inevitable disruption. You will find no nation throughout human history which survived the corruption of indulgence and permissiveness.

"Rome perished. The glory of Greece collapsed. France, because of the indulgent lives of its citizens, turned soft and gave way to the first Nazi assault. One of their most famous generals himself wrote that the reason for their weakness was the inner erosion of character.

"Spengler foresaw the downfall of Western civilization and said that other lands would in the future see great cultures arise. Perhaps the East will be one of the first to return to its ancient heritage. This will not come by worshipping at the false shrine of misguided civilizations. But the decline of one civilization can awaken men to the divine plan and inspire them to follow it; and so by means of this sublime truth, to found an entirely new social life on sound foundations."[6]

Today the two advanced block of East and West see their destruction in their own creation 'atom'. Both fear each other. Both apprehend an atomic assault against each other. They find no way out. They meet and disperse without any tangible agreement. What is wrong behind all these deliberations? They lack nothing. Both are civilized nation-blocs. What is lacking, is 'morale'. None of them is ready to rely

6. Lari, S.M.R. Musavi, "Western Civilization through Muslim Eyes", 1977, F.J. Goulding Guildford GU25 LR, p. 58.

in other's words due to their moral bankruptcy. Science is unable to restore this gem. It is only a true religion which can revive human values in man.

Voltaire, who at the beginning was one of Islam's most obdurate opponents and poured scorn on the Prophet, after his 40 years of study of religion, philosophy and history, frankly said: "Muhammad's religion was unquestionably superior to that of Jesus. He never descended to the wild blasphemies of Christians, nor said that one God was three or three Gods were one. The single pillar of his faith is the One God. Islam owes its being to its founder's decrees and manliness; whereas Christians used the sword to force their religion on others. Oh Lord ! if only all nations of Europe would make the Muslims their models."[7] Enemy returns to his foe as his friend aspiring the entire Europe to follow his suite.

At another place Voltaire writes, "Muhammad was a great man and a great trainer of great men by his example of virtue and perfection. A wise lawgiver, a just ruler, an ascetic prophet, he raised the greatest revolution earth has seen."[8]

Tolstoi wrote: "Muhammad needs no other claim to fame than he raised a barbarous people out of their diabolical customs to untold advances. His Canon Law with its intelligence and wisdom will come to be the world's authority."[9]

Islam is again ready to reform the barbarous West.

The Lord of all declares: "*Howallazi ba'asa fil-Ummiyina Rasoolan, yatlu 'alaihim ayatihi, wa yozakkihim, wa yo'allimohullimohomul Kitaba wal Hikmah; wa in-kanu min qablo lafi Zalalim Mobin.*"[10] (Allah is that sent among ignorants a messenger from among themselves, who read for them his verses, and purified them, and (then) taught them the Book and Sciences; and before it they were in complete disarray.) The Prophet of Islam was confronted with the toughest tribes, which did not see a prophet for about 35 centuries after Ismail

7. Ibid.
8. Lari, S.M.R. Musavi, Ibid, p. 58.
9. Ibid.
10. Qur'an, Sura 'Jum'a', v. 2.

(PUH). This long span of darkness rendered them the most barbarous. And it was the most intelligent and logical system of education, bestowed by the Creator of man and adopted in its true spirit by Mohammad (PUH), which won the hearts and minds both of the Pagan Arabs. It is not only the philosophy but his exemplary moral background of truthfulness, mildness, forbearance. steadfastness and high-sightedness which helped in making the tough ground arable for sowing the seeds of nobility and reason. From his very childhood Mohammad (PUB) was known as 'truthful' and the Meccans called him 'Ameen' (trustworthy) and used to keep with him their ornaments and jewels even after declaration of prophethood. When he recited the *ayahs* of Qur'an before them, nobody could say that it was his creation—rather they said it was against their and their forefather's belief. The Holy Prophet tackled this problem in many ways and persistently tried to find way into their hearts through logical reasonings and courteous approaches. During ten continuous hard years' stay in Mecca he was able to attract over a hundred persons towards his camp, whereas Noah having five centuries' record of continuous preachings on the same land could find only a few men aboard his Boat. In Medina the Holy Prophet found a softer ground and it was this city he triumphed with marvellous success during the succeeding thirteen years when he was able to capture the hearts of the entire Arabian Peninsula.

The special feature of the Islamic Laws is its compatibility with the Laws of Nature. The curriculum laid down for Mohammad comprised of three stages :

(a) Da'wat-e-Haque —Call to reason and Divine Truth.

(b) Tazkia-e-Nafs — Purification of thoughts and manners.

(c) Ta'lim-e-Kitab wa Hikmah —Inculcation of the laws of survival and its benedictions;

cautioning against the losses of deviatian; and
laying foundation of peace and progress through coachings in sciences and social & political laws.

Before going into explanations of the above curriculum, it seems expedient to caution that the word 'ummiyin' (ignorants) used for Meccans should not be misconstrued to mean 'literal ignorance'. Mecca being the capital of Hejaz (now Saudi Arabia) and having the stature of the Holiest City, from time immemorial, of Arabian Peninsula, after Palestine, had a formidable population of literate and well-versed people. The Arabs of Mohammad's time in general and the Meccans in particular were literate enough inasmuch as they considered the non-Arabs to be *'Ajam* (dumb). Among them were many top-ranking poets and litterateurs. Even their ladies talked in versatile poetic diction. Despite the fact Qur'an brands them 'ignorant' because of their deviation from the right path and because of their carrying certain dangerous notions about self, under which they used to commit brutalities just as today some of the so-called advanced countries are doing.

Now let us come to the point of Islamic curriculum. As already said, it has three stages—Da'wah, Tazkia-e-Nafs and Tallim-e-Ilm o Hikmah.

Da'wah—Call to Truth and Reason.

By nature man is 'reason-oriented'. A plain and conscious brain when confronted with an unbiased and unselfish call to reason, feels little repugnance from within; and repetition of the truth appeals to his conscience and ultimately wins his concurrence within a short while. Thus a peaceful call to reason achieves what oppressive measures or measures against the innate nature of man are unable to achieve over centuries. This form of education is, in other words, called *'Targheeb'* (persuasion). The special feature of this form of teaching is that it has strong effects on human wisdom, whereas all other forms of teaching or propaganda which are against the nature of man have little and temporary bearing and it vanishes as soon as the compulsive forces become weak. The second feature of 'Targheeb' or 'Da'wah' is that it does not require maintenance of military force or a band of spies. Once the heart is changed, no need of guarding or enforcing. The third feature of 'Targheeb' is that once it gains ground in human heart, it inculcates a sense of self-respect, self-control, responsibility towards family, society and towards the Lord and love for all.

Tazkia-e-Nafs—Purification of thoughts and manners.

A new-comer to a camp requires training into the discipline and manners of the new philosophy and removal of the past ignorance and disorders manifest in his thoughts and manners. This training, in Islam, is called 'Tazkia-e-Nafs' (purification of thoughts and manners). After switching over from a disorderly system to a divine philosophy such a training becomes essential. Just as a wise potter before doing oil-painting and printing cleans his raw pot in order to make it worthy to accept glaze and prints easily and finely, in the like manner a wise leader of a revolution tries his best to make his followers apt to imbibe the revolutionary messages, laws and customs both internally and externally in order to constitute a group of noble and true followers and a formidable force against devil designs of the enemies of humanity. This curriculum forms the backbone of the Islamic philosophy, and it is most vulnerable to the evil designs of devilish forces. The whole scheme of morality, which is the main theme of Islam, bases on 'Tazkia-e-Nafs'. It is a very delicate and the most important faculty of Islamic education. Hence the Muslims all over the world have always been most sensitive in respect of 'Akhlaque' (morality), and they must remain so if they have at all to protect their entity as Muslims. Piety (*taqwa*), *nemaz*, *roza* (fasting), *hajj*, *zakat*, *khums*, *jihad* are the various courses of training under this discipline. *Namaz* means a five-time meet to pay respect to the Lord and attendance before the leader. Besides this, it carries many hygienic, social and moral benefits. *Roza* (fasting) means purification of body and soul. It is one-month compulsory yearly refresher course of alertness against adversities and natural calamities. It has also a calculated scheme for thrift aimed at removing hunger and poverty from the society. *Hajj* is compulsory once in life provided one has the requisite means to bear expenses. It is a universal get-together of the servants of God at a particular place of worship. *Taqwa* (piety) and *Qurbani* (sacrifice) are the two main spiritual goals of this ritual. This ritual has also some important political significances—(1) realisation of the fact that believing population of the entire world is one and the same, and none has supremacy or privilege over the other in the eyes of God; (2) they must meet each other, try to know their social, economic and political problems, discuss their way-outs, resolve their differences in the name and at the Sacred Place of Allah; and (3) to express disapproval and hatred against the devilish forces of oppression and tyranny. All these lessons are included in the process of *Hajj*. *Zakat* is an Islamic tax. In the absence of an Islamic government, pietiful *Faqih* (theologian) has the right to collect this tax and expend it in the betterment of the believers. *Khums* is also a tax, exclusively earmarked for Aal-e-Rasool (descendants of the Prophet). *Jihad* is a practical device for counteracting the evil forces. It is compulsory for all able bodied, adult and sane male believers—women, ill persons and insane men are excluded from the duty of jihad-bi-saif. It is mainly of two kinds—first *jihad-bin-nafs* (fight against one's own evil desires) and second *jihad-bis-saif* (fight against enemies of Islam, brutals and tyrants). The first kind of *jihad* is the best and compulsory for all—male and female. The second form of *jihad* is allowed for defence of self, nations, religion and in help to the oppressed against a tyrant ruler. And the soul of all these courses is PIETY (*Taqwa*). One must note that God is Himself JUSTICE, and he abhors injustice and oppression. Islam does not allow offence against a peaceful entity or nation. It must be noted that the cost of life even of a non-believer is beyond imagination. God wants peace and harmony. Nobody is allowed to attack a peaceful nation in the name of religion, and this is called 'hypocrisy' which is punishable ever graver than a non-believer. *Jihad* is allowed or permissible only under the direction of a pietiful *Faqih*.

It must be noted that the above-mentioned two faculties are compulsory for each Mo'min (male believer) and Mo'mina (female believer). The third stage, i.e. Ta'lim-e-Kitab wa Hikmah, is not compulsory for all. In this connection Qur'an has said that there should be people from every ground who should leave their houses for receiving light, and thereafter guiding people towards the right path.

Ta'lim-e-Kitab wa Hikmah

This faculty of education is not compulsory for all. Selected and able persons should acquire the knowledge of Qur'an and Sunnah along with different physical sciences and philosophical truth so that they may guide their people towards the Path of Allah. Because education of physical and spiritual both sciences is compulsory for all male and female believers, it is the duty of *Ulema* to enlighten them in these faculties according to their needs and worth. The needy is directed to approach *Ulema*. Ulema have not been troubled to approach the people. To sit in the company of an Alim and to look towards his face carries reward. Ulema have been stopped from asking remuneration for enlightening people or preaching, but at the same time the people have been directed to look and to cater to the necessities of life of their Ulema according to their position, i.e., higher than the people. That society has been said to be curseful whose Ulema are compelled for begging or remain hungry.

'Ilm' is priceless jewel. The custodians of 'Ilm' are the trustees of God and His prophets. Ulema's position in the society is just like Prophet's position in *Ummah*. This position is certainly not for *ghair-muttaqi* (impious) ulema.

During the Middle Ages, the Muslim culture and learning was superior to Western civilization. The Muslims translated many books into Arabic and thousands of their books were translated into Roman, French, German and English languages. This spirit unfortunately did not continue beyond Abbassite period. Islamic education flourished commendably during Abbassite dynasty and both male and female took interest in religious as well as scientific education.

The Qur'an says: "They are losers who besottedly have slain their children by keeping them in ignorance." (Qur'an : 6: 41) This created a universal desire for education and learning among its followers and so within a short period a nucleus of educational institutions was formed.[11] The Prophet once said, "To seek knowledge is duty for every Muslim man and woman." Another tradition of the Prophet asserts, "He who goes out in search of knowledge is working in the way of God, till he returns", and, "Search after knowledge even if it be in China", also reveals the value of education and learning in the eyes of God. While revealing the importance of knowledge and wisdom, the tradition dishonours *jehl* (ignorance). The four things which the Prophet commanded his followers to do for their children are : (1) to circumcise them, (2) to inform them of the principles of their religion, (3) to educate them properly, and (4) to marry them off when they reach the proper age. Thus we see that in Islam education is given an important position in the life of the people.

The importance of education, learning, knowledge and wisdom also becomes quite clear from the fact that the first revelation to Mohammad began with the word 'Iqra', which means 'Read'. One day he (Prophet Mohammad, was asleep in the cave when the Angel Jabrail appeared with a book in his hand and said to him 'Read'.[12]

One Hadith (tradition) declared, "Men of letters cannot be equated with those without learning and education." Likewise in another tradition distinction between 'Ilm' (knowledge) and *jehl* (ignorance) has been presented as, "Ilm is life and jehl is death."[13] This reveals that an ignorant or illiterate man is like a dead person who cannot see the things around him in its right perspective. Further, defining 'Ilm' the Prophet said, "Al-Ilmo Ilmane—Ilmul Abdan wal Ilmul Adyan." (Knowledge is of two sorts—knowledge of physical bodies and the knowledge of spiritualism). Thus the Prophet covered all the faculties of knowledge and education in making their

11. Ali Amir, "The Spirit of Islam", p. 362.
12. Hasan-al-Ameeni, "Islamic Shi'ite Encyclopaedia", Vol. I, p. 148.
13. Shustry, pp. 121-22.

acquisition obligatory for both men and women believing in Islam. Prophet himself imparted knowledge about the Earth, the Sky, the celestial world; about physical bodies and about the spiritual facts and duties. The mosques became the place of worship, a centre of education and a court of justice. As reported by Shustry, the mosque at Cairo was daily visited by about five thousand men to attend lectures on various subjects."[14]

Undoubtedly the Abbassite Kholafa were fond of art and culture and they devoted at large in the acquisition and propagation of varied types of knowledge. Their contribution towards physics, chemistry, medical science, art and culture is admitted. But it is wrong to say they were true to the religious teachings. It was Imam Jafar as-Sadique, Imam Abu Hanifa, Imam Malik, Imam Shafie, Imam Ahmad bin Hanbal who contributed a lot to various faculties of knowledge. And because all these renowned personalities happened to be in the period of Abbassite dynasty, the antagonists of Islam related all these academic progresses to the dynasty itself. Abbassite Kholafa were in most of the cases enemical to the real custodians of prophetic teachings. They imprisoned Aimma-e-Ahle-Bait very off and on, and in many cases they killed them by poisoning. They stripped Imam Abu Hanifa and killed him, only because he was not ready to give 'fatwa' in favour of the Khalifa who wanted to marry the young and beautiful daughter of his concubine. The British historians have found the Abbassite period most suitable for their treacherous plans against Islam and Muslims of the world. This is why they have been very praiseworthy of this dynasty. The second reason of their praise was because the Abbassite Kholafa gave Europeans free access to their treasures of book and they enriched their peoples by translating Arabic books in European languages, in return whereof they were kind to translate a few Roman books on astronomy, philosophy and medicine into Arabic language. Three hundred books of Jabir bin Hayyan (an

14. Maulana Syed Ali Naqi, "Islam ki Hakimana Zindagi" (Urdu), 3d Edition, p. 57.

intelligent disciple of Imam Jafar Sadique) alone were translated from Arabic to the French, Roman, English and German languages. At the time when Abbassite Kholafa were engaged in fighting with dooming Umawwi dynasty, Imam Mohammad Baqir and Imam Jafar Sadique got a favourable time to propagate the prophetic teaching alongwith astronomy, medicine, physics, chemistry, biology, etc. among Muslims. About 4,000 disciples of Imam Sadique engaged throughout the year in collecting knowledge from this Apostle of God. They loaded thousands of camels with their countries. Jabir was one of the few closest disciples of Imam Sadique, who acquired the utmost from the Imam. He wrote more than five hundred books, of which three hundred were available to the Abbassite Caliphs and were made a gift to the Europeans.

It was during the period of Imam Sadique when education was divided into two broad disciplines of '*Manqulat*' and '*Ma'qulat*', and these two disciplines were sub-divided into various faculties as given below in tabular form.

Education

- *Manqulat* (Traditional Sciences)
  - *Tafsir* (Exegesis)
  - *Hadith* (Tradition)
  - *Fiqh* (Law)
  - *Tarikh* (History)
  - *Adab* (Literature)
- *Ma'qulat* (Rational Sciences)
  - *Mantiq* (Logic)
  - *Hikmat* (Philosophy)
  - *Tibb* (Medicine)
  - *Riazi* (Mathematics)
  - *Haiyat* (Astronomy)

A few books of Indian scholars were also translated into Arabic. These were mainly on medicine, astronomy and arithmetic.

The publication division of the Ministry of Information and Broadcasting, Government of India has collected information about contributions of Muslim scholars during medieval period, in India. It is, no doubt, a very systematic collection giving an account of academic activities of Indian Muslims during Lodi and Moghal periods.

According to the said publication,[15] the traditions of Muslim education as they had developed under the 'Abbasids of Baghdad were the nucleus of the Muslim educational system in India. They were transplanted in India by the literature and scholars of Muslim lands after the Mongols had overrun them. Within a century of its foundation, the Sultanate of Delhi came to occupy an unrivalled place in the sphere of Muslim education. During the reign of 'Alauddin Khalji (A.D. 1296-1316), scholars of Bukhara, Samarqand, Iraq and Khwarazm looked to India for guidance and inspiration in academic matters. Amir Khusraw regarded Indian learning superior to that of such centres as Ray, Isfahan and Rum. According to Dia-ud-din Barani, the scholars of this country attained the stature of Ghazali and Razi. According to an Arab traveller of the 14th century, Delhi alone had one thousand *madrasahs*.

The basic feature of Muslim educational system was that it was traditional in spirit and theological content. Its main purpose was to stabilize a body of beliefs. The curriculum was broadly divided into two categories: the *manqulat* and the *ma'qulat*, the former dealing with traditional and the latter with rational sciences. Exegesis (*Tafsir*), Traditions (*Ahadith*), Law (*Fiqh*), History and Literature came under the category of traditional sciences; Logic (*Mantiq*), philosophy (*Hikmat*), Medicine (*Tibb*), Mathematics (*Riyazi*) and Astronomy (*Hai'at*) were treated as rational sciences. In the early stages the study of the traditional sciences was emphasized, but gradually the rational sciences began to receive greater attention. But this emphasis on

15. "India: Society, Religion & Literature in Ancient & Medieval Periods", Publication Divn., Ministry of Information & Broadcasting, Govt. of India, 1979, p. 126.

maq'ulat did not lead development of the experimental and inductive methods, which alone could pave the way for scientific and technological advancement.

The institution which provided elementary education were known as *maktabs*, while those of higher learning were called *madrasas*. While the maktabs were generally run by public donations, rulers or nobles maintained the higher centres of learning. One comes across the following types of institutions during this period: (a) those established and maintained by the rulers or the nobles; (b) those established by individual scholars with the help of public donations and state assistance; (c) those run by individual scholars exclusively without any outside help; (d) those attached to mosques funds; (e) those attached to tombs and financed from their endowments; and (f) those attached to the hospices (*khanqahs*) of Sufi saints. The Mu'zzi, the Nasiri and the Firuzi madrasahs of Delhi, the madrasah of Bibi Raji of Jaunpur, the madrasah of Mahmud Gawan in Bidar, and the madrasah of Abul Fazl at Fatehpur Sikri were some of the most renowned centres of higher learning established by the rulers and nobles. Among the institutions established by individuals, the madrasah of Sadiq Khan in Gujarat, Maham Anaga, and Mirza Abdur Rahim Khan-i-Khanan in Delhi, Shihabuddin Daulatabadi at Jaunpur and Qutubuddin Sihalwi at Lucknow deserve particular mention. Mutahhar has given a vivid account of Firuz Shah's madrasah at Delhi. It was a double-storeyed building standing on the bank of the Hauz-i-Khas surrounded by a beautiful garden. Besides numerous lecture-halls, there were spacious hostels for the visitors and a big congregational mosque. The government met all the expenses of the students, including boarding and lodging.

The *Sirat-i-Firuz Shahi* gives the following list of 14 subjects which were taught in the madrasahs established by Firuz Shah Tughluq: (1) *Figh* (Jurisprudence), (2) *Qir'at* (Method of recitation, punctuation and vocalization of the text of Qur'an), (3) *Usul-i-Kalam* (Principles of Scholastic Theology), (4) *Usul-i-Fiqh* (Principles of Jurisprudence), (5) *Tafsir* (Exegesis), (6) *Ahadith* (Traditions of the Prophet), (7) *Ma'ani-wal-Bayan* (Rhetorics), (8) *Nahw-wa-Sarf* (Syntax and Etymology), (9) *'Ilm-i-Nazar* (Science of observation), (10) *'Ilm-i-Riyazi* (Mathematics), (11) *'Ilm-i-Tab'i* (Natural Sciences), *'Ilm-i-Ilahi* (Metaphysics), (13) *'Ilm-i-Tibb* (Medicine), and (14) *Tahrir-wa-Khat* (Calligraphy).

From the time of Iltutmish (A.D. 1211-1236) to the days of Sikandar Lodi (A.D. 1489-1517) traditional subjects (*manqulat*) occupied a more important place than the rationalistic subjects (ma'qulat). A change, however, took place when Shaikh Abdullah and his brother Shaikh Azizullah of Multan came to Delhi at the invitation of Sikandar Lodi. They introduced the study of philosophy and logic in the curriculum of the day, and thus reduced the religious bias of the existing system. The Hindus now took to learning the Persian language, and a Hindu scholar, Brahmana by name, instructed Muslims. The next significant step in the direction of making the Muslim system of education more rationalistic was taken by Humayun whose madrasah in Delhi laid greater emphasis on the study of mathematics, astronomy and geography. Significant though these steps were, they did not bring about any fundamental change in the content and character of the Muslim education in India.

Akbar attempted to reorientate the educational system by introducing subjects like logic, arithmetic, mensuration, geometry, astronomy, accountancy, public administration and agriculture into the curriculum. Fathullah Shirazi displayed keen interest in mechanical and technical education and under his inspiration Akbar built a workshop near his palace and personally supervised its work. This attempt at placing the educational system on a more secular and scientific basis does not seem to have found much favour. A few state-managed institutions changed their syllabii under Akbar's influence, but the general pattern of Muslim education remained unaltered. Probably the orthodox revival, which set in after Akbar, checked the growth and development of the educational system on the lines indicated by him. The syllabus prepared by Maulana Nizamuddin in the middle of the 18th century popularly known as *Dars-i-Nizami*, merely consolidated the medieval system of education. It is true that some nobles like Danishmand Khan did display interest in the western methods of enquiry, investigation, observation and experiment, but their efforts remained purely personal and did not have any impact on the general system of Muslim education.

Instruction in Muslim madrasahs of the middle ages was based on memorization, discussion and writing out the lessons taught. Seminars were considered an integral part of education and students of the higher classes had to master the art of casuistry.

LITERATURE

Urdu

Urdu emerged as an independent language only towards the end of the 14th century A.D. Its base was *Khadi-Boli*, which has been styled by some of the earlier writers as Zuban-i-Dihlawi or Hindustani. It assumed a new character by absorbing words and idioms and also the literary forms and themes of Persian, which had itself imbibed Arabic and Turkish elements. It was thus a mixed language, and served as a fit medium of intercourse between the people of India and the Muslims who came from Islamic countries and made India their home. Strange though it may appear, the cradle of Urdu literature was the South where it had gone with the soldiers of Alauddin Khalji and Muhammad Tughluq, and flourished in the quieter environment of the kingdoms of Bijapur and Golconda. In its own homeland, Delhi and its neighbourhood, reigned Persian, the court language of the Mughals.

The earliest available work in Dakhni Urdu is Me'rajul-Ashiqin, a mystical prose treatise written by saint Gesu Daraz in the beginning of the 15th century A.D. A few more works are also traceable, but their language is much too archaic. On the break-up of the Bahmani kingdom, Urdu received adequate patronage at the courts of the Adil Shahi rulers of Bijapur and the Qutb Shahi rulers of Golconda in the 16th and 17th centuries A.D. Among the writers of Bijapur the two mystics, Shah Miranji Shamsul Ushshaq (d. A.D. 1496) and his son Burhanuddin Janam (d. A.D. 1582) deserve special mention—the former wrote two fine poems *Khush Namah* and *Khush Noghz* and the latter *Irshad Namah* and *Wasiyat-ul-hadi*. One may question their literary merit, but their linguistic significances is beyond doubt. The literary activity in Golconda was distinctly richer. The rulers were not only patrons but also literary crafsmen of a high order. Muhammad Quli (A.D. 1580-1612) was a great poet, and he brought Urdu poetry out of the obscure groves of the mystics into the open sunshine of normal life. The other important writers of Golconda were Mulla Wajahi and Ghawasi. Wajahi occupies an important position among the authors of poetical romances and masters of prose. Ghawasi is the author of two famous *masnawis*, *Saif-ul-muluk* and *Tuti Nama*.

Deccan was conquered by the Mughals but Urdu flourished under the patronage of the court. Of the early poets Wali played a remarkable role in giving the final shape to Urdu by substituting the idiom of Delhi for that of Dakani and hence he is called the 'Father of *Rekhta*'. Urdu literature came to the North from the Deccan in a developed form, and soon became popular. Hatim founded the Delhi school of poets who sought to purify the language by excluding the unfamiliar words and expressions of the Dakani. Gradually an elegant literary language emerged in the works of Mirza Jan-i-Janan Mazhar of Delhi (A.D. 1699-1781). Mir Taqi of Agra (1720-1808), Muhammad Rafi Sauda (1713-1780) and Mir Hassan (1736-1786). Sauda tried successfully all forms of verses—he excelled both in *ghazal* and *qasidah*, but he was a master of satire. None could depict better the world of the decadent Mughals with such brilliant fury. Mir was a lyricist *par excellence*. No Urdu poet has ever touched the deeper chords of human heart with a more delicate hand. His contemporary and namesake Mir Hasan was the greatest *masnawi*-writer in Urdu. Mir Dard was essentially a mystic. He sang of the divine love with great fervour in short metres. This was in a way the golden age of Urdu poetry when classical standards in *ghazal*, *qasidah* and *masnawi* were set. Mirza Ghalib was the last and the foremost poet of the medieval period who elevated Urdu poetry parallel to any other contemporary language of the world. Akbar Illahabadi and Sir Mohammad Iqbal and Josh Malihabadi were the pioneers of Urdu poetry who fought the war of independence through poems and mobilised public opinion against the

British rule. Shaad Azimabadi, Mir Anis and Mirza Dabeer Lucknawi were the pioneers of *Marsiagoi*. Pandit Brij Narain Chakbast Faizabadi, Mir Munis Lucknawi, Zaar Azimabadi, Danish Azimabadi and Hosh Azimabadi followed Mir Anis and Mirza Dabeer successfully in *Marsiagoi*. Shamsul Ulema Nazir Ahmad, Minto, Allama Shibli, Sir Syed Ahmad, Munshi Premchand, etc. are the master-piece prose writers.

Arabic

In the first few centuries after the rise of Islam, Arabic was the dominant language of the Islamic world, which extended from China to Spain. It was the language of religion and theology as well as learning and scholarship. It was only natural that with the establishment of Muslim power, increasing attention should be paid to the cultivation of the language in India. The Arabs conquered Sind in the 8th century and made it a flourishing colony of the Muslims, with Bhakkar, Tatta and Multan as important centres of learning.

Sind was a great centre of traditionists and literary men down to the 18th century A.D., but very few of their works have come down to us. Abu Ata Aflah al-Sindi, the first poet, Abu Hafs Rabi bin Subayh (d. A.D, 716), and Abu Ma'shar Najih bin Abdur Rahman (d. A.D. 786) were the prominent scholars of the 8th century. Among the later theologians and scholars may be mentioned the great saint Bahauddin Dhakariya Multani (d. A.D. 1262), Abu Hanifa al Sindi, the Qazi of Bhakkar, Abu Tayyab al-Sindi, Shaikh Hamid bin Abdullah (d. A.D. 1600), Abul Hasan bin Abdul Hadi (d. 1725), Mohammad Hayat al-Sindi (d.1749) and Haji Hashim (d. 1760). Some Arabic works of original merit were written in India under the patronage of the Ghaznavids (A.D. 962-1186). The great Iranian scholar Abu Raihan Alberuni (d. A.D. 1048) came to India, studied Hindu culture and Sanskrit literature and wrote in A.D. 1030 his famous work on India, *Kitab-ul-Hind* or Indica, which brought Indian philosophies and science to the knowledge of the Muslims. Among his other notable works are *Qanun-i-Masudi*, a treatise on astronomy, and *Jawahir fil-Jawahir*, a book on minerology, both dedicated to Sultan Masud of Ghaznawi. It was this Sultan that had made Lahore the capital of the Ghaznavid dominion, east of the Indus, and it came to be known as Little Ghazni. The first *muhaddis* (traditionist) and *mufassir* (commentator) Mohammad Ismail (d. A.D. 1056) settled down in Lahore during his reign.

When Delhi became the capital of the Muslim rulers of India under the Sultan of Delhi (A.D. 1206-1290), it assumed great importance in the literary circles of the East. In the time of Iltutmish several scholars sought refuge at Delhi after the sack of Bukhara by Chingiz Khan. Raziuddin Hasan al-Saghani (d. A.D. 1252), a prominent traditionist and philologist, was attached to his court as an ambassador of the Abbasid Caliph An-Nasir (d. 1220 A.D.). He was the author of a scientific dictionary, the *Lubab-ul-Zakhirah*, and of a compendium of tradition, the *Mashariq-ul-Anwar*, which are still reckoned as standard works in Arabic. Unfortunately some of the other works of this period by authors like Shaikh Hamiduddin Nagauri (d. A.D. 1274), and Shaikh Jamal Hanswi (d. A.D. 1265) have not come down to us in full, but are still considered as the first-rate contributions of the time.

During the Khalji period (A.D. 1290-1320), Shihabuddin Sadrnashin, a contemporary of Nizamuddin Auliya, Shamsuddin Muhaddis Dehlawi who came from Egypt to Multan, Saifudnin Hindi (d. A.D. 1315) and Amir Khusru (d. A.D. 1325) contributed a great deal to Arabic literature. Some of these writings have been preserved for posterity. Ziauddin Barani, the contemporary historian and author of the Tarikh-i-Firuz Shahi, gives a glowing account of the literary patronage of the Khaljis.

Muhammad bin Tughluq who reigned from A.D. 1325 to 1351, endeavoured to revive Arabic, but his efforts bore little fruit. His successor Firuz, however, had the good fortune of being the patron of scholars like Maulana Khwajagi, the teacher of Shihabuddin Daulatabadi (d. A.D. 1445) and the author of *Al-Irshad* and *Sharh-i-Hindi* on Arabic syntax; Qazi Hamiduddin Dihlawi, the author of commentary on *Hidayah*; Husamuddin Dihlawi, the author of *Al-Bahr-ul-Zakhirah*; Ahmad Thanesari, the composer of the *Qasidat-ul-Daliyah*;

and Abdul Muqtadir, the author of the *Qasidat-ul-Lamiyah* composed in reply to the famous masterpiece, the *Lamiat-ul-Ajam.* The great Arabic dictionary, the *Qamus* of Majduddin Firuzabadi, reminds us of the patronage of this Sultan to Arabic lexicography.

The Lodis (A.D. 1451-1526) made Agra the capital of their empire and many authors were attracted to it. Abdullah Tulambi, the first Indian scholar of Islamic philosophy and Rafiuddin Shirazi, a pupil of Muhaq-qiq Jalaluddin Dawwani in philosophy and of the great traditionist Sakhawi in Hadith, came to Agra and contributed much to Islamic studies. Abdul Fath of Thanesar, one of the teachers of Abdul Qadir Badauni, and Abdul Fazail Sa'duddin of Delhi also wrote important books on theology.

Apart from the patronage of the ruling kings at the centre, the provincial dynasties of India also helped the cause of Arabic learning in their own territories and their contributions were of no mean importance. The governors of Bengal had their seats at Lakhnauti, Murshidabad and Buhar, a village in the district of Burdwan. These places became famous as centres of learning before the Mughal period.

The Sharqi kings of Jaunpur (A.D. 1394-1484) patronized scholars like Qazi Shihabuddin Daulatabadi and Maulana Ilahdad of Jaunpur. From Jaunpur hailed Syed Muhammad Jaunpuri (d. A.D. 1505), the founder of a sect of Islam called the *Mahdawiyah*, whose adherents are found even now in different parts of India. Later on, during the Mughal period, many scholars and writers arose from Jaunpur, viz., Abdul Awwal (d. A.D. 1560), Mulla Mahmud (d. A.D. 1651), the philosopher, Abdur Rashid (d. A.D. (1672), and the great Mulla Ahmad Jiwan (d. 1718), one of the teachers of Aurangzeb, who was the author of *Tafsir-i-Ahmadi* and *Nurul Anwar*. The *Fatawa-i-Alamgiri*, compiled during the reign of Aurangzeb, is a signal contribution to Muslim canon law by Mulla Hamid, Muhammad Husain, Jalaluddin and other Jaunpur scholars.

Ahmadabad, the capital of the Sultans of Gujarat (A.D. 1407-1572), was founded by Ahmad Shah I. It rose into prominence on a seat of learning. Nuruddin Shirazi, a pupil of Syed Sharif Ali bin Muhammad, and Wajhuddin

Muhammad Maliki, the Malikul Muhaddaseen, gave great impetus to the study of Hadith among the Muslims of Gujarat. Ibnud-Dammanini (d. A.D. 1424) of Egypt came to India and composed some of his famous works under the patronage of the kings of Gujarat. Other important contributors are Ali ibn Ahmad Maha'imi (d. A.D. 1432), the author of the well-known commentary on the Qur'an, the *Tafsir-ul-Rahman*; Mohammad bin Tahir Patani (d. A.D. 1578), the author of *Bahr-ul-Anwar*, an important dictionary of the Hadith; Sirajuddin Umar Ulugh Khani al-Makki, commonly known Hajjirud-Dabir, the writer of the standard history of Gujarat, known as *Zafar-ul-Walih, bi-Muzaffar wa Alih*.

Before the advent of the Mughals, the kingdoms of the Deccan also played a great part in the dissemination of Islamic learnings and the growth of the Arabic literature. Among the great Deccani scholars may be mentioned the great saint Syed Muhammad al-Husaini Gesu-daraz, known as Khwajah Bandah Nawaz of Gulbarga, Hasan bin Ali Shadkam (d. A.D. 1636), Zainuddin al-Ma'bari, Ibn Ma'sum, the author of *Tuhfatul Mujahidin* and Mulla 'Abdu'n Nabi, the author of *Dastur-ul-Ulama*.

During the Mughal period great impetus was given to Arabic literature. Of the writers of the time may be mentioned Faizi, the writer of a commentary on the Qur'an, the *Swati-ul-Ilham*. Prominent among the contributions are Al-Muttaqi Ali ibn Husamuddin al-Burhanpuri (d. A.D. 1567) great compendium of the whole corpus of the Hadith, *Kanz-ul-Ummal*, Abdul Haque Dihlawi's (d. A.D. 1642) *Ashirat-ul-Lama'at*, the famous commentary on the *Mishkat*; Syed Abdul Awwal Jaunpuri's (d. A.D. 1560) *Faiz-ul-Bari*, commentary on the *Sahi-ul-Bukhari*; Shaikh Abdul Hasan Sindi al-Kabir's glosses on the six canonical works of tradition; Shaikh Ahmad Sirhindi, the Mujaddid-e-Alf-i-Sani's (d. A.D. 1615) polemical critical works; Mulla Mahmud Jaunpuri's *Shams-ul-Bazigah*, Qazi Muhibullah Bihari's *Sullam-ul-Ulum*, a standard work on philosophy and its commentaries; Mirak Abdul Baqi Thattawi's *Ashkal-ul-Jadidah* on mathematics; Fariduddin Dihlawi's *Zij-i Shah Jahani* on astronomy; Abdul Hakim

Sialkoti's glosses and treatises on various literary and philosophical texts; Shaikh Nizamuddin Sahili's commentaries and glosses; Muhammad Ali al-Sanawi's famous dictionary of technical terms, the *Kashaf-i-Istilahat-ul-Funun*, written in 1743; Shah Waliullah Dihlawi's masterpiece on theology, the *Hujjat-ullah al-Balighah*; Shah Abdul Aziz and Shah Abdul Qadir's commentaries and translations of the Qur'an; Mir Ghulam Ali Azad Bilgrami's *Subhat-ul-Marjan* and *Saba'-Sayyarah*; Maulana Bahrul Ulum Fazl-e-Haqq Khairabadi's contributions; Zubaid's *Taj-ul-Arus*, a standard dictionary of the Arabic language, and Maulana Abdul Hai of Lucknow's *Nuzhat-ul-Khawatir*, a dictionary of the biography of Muslim authors, *Jannat-ul-Mashriq* and *Ma'ariful Awarif*.

From the foregoing account it will be seen that India had its own share in enriching Arabic literature. During the middle ages there were many active centres of Islamic studies and Arabic learning throughout the country. In the 14th century Khusraw regarded Delhi as superior to Baghdad in Arabic scholarship. On the whole, however, although India produced commentaries, super-commentaries, glosses and annotations of the works of the earlier authors and a number of competent works on philosophy, traditions, linguistics and philology, the quantum of original work in Arabic was small, and in poetry and creative literature the contribution was meagre.

Persian

The beginnings of Persian literature in India go back to the Ghaznavids and the Ghurids. The eminent poets of Indian origin at the time were Abul Fari Runi (alive in A.D. 1098) Mas'udi-Sa'di-Salman (d. A.D. 1131) and Shihabi-i-Muhmira (d. c. A.D. 1295).

The cultivation of the language received great impetus under the patronage of Qutbuddin Aibak, Iltutmish and Ruknuddin. Among important historical works of the time may be mentioned the following: the *Taj-ul-Ma'asir* of Hasan Nizami Nishapuri, the *Chach Namah*, an early history of Sind, by Ali bin Hamid bin Abi Bakr al-Kufi (d. after A.D.

1216), the *Jami'ul-Hikayat,* a compendium of historical anecdotes, by Sadiduddin Muhammad Awfi Bukhari (d. after A.D. 1230), and the *Tabaqat-i-Nasiri* by Minhaj-us-Siraj. There were important works in other fields also. Bukhari referred to above compiled the *Lubab-ul-Albad,* the first extant Persian anthology. Fakhr Mudabbir (d. after A.D. 1210) compiled the *Adab-ul Harb wal Shuja'at,* a manual dealing with the science of warfare. Abu Bakr al-Kashani translated and revised the *Kitab-us-Saydana* (Book of Drugs) of Alberuni about A.D. 1215.

The age of the Khaljis was a glorious period. According to Barani, the famous contemporary historian, "there lived at Delhi scholars of such eminence and calibre as were not to be found in Bukhara, Samarqand, Tabriz and Isfahan and in their intellectual accomplishments they equalled Razi and Ghazali. Under every stone lay hidden a precious gem of literary excellence." In the midst of a host of literary artists, the two outstanding persons were Amir Khusraw (A.D. 1253-1325) and Shaikh Najmuddin Hasan, popularly known as Hasan-i-Dihlawi (d. A.D. 1327). The former is the greatest figure in the world of Persian literature in India. He was a prolific and versatile writer of genius who is said to have composed about half a million verses and 99 works on different subjects. His five literary masterpieces of the *Khamsah,* composed as a rejoinder to the *Khamsah* of Nizami, were *Mutla-ul-Anwar, Shirin Khusraw, Laila Majnun, Ayina-i-Sikandari* and *Hasht Bahisht.* These were dedicated to his great patron Alauddin Khalji. His five Diwans, *Tuhfat-us-Sighar, Wast-ul-Hayat, Ghurrat-ul-Kamal, Baqiya-Naqiya* and *Nihayat-ul-Kamal,* written at various stages of his life, show the development of his lyrical talent at best and give him a place next to Sa'di of Shiraz, his great contemporary. Since Khusraw enjoyed the patronage of successive rulers of Delhi, his writings have great historical value. His *Khaza'in-ul-Futuh* described Alauddin's conquests. The Tughluq-Namah depicts the rise of Ghiyasuddin Tughluq. The Qiran-us-Sa'dain is the story of the meeting between Sultan Mu'izzuddin Kaiqubad of Delhi and his father Nasiruddin Bughra of Bengal in A.D. 1288. His Miftahul Futuh (A.D. 1291) gives an account of the four victories of Jalaluddin Khalji's reign. The Duwal Rani-wa-Khizr Khan or 'Ishaiyah is a poetical narrative of the love adventure of Khizr Khan, son of Sultan Alauddin Khalji and Devala Rani, daughter of Rai Karan, the Raja of Gujarat. The Nuh-Sipihr contains a poetical description of Qutubuddin Mubarak Shah Khalji's reign, and gives a glowing account of things found in India.

Hasan-i-Dihlawi, the friend and contemporary of Khusraw, was also an eminent poet, and the quality of his *ghazals* won him the name of Sa'di of India.

In the time of the Tughluqs many famous historians and poets adorned the court of Muhammad Tughluq. The historical works of Ziyauddin Barani (b. A.D. 1285), the poetical writings of Mutahhar, the *masnawi* of Abu Ali Qalandar (d. A.D. 1324), the Futuhat-i-Firuz Shahi by Sultan Firuz Shah Tughluq himself, and the Tarikh-i-Firuz Shahi of Shams-i-Siraj 'Arif, are of importance. The transfer of the capital from Delhi to Daulatabad had the effect of extending the influence of Persian literature and culture to South India.

There was considerable activity under the Syeds and the Lodi Kings also. Shaikh Jamali Kambo (d. A.D. 1536), the greatest poet of the time, composed the *Siyar-ul-Arifin* and the *masnawi Mihr-wa-Mah*. Syed Mu'inul Haqq wrote a genealogical account of the Syeds of Bhakkar. Ibrahim Qiwam Faruqi compiled a lexicon known as Farhang-i-Ibrahim. Philosophical studies were specially promoted by the arrival at Delhi of Shaikh Abdullah Tulambi and Shaikh Azizullah from Multan. Yahya bin Ahmad Sirhindi and the great Sufi Abdul Quddus Gangoh were other prominent litterateurs. Azizuddin Khalid wrote a treatise on natural philosophy, the Dala'il-i-Firuz Shani, and Abdul Aziz Shams of Thanesar a treatise on music and dancing.

In South India, the influx of eminent poets, scholars, saints, artists and calligraphers from Persia turned Gulbarga into a virtual capital of a Persian prince. The founder of the Bahmani kingdom, Sultan Alauddin Bahman Shah, was a great patron of learning. 'Isami composed Futuh-us-Salatin in A.D. 1349 and dedicated it to him. Firuz Shah Bahmani and Alauddin Ahmad Shah II Bahmani were also great patrons, and the latter was himself a great poet. The reign of Muhammad Shah (A.D. 1463-1482) brings us to one of the greatest figures of the history of the Deccan, Khwajah Jahan Mahmud Gawan, his illustrious Wazir, whose glorious achievements, literary productions and educational institutions remain as historic monuments of the period. Khawajah Ubaidullah Ahrar (d. A.D. 1491), the great saint of the Naqshbandi order, Sharafuddin Ali Yazdi Dawwani (d. A.D. 1502), who wrote the Shawakil-Hur, and many other scholars under his patronage. The Wazir himself was a writer of no mean merit.

The Adil Shahis of Bijapur (A.D. 1490-1686) and the Nizam Shahis of Ahmadnagar (1490-1633) have also left a great mark. Their courts were full of talented authors and poets like Malik Qummi (d. A.D. 1615), Nuruddin Zuhuri (d. A.D. 1616), Sanjar-i-Kashani (d. A.D. 1612) and Atashi. Zuhuri is by far the most distinguished of the poets of this period and exerted considerable influence over later poets. Several historical works were also written under the patronage of these rulers: the *Burhan-i-Ma'asir* by Syed Ali bin Azizullah Tabatabai, the Tazkirat-ul-Muluk on the Adil Shahis by Rafiuddin Ibrahim Shirazi (d. after A.D. 1611), the Futuhat-i-Adil Shahi (c. A.D. 1644) by Fuzuni Astrabadi, the Muhammad Namah on Muhammad Adil Shah (A.D. 1627-1657) by Mulla Zuhuri, the Tarikh-i-Ilchi-i-Nizam Shah by Khwar Shah bin Qubadal Husaini, and the Gulshan-i-Ibrahimi by Firishta Muhammad Qasim.

In the Qutb Shahi court at Golconda, Mir Muhammad Mu'min Astrabadi (d. 1580 A.D.), the chief Wazir of Muhammad Quli and Muhammad Qutb Shah, was a great patron of Persian scholarship. He was himself a noted poet and one of his technical brochures deals with weights and measures and distances according to Muslim law. His protege Mirza Muhammad Amin Shahristani styled Mir Jumla and Allamah Ibn Khatun were also well-known administrators, poets and scholars. Of the other poets and men of learning patronized by the Qutb Shahis may be mentioned Malikush-Sho'ara Mulla Mu'in Mirak Sabzwari, Rukn-i-Masih. Sirajuddin Arif, Ghiyasuddin Isfahani, Mir Hasan Askari and Muhsin Hamadani.

The foundation of the Mughal empire in India heralded the dawn of a new era in the history of Indo-Persian literature. The Mughal emperors were not only great patrons of art and literature, many of them were themselves litterateurs in their own rights.

Babar wrote his own biography, Tazuk-i-Babari, in Turkish which was later translated into Persian by Abdur Rahim Khan Khanan. In the time of Humayun and his successor, many sholars and poets were attracted to India, and they gave an impetus to the afflorescence of Persian literature, Humayun himself was a poet of merit, his brother Kamran was a poet and his sister Gulbadan Begam was a prose-writer who composed Humayun Namah, Muhammad al-Miskini compiled his encyclopaedia of Islamic sciences called the *Jawahir-ul-Ulum-i-Humayuni* in A.D. 1539 and Yusufi Yusuf bin Muhammad Harati wrote in A.D. 1533 the *Badali-ul-Insha*, a treatise on the epistolography. Poets like Shah Tahir Dakhni (d. A.D. 1545), Damiri Bilgrami (d. A.D. 1594) and Khwajah Husain Marvi (d. after 1572) adorned his court.

The age of Akbar (A.D. 1556-1605) was indeed a brilliant epoch in the history of Indo-Persian literature. Under him Agra could justly claim to be the literary metropolis of Central Asia. A host of poets from all parts of Persia flocked to his court, amongst whom Ghazali Mashhadi (d. 1572), Jamaluddin (d. 1591). Urfi Shirazi, Sanai Mashhadi, Zuhuri Turshizi and Mulla Husain Naziri Naishapuri are the most prominent. Faizi (d. A.D. 1595), was the most eminent among the numerous poets mentioned by historians. In the field of history the outstanding works are the *Akbar-Namah* and the *Ain-i-Akbar* of Abul Fazl, the *Tabaqat-i-Akbari* of Mulla Nizamuddin Ahmad Harawi, the *Nafa'is-ul-Ma'asir* of Mir Alauddaulah Qazwini and Abdul Haqq Dihlawi's *Zikr-ul-Muluk*.

The tempo of progress was maintained under Jahangir and Shah Jahan. Abu Talib Amuli (d. A.D. 1626) was the Malikush Sho'ara of Jahangir's court, and Abu Talib Kalim (d. A.D. 1651) was the poet-laureate of Shah Jahan. Besides Kalim, the other great poets, such as,Qudsi Mashhadi (d. A.D. 1645), Chandrabhana Brahmana (d. A.D. 1662) and Muhammad Ali Sa'ib (d. A.D. 1677) adorned Shah Jahan's court. Of the historical writings of the two reigns may be mentioned *Tazuk-i-Jahangiri* by the emperor Jahangir himself, *Iqbal-Namah* of Mu'tamad Khan, Mulla Muhammad Ma'sum Bhakkari's *Tarikh-i-Sindh*, Muhammad Murad's *Siyar-i-Bilad*, Alauddin Isfahani's Tarikh-i-Bangala Sikandar bin Muhammad Manjhu's *Mir'at-i-Sikandari*, and Malik Haidar's *Tarikh-i-Kashmir*. Shah Jahan's reign is described in a number of works, e.g. Padbah-Namash of Abdul Hamid Lahori and Muhammad Waris and Shah Jahan-Namah of Muhammad Salih Kanbo.

As regards Aurangzeb, the emperor was himself a great scholar devoted to scholarly pursuits. His letters or the *Ruq'at* reveal the depth of his learning and his command over the Persian language. Several other great works werè produced under his aegis: Aqil Khan Razi's *Zafar Namah-i-Alamgiri*, Mirza Muhammad Kazim's *Alamgir-Namah*, an official history of the first ten years of the reign, Muhammad Saqi Musta'idd Khan's *Ma'asir-i-Alamgiri*, Muhammad Rafi Khan's *Hamla-i-Haidari* composed on the lines of the Shah-Namah of Firdawsi, Muhammad Afzal Sarkhush's biography of poets called the *Kalimatush-Shu'ara*, Muhammad Waris's *Badshah-Namah*, Ni'mat Khan Ali's *Waqai-i-Hyderabad*, a chronicle of the siege of Golconda in A.D. 1686 written in prose and verse and Bakhtawar Khan's *Mir'at-ul-Alam*. The *Tarikh-Shah Shuja'* by Muhammad Ma'sum also belongs to this period.

Rai Bindraban and Isar Das wrote the *Futuhat-i-Alamgiri* (A.D. 1696). Bhimsena completed the *Dilkusha*, an account of Aurangzeb's reign; Munshi Sujan Rai compiled his famous history, the *Khulasat-ut-Tawarikh*; and Mirza Khan Fakhruddin completed the *Tuhfat-ul-Hind*, an encyclopaedic work dealing with Hindi literature in a variety of subjects.

Another very remarkable personality of the period is prince Dara Shukoh, who has contributed a great deal to the mystical literature of India and has earned a wide reputation for the catholicity of his views and for his efforts in harmonizing Islamic and Hindu religious ideals. Of his works may be mentioned the *Safinat-ul-Auliya*, a collection of the biographies of Sufi saints, the *Sakinat-ul-Auliya*, a biography of his two preceptors Mulla Shah Muhammad Badakhshani and Miyan

Mir or Mullah Jiw; the *Hasanat-ul-Arifin* and *Majma'ul-Bahrain*, containing his philosophical and religious ideals; and the *Sirr-i-Akbar*, containing a translation of fifty-two Upanishads.

A noteworthy attempt of the times was to create mutual understanding between the Hindus and Muslims. Reciprocity of learning and exchange of knowledge were advanced through translations from Sanskrit and Hindu into Arabic and Persian and *vice-versa*.

Among the important Sanskrit texts rendered into Persian the following be mentioned : *Atharva Veda, Mahabharata, Hari Vamsa, Ramayona, Upanishads, Yoga Vasistha, Lilavati, Puncatantra* and *Rajatarangini*.

Apart from religious and philosophical literature, story-books and scientific treatises were translated.

One or two special aspects of the literature may also be mentioned. Firstly, there is a vast literature in Persian left by the Sufi saints, and it is of great value both from the religious and literary points of view. A brief account of it is to be found in the section on the religious movements among Muslims. There are again innumerable anthologies and collections of biographical sketches of poets, and these give a clear picture of the literary climate of the different periods. Finally, the contribution of India to Persian lexicography is particularly significant, since this was a field neglected by the scholars outside India. Of the many works on the subjects, mention may be made of the *Burhan-i-Qati'*, *Chiragh-i-Hidayat*, *Farhang-i-Jahangiri*, *Farhang-i-Rashidi*, *Ghiyasul Loghat*, *Farhang-i-Anand Rai*, *Muntah-ul-Arab*, *Mustalihatush Sho'ara* and the *Muntakhab-ul-Lughat*.

Science

Since scientists were patronized by kings and chieftains, those branches which were of value to the latter developed to a greater extent, viz., Astronomy, Astrology and Medicine; and Chemistry, Botany and Zoology as adjuncts to Medicine. Development of Zoology was also due to their interest in horses, falcons and hunting.

Astronomy

The main purposes for acquiring astronomical knowledge were working out a calendar, fixing the dates of seasons and festivals, navigation, calculation of time and casting of horoscopes.

The main observatories continued to be at Ujjain, Varanasi, Mathura and Delhi. The first two were ancient centres. Firuz Tughluq had set up a few observation posts at Delhi. These were reorganised on right lines in the time of Humayun, and were developed by Raja Sawai Jai Singh II of Jaipur in the reign of Muhammad Shah. An observatory was set up at Daulatabad by Firuz Shah Bahmani under Hakim Husain Gilani and Syed Muhammad Kazimi, Shah Jahan's desire to build an observatory for Mulla Mahmud at Jaunpur did not materialise.

A remarkable chain of observatories was, however, erected by Raja Sawai Jai Singh II of Jaipur. Those at Delhi and Jaipur were started in 1718 and completed in A.D. 1734. The observatories constructed at Ujjain, Mathura and Varanasi no longer exist. These were masonry instruments erected in preference to small metallic ones for the sake of accuracy in measurements. On the basis of the observations carried out at these observatories *Zij-i-Jadid-i-Muhammad Shahi* was compiled.

The chief instrument for observation was the astrolabe which reached its zenith in the 17th century; about 40 astrolabes of the period are extant. Lahore seems to have been the major centre for the industry where about 29 were made. Of the astrolabe makers we have an account of one family from the time of Humayun to Aurangzeb. Besides the astrolabe, various types of quadrants and armillary spheres were in use.

Numerous instruments were developed by Sawai Jai Singh, and most of these were of masonry. The reason was: "But finding that brass instruments did not come up to the ideas which he had formed of accuracy, because of the smallness of their size, the want of divisions into minutes, the shaking and wearing of their axes, the displacement of the centres of the circles, and the shifting of the planes of the instruments, he concluded that the reason why the determinations of the ancients such as Hipparchus and Ptolemy proved inaccurate, ...therefore he constructed...instruments of his own invention...of stone and lime, of perfect stability, with attention to the rules of geometry, and the adjustment to the meridian, and to the latitude of the place, and with care in the measuring and fixing of them to remove the inaccuracies and overcome the other limitations."

Both lunar and solar calendars were in use; based on them were a number of calendars depending upon the language of the writer or the country of his origin.

Time was measured either by count of respiration projected to day or year or by the division of day and night in equal parts. Sun dials and clepsydra were also developed to measure time. The general divisions were:

60 Til	1 Bipal
60 Bipal	1 Pal
60 Pal	1 Ghazi
60 Ghazi	One day and night

i.e., each ghazi was roughly equal to modern 24 minutes. Roughly 7 *ghazis* were equal to one *pahara.* A day and a night comprised 8 *pahars.*

Earth was considered to be flat or a solid sphere; its rotation though discussed was refuted, and the geocentric theory was generally accepted. The phenomenon of seasons was explained on the basis of revolution of the sun, and in general the Ptolemaic scheme was in vogue.

Most of the books of the time were commentaries on earlier works, mostly of Tusi, Al-Kashi and other astronomers, or translations from Sanskrit works. Of the Sanskrit works mention may be made of the Tables of Makaranda (A.D. 1478), *Tithyadipatra* or *Grahalaghava* of Ganesa (A.D. 1528), and *Tajikanilakanthi* (*c.* A.D. 1587) which gives the astronomy of Arabo-Persian School. Three astronomical tables were produced : *Zij-i-Shah Jahani* (A.D. 1628) by Fariduddin Masud bin Hafiz Ibrahim Dihlawi) (d. A.D. 1629). In the reign of Shah Jahan, Malajita, on whom the emperor had conferred the title of Vedangaraya, compiled *Parsiprakasa* (A.D. 1643). It deals mainly with conversion of dates, *Zij-i-Jadi-i-Muhammad Shahi* was written over a century later by Raja Sawai Jai Singh II of Jaipur and it is by far the most outstanding book of the period.

Mathematics

Before the period began, two outstanding Indian mathematicians had made major contributions—Sridhara (b A.D. 991), author of *Ganita Sara*, and Bhaskara (12th century), author of *Lilavati Bija Ganita* and *Siddhanta Siromani*. *Ganita Sara* deals with multiplication, division, square root, cubes, fractions, zero, natural numbers, partnership, mensuration and shadow reckoning.

Bhaskara's *Lilavati* covers notation, operation with integers, fraction, commercial rules, interest, permutation and combination and algebra. *Bija Ganita* directed numbers, negative quantities (unknown quantities are designated with colours), and simple and quadratic equations. In *Siddhanta Siromani*, Goladhyaya deals with spheres.

Some of these works along with the works from Central Asia, Iran and West Asia were translated into Persian. For instance, *Lilavati* was translated by Faizi in A.D. 1587 and *Bija Ganita* by Araullah Rashidi in the 8th year of Shah Jahan's reign. There were other translations and commentaries too. All these exerted great influence.

Riyazi (Mathematics) during the period comprised Hisab (Arithmetic), Hindsah (Geometry), Hai'at (Astronomy) and Musiqi (Music).

The works frequently used were those of Bahauddin Amuli (16th-17th century), Nasruddin Tusi (13th century), Arraq (11th century), and Al-Kashi (15th century). Amuli's *Khulasatul Hisab* was used throughout the period and seems to have been the most popular. In Sanskrit Narayana

Pandit's *Ganita Pali Kaumudi* (A.D. 1356) and Nayana Sakba's *Ukarathya Grantha* (A.D. 1731) are worth mentioning.

In Arithmetic, the study covered positive integers, fraction, rule of three, method of trial and error, mensuration, measurement of weight and calculation of distances.

In Algebra, the general development was on the lines laid down by Al-Khwarazmi, Bhaskara and Amuli. Asmatullah Saharanpuri (17th century) contributed to the knowledge of quadratic equations.

In Geometry, Euclid's translations were the most commonly used, and a large number of commentaries were written on them. Of these two *Sharh-i-Uqlidis*, one by Mir Muhammad Hashim (17th century) and the other by Maulavi Muhammad Barkat (18th century) are the important ones, and make substantial contributions to the theory parallel postulate.

Another illustrious family contributed considerably to the development of Mathematics by way of translation of commentaries—Ustad Ahmad al-Mi'mar Lahori, his sons Ataullah Rashidi and Lutfullah Muhandis, and Muhandis's two sons Imamuddin Riyazi and Khairullah Rashidi translated *Bija Ganita*, while Riyazi is said to have written 25 books on various subjects, particularly on Mathematics and Astronomy.

The general course of development was by way of preparing summaries of or commentaries on earlier works, rather than of developing new techniques, concepts or notations. The application of Mathematics was mostly limited to Astronomy. Its use in drawing magical squares, alchemy and astrology called for intellectual resourcefulness.

Chemistry

The general ideas in the field were alchemical. There were four elements—Fire, Earth, Air and Water—with four qualities (*khawass*) hot, dry, moist and cold. There were neither any definite ideas regarding chemical combination, nor any understanding of the chemical nature of substances. The wide interest in the philosopher's stone and elixir of life gave rise to charlatans and adventures.

Weights and balances, the first requisite of Chemistry, were crude and rudimentary. The bases of weight measurements were seeds, poppy, black and white mustard, barley, *gunja*, *ratti* and *masa*. The standardization carried out in respect of weights of higher denominations could hardly have any relevance to Chemistry. The theory of Chemistry was alchemical and in close association with Astrology, and its application was limited to medicine and industrial processes, there being no proper relation between the two. The stage had not been reached when it could develop as an independent branch of science to study matter and to investigate its chemical composition.

Various compounds of mercury and arsenic and also extracts and decoctions from different herbs were used in medicine. Although a large number of compounds were prepared or isolated from organic substances, hardly any attempt was made to identify or name them. They were just referred to in connection with processes of drug manufacture.

There were no doubt references to a large number of manufacturing processes, but the approach was empirical and no attempt was made to standardize the processes. Those engaged in the field occupied a low social status, the equipment used were crude and the processes adopted were elementary.

Mineral acids were used. Making of both fire-works and weapons was well known. Mention may also be made here of the glazed tiles and pottery made during the period. Further, technical skill combined with chemical knowledge was of a high standard, but the knowledge remained only at an empirical level, codified into a set of practices which were to be followed if good results were to be achieved. There was no scope for freshness of outlook or innovations. No doubt some of the manufactures reached the highest standards of quality and excellence, but what is regrettable is that there was little attempt at standardization or systematic efforts to find ways and means of increasing output.

Knowledge was handed down from father to son, or teacher to student. Except in medicine, there was no development of technical literature as such, and much of the stagnation was perhaps due to failure in developing this medium of transmitting knowledge. The few works that have come down are of an alchemical nature, or deal with preparation of medicines. Of them, mention may be made of *Rasaratnasamuccaya*, *Rasarajalaksmi* and *Rasasara*. In the 17th century, Mulla Mahmud Jaunpuri wrote *Hikmat-ul-Balighah* and its commentary *Ash-Shams-ul-Bazighah*. *Majmu'at-us-Sana'i* of Mir Yahya (A.D. 1624) is an illustrated encyclopaedia of crafts, and deals with manufacture of precious stones, dissolving of metals, polishing of glass and colouring of wares, and a number of other processes

Metallurgy

The general emphasis throughout the period remains on the use of metals and alloys for making of armament or decorative objects, and in neither field any significant technological advance seems to have been made.

Cannons and guns were made of brass, bronze, iron and steel. These were generally used in India from A.D. 1400 onwards. The mining and casting processes were crude, and there were no visible efforts at improvement of quality or at reducing cost. Babur in *Tuzuk-i-Baburi* gives an account of the casting of cannons: around the mould, furnaces were erected, with channels to mould; the metal (copper in this case) was melted and allowed to run into the mould, till it was full, and then it was allowed to cool. The weight of a giant size cannon was 30.48 to 47.76 tonnes, length 9 44 m., and the bore 0.475 m.

The earliest use of iron in construction seems to have been in the Sun temple at Konarak (9th century) where it was used in making beams. The composition of the beams is very similar to that of the famous Iron Pillar at Delhi, but unlike the latter the beams of the Sun temple have rusted.

An early 19th century account of smelting of iron and making of steel throws light on the primitive techniques.

According to Voysey, a cake equivalent to the weight of 110 rupee coins was sold for half a rupee.

Coating of copper utensils with tin came into vogue and gained much currency; according to some it was introduced round about A.D. 1300. Abul Fazl refers to tinning of copper vessels for use in the royal household of Akbar.

The lead alloy Bizari (8:2:1 copper, lead and tin) was used mostly for articles of decorative character. White and coloured enamels were also developed and used.

Medicine

Medicine covered a wide range of subjects including dietetics and food technology. The main emphasis was on diagnosis of diseases and their cure. Diagnosis was based on observation of the general condition of the patient and examination of pulse and urine. Though non-quantitative and non-chemical, the great progress made in the development of these techniques was of immense value. A Persian treatise of the 17th century widely used in India, *Tuhfat-ul-Mu'minin* by Muhammad Mu'min Husaini Tunkabuni, discusses in detail differences of opinion amongst physicians regarding drug action.

There were specialized treatises on diseases such as fevers and particular organs of the body such as eyes and stomach. *Nurul-Uyun* by Zarrin Dast (A.D. 1087) deals with the constitution of the eye and its diseases which can be seen and those cannot, and also suggests prophylactic measures for the latter. The use of spectacles was known, the earliest reference being of 16th century.

There is no conclusive evidence to show that dissection was practised. There are, however, a few treatises on anatomy of the human body, describing in detail the bones, nerves, veins, arteries and muscles and various organs. Something of this knowledge was based on earlier treatises written outside India. In this connection Al-Baidawi's *Mukhtasar dar Ilm-i-Tashrih* (13th century), Muhammad Riza's *Riyaz-i-Alamgiri* (17th century), *Ta:hrih-ul-Badan* (15th century), and Abdur

Razzaq's *Khulasat-ul-Tashrih* are worth mentioning. The last one incidentally is fully illustrated. These authors knew the difference between veins and arteries, but had no idea of the circulation of blood.

But Jabir bin Hayyan (A.D. 8th century), a disciple of Imam Jafar Sadique, in his book *Maghz-i-Mutafakkir-i-Jahan-i-Shia*'[16] has recorded an interview of Mufazzil bin Umar with Imam Jafar which explains the circulation and impurity of the blood and their effects on health and disposition of man. Abu Ali Senna has also given a chapter on Blood Circulation in his 'Qanoon'. (Perhaps the compiler of the Book 'India—Society, Religion and Literature' has no idea about these books.)

Bhuwa bin Khwas Khan's *Ma'dan-ush-Shifa-i-Sikandar Shahi* (A.D. 1512), written at Delhi for Sikandar Shah Lodi, is based on Sanskrit sources, and uses Sanskrit terms extensively.

In the nature of things, physicians were quite occupied by poisons and their antidotes, and a number of treatises deal with these. The antidotes were both of mineral composition as well as of alkaloidal nature.

A number of treatises of the period show the care and thought given to dietetics. There was knowledge of food preserves, both of pickling and use of sugar syrups (*morabba* and *sharbat*). But the knowledge did not go deep enough and lead to the understanding of the constituents involved in preservation.

In the practice of medicine, considerable knowledge was accumulated relating to description of medicinal plants and their properties, preparation of decoctions and extracts, study of the effect of drugs on human body, chemical processes connected with it—extraction, distillation, evaporation, drying, etc.

Curiously, oils and perfumes also were a part of medicine, and medical lists give details about their preparation for their use, and their benefits.

General regard for sanitation was part of the medical

16. Alwaiz Monthly, March 1984, pp. 36-37, Lucknow.

practice and various directions in this respect are given, such as in *Riyaz-i-Alamgiri* of Muhammad Riza.

The knowledge and practice of medicine at the time reveals a strong and vigorous tradition.

There are a few references to hospitals, but the practice of medicine was highly individualistic. The individual practitioners, however, distinguished, could not command resources to effect great improvements, either in basic knowledge or on the organization side.

Engineering and Technology

Besides the sciences described above, there was considerable development in engineering, mainly civil, as is evident from various constructions of houses, mausoleums, mosques, bridges, dams and canals. There was some progress also in technology, particularly textiles, ceramics and metallurgy. There is some evidence to indicate the windmills, telescopes, cranes and automatic firing guns were developed as toys. Watermills were in use, but not extensively. Lack of development of printing technology is one of the most significant facts with very far-reaching consequences.

The developments of this period (A.D. 1206-1761) can only be appreciated fully in the context of the developments in contemporary Europe. In making a comparative evaluation one becomes intensely aware that these developments were in a very limited framework, unaware of and impervious to contemporary developments in spite of direct contacts with Europe. It is amusing that the emissaries of Raja Sawai Jai Singh did not bring back the books of Copernicus, Galileo and Newton, but only of De la Hire. The lack of awareness was the same in other fields too.[17]

Like men, Muslim women have also the tradition of learning from the very beginning. A lot of women in India at different stages of history have attained distinctive positions in the field of education. But it was confined mainly to

17. "India,—Society, Religion and Literature", 1981, pub. by Govt. of India, Ministry of Information and Broadcasting, pp. 126-29, 135-36, 159-69 & 170-78.

princesses and upper class ladies. This class employed the Atalique (teachers), males or females, with boarding and lodging facilities, preferably learned relations. Females generally did not go to attend the academic institutions where co-education was imparted on account of seclusion and purdah. At best it was permissible till the elementary level Society accorded an honourable place to educated women, some of whom rose to the eminence of being King's advisers and counsellers by dint of sheer merit.

Though ladies in medieval India did not accomplish that much of excellence in literary education as Muslim ladies of Baghdad and Spain, however, there were luminaries like Razia Sultana, Mehr Angez, Islam Khatun, etc.[18] A survey of contemporary literature reveals the state of learning and status acquired by Muslim women in the sphere of religion, politics, medicine, etc.

In Moghal period too female education was not ignored. Special care was taken of the schooling of Moghal princesses. They were imparted lessons in religion, literature, arithmetics and sometimes they were also initiated into warfare and fine arts, etc. Chand Bibi, Gulbadan Begum, Nur Jahan, Jahan Ara, Sahibji, Gulrukhi, Salima Sultana, Zaibun Nisa, Zinat-un-Nisa, Mumtaz Mahal, etc. distinguished themselves in the sphere of literature and politics. Akbar established a madrasa for girls attached to his fort at Fatehpur Sikri.[19]

With the rise of English and fall of Mughals, socio-cultural life of Indian Muslims was badly affected. In order to protect their identity, Indian Muslims thought it best to spread mass education. But the Muslim intelligentsia could not decide unanimously on the form and content of education. Two main viewpoints emerged—one argued for the traditional religious education and the other favoured a secular and modern education of western model. The protagonists of

18. Rashid, A., "Society and Culture in Medieval India", Firma K.L. Mukhopadhya, Calcutta, 1969, pp. 143-144.

19. Ali, S. Nausha, "Musalmanan-e-Hind-o-Pakistan ki Tarikh-e-Ta'leem, Karachi, Suleman Academy, 1963, p. 286.

the former set up Darul-Uloom, Deoband, and the latter founded the Muslim University at Aligarh. The differences in the policy of education created a gulf and hampered the growth of Muslim education. But the Khilafat Movement of 1920 played an important role in uniting the Indian Muslims. Muslims from all walks of life assembled and gave a second thought for adopting a moderate educational policy. This resulted in the establishment of two more universities making the total number of Muslim centres of education four: Muslim University, Aligarh, as a secular seat of learning tending to modernity; University of Darul-Uloom, Deoband as a purely religious one; University of Nadwat-ul-Ulema, Lucknow as more a religious and less a worldly teaching centre; and lastly Jamia Millia Islamia, Delhi as more a worldly and less a religious institution. Later on a fifth University took shape as Jamia Usmania on the pattern of Muslim University, Aligarh.

Sir Syed Ahmad Khan, founder of A.M.U. would be remembered for all time to come for his leadership in the field of modern education among Indian Muslims. It was mainly concerned with the development of rational outlook in respect of Western education and creating a taste in Muslims for a modern scientific education imparted in an Islamic setting. The Aligarh movement launched by Sir Syed was a watershed in the history of modern education of Indian Muslims, which attracted a large number of Muslim youths, both male and female, from all corners and sections of India.

Dr. Sir Mohammad Iqbal, the renowned Islamic poet, the philosopher and the reformer of the 20th century, also realised the importance of modern scientific education, but, at the same time he was of the firm opinion that Islamic ideals were essential for a Muslim to build his character and to preserve his ego. Thus Iqbal's philosophy presented a fusion of Islam and modernism in presenting a system of education. Such a synthetic educational philosophy of Dr. Iqbal made a profound impact on the Indian Muslims and their educational policies.

The educational movement started by Sir Syed and its philosophy put forward by Dr. Iqbal gave impetus to the origin and growth of educational institutions for Muslim boys and girls in different parts of India by the end of the first decade of this century.[20] The Muslim Girls School in Lucknow was founded by Karamat Husain. The Begum of Bhopal pursuaded people send their daughters to schools where adequate provision was made for purdah. In Aligarh, Begum Abdullah went from house to house requesting people to send their daughters to the school started by her. In Patna, too, Badshah Nawab Rizvi started a girls school known as B.N.R. Training School (now a College), and the Muslim Educational Committee opened a boys school known as Mohammedan Anglo-Arabic Oriental School at Patna City. Likewise, Anjuman-e-Islam of Bombay and Muslim Educational Society of Madras, etc., started schools and colleges in their respective states. Now-a-days, most of the Islamic schools which give Islamic Ethics-oriented education, have also started teaching both Hindi and English so that the children may be able to compete with others and may not fall back in the democratic set up of competition. Referring to this fact Amir Ali states, "There is no demand now for Arabic or Persian education. A strong desire has grown up among all the sections of Mohammedan community for the study of English language and literature.[21] These attempts proved fruitful in turning people's faces towards education.

For the Indian Muslims, Urdu has got very important place. It expresses community sentiments and has achieved religious significance. It is the mother language specially of the Muslims of Bihar, Uttar Pradesh, Madhya Pradesh, Jammu and Kashmir and parts of Maharashtra, Andhra Pradesh and Karnataka. In Bihar Urdu has got the status of second official language and now Uttar Pradesh is trying to follow Bihar.

20. Brijbhushan, Jamila, "Muslim Women in Purdah and Out of It", Vikas Pub. House Pvt. Ltd., New Delhi, 1980, p. 99.

21. Ali Amir, "Mohammedan Education", in 'History of Education in Bihar' by Roy Bahadur Bhagvati Sahay, United Press Ltd., Bhagalpur, 1928, p. 300.

Unfortunately, even all these could not accelerate the growth of general education among Muslim youths of the first three or four decades of the 20th century. What to tell about the female education, the males also were very shaky about the higher education. Shukla makes responsible to two main factors—(1) migrating of a large number of educated elite to Pakistan, and (2) continued communal hatred.[22] These facts reveal that from the lack partly of desire and partly of recourse and, of course, due to new socio-political developments, Muslims are lagging behind in the pursuit of education. Abid Husain suggests, "To remove this the organized campaign, such as Sir Syed had started to break the spell of the so-called religious prejudice of Muslims, against English education is required."[23]

In a secular democratic system like India, competition is the only way to survival. The modern age is a fast-running age. Whoever will strive to have pace with the age, he will survive; and those lagging behind, will be left back far behind others. The time and tide wait for none. If Muslims, as a community, have to maintain equi-status in the greater Indian society, they must strive for having pace with others in all walks of life—especially education, which is the pivotal force of all success in life. This understanding was evoked among the Muslims by the enlightened leaders like Sir Syed Ahmad Khan with good results. The Muslims who were afraid of English system of education due to anti-British clergical propaganda, started realising importance of the modern education when they were assured of equal importance of religious teachings vis-a-vis modern teaching. Sir Syed Ahmad Khan established a college at Aligarh with a new system of education combining both Islamic Fiqh and modern sciences, which had a quick and encouraging impact on the outlook and attitude of the Muslim community inasmuch as the Aligarh College grew, within a very short span of time, into a Muslim University. Dr. Zakir Husain established another

22. Shukla, Ibid., p. 212.
23. Abid Husain, "The Destiny of Indian Muslims", pp. 232-233, Asia Publishing House, Bombay, 1965.

University in Delhi known as Jamia-e-Millia with a view to integrate the national spirit with that of religious spirit, and introduced the same syllabii as introduced in the Muslim University. The third University was established on more or less the same line in Hyderabad known as Jamia-e-Usmania. These efforts of the enlightened Muslim leaders of the country gave an impetus to the educational reform and, by and by, it took the shape of an educational revolution among the Muslims of the country. During the last three decades the attitude of the Muslims of India has well reconciled with the modern demands and both boys and girls of this community have accepted the necessity of modern and formal education. Majority of the urban Muslims send their wards to institutions imparting formal education. This new trend is expected to change the attitude, norms and values with regard to modern and formal education, which we shall analyse in the light of the data obtained from the field in respect of education.

But, before analysing the data, it is worthwhile to give the views of educationists and social scientists about the impact of education in general and that of formal education in particular on individuals and on society. Education in general and formal education in particular has been regarded as a powerful force of social change and social development. The pre-literate societies were immobile and more or less in a state of stagnation due to lack of education. The traditional societies were near-immobile societies showing a very slow process of change due to educational backwardness and confining it to the privileged class of traditional society. With the rise of industrialism and technological achievements, education also expanded and the concept of mass education developed in the modern age. As a result of the development of the idea of mass literacy and mass education the importance of education was recognized and it is regarded as one of the powerful factors of social change. The entire social structure is undergoing significant changes under the impact of spreading and expanding education. In the words of Broom and Selznick, "Today education is more important in size and scope than ever before in human history. In earlier times the educated man was economically unproductive; today productivity depends on wide distribution of specialised skills. Modern political systems, too, call for mass education. Effective participation in a modern society requires heady investment in educational institutions.

"Like the broader process of socialisation itself, education has a dual significance. It is person-centred and society-centred. Education enhances the capabilities of the individual and contributes to his self-reliance; at the same time, education does symbolic and practical work for the social system. The need to balance these functions, personal and social, poses perennial issues of education."[24] This remark of Broom and Selznick suggests that education is significant both for individual and societal growth. On one hand it helps in the development of individual's personality and on the other it contributes to social development and social progress. The functions of formal education perform five functions of (1) cultural transmission, (2) social integration, (2) innovation, (4) screening and allocation, and (5) personal development as given by Broom and Selznick.[25] The functions of social integration, innovation, screening and allocation and personal development form the key role of education in the process of social change and social development. Referring to the social integration role of formal education, Broom and Selznick observe, "Formal education is a major agency for transforming a heterogeneous and potentially divided community into one bound together by a language and a sense of common identity. The rise of national states in Europe, for example, are aided by the creation of systems of public education."[26] In the same way, referring to the functions of formal education's role of screening and allocation, the authors remark, "The allocating function tends to bring the educational system into close co-ordination with government and industry. In a period of rapidly changing technology, the school system runs the risk of turning out

24. Broom, Leonard and Selznick, Philip, 'Sociology', p. 339.
25. Ibid., pp. 339-40.
26. Ibid., p. 340.

students who are ready for yesterday's jobs rather than today's or tomorrow's."[27] The remarks clearly suggest that through generating inter-generational mobility, education contributes to development of personality as well as generational gap. Moreover formal education helps in acquainting younger generation with new skills and modern technological knowledge and develops disciplinary atmosphere in the educational institutions. The disciplinary function of education is significant in changing attitudes, behaviours and ideas of the individuals receiving formal education. As pointed out by Broom and Selznick, "In addition to providing intellectual discipline and the opportunity to specialised subject-matters, the school is often a place of transition from a highly personal to a more impersonal world; habits are learnt, such as punctuality, that may be necessary in a time-conscious society."[28] It appears from these remarks that education performs significant functions in the development of personality as well as in the development and progress of society, whether it is the development in society or of human personality, changes are bound to take place in social life.

Analysing the concept of education, Brookover and Gottlieb have pointed out that education may be regarded as "the process of teaching and learning expected patterns of human conduct."[29] It includes any social behaviour that assists in the induction of the child into membership in society or in behaviour by which the society perpetuates itself through the new generation.[30] It appears from these remarks that education is a process which is synonymous with the process of socialisation. According to Durkheim, education is a methodical socialisation.[31] Whether education is socialisation

27. Ibid.
28. Ibid.
29. Brookover, W.B. and Gottlieb, D., 'A Sociology of Education' p. 16.
30. Ibid., pp. 16-17.
31. Durkheim, Emile, 'Education and Sociology'.

in general or a methodical socialisation, it is evident that education helps in the development of personality and in acquainting the younger generation with the culture of the society. It is also important to point out that education—a specific form of socialisation—is instrumental not only in maintaining the culture through the process of transmission of culture but it is also helpful in the transformation and creation of culture. This function of transforming or creating culture results in the development of new trends, patterns of behaviour, ideas, attitudes and forms of social relationship of the next generation. In this way education plays a significant role in developing social life and in generating or accelerating the process of social change.

Analysing the concept of education and its functions, F.J. Brown has pointed out, "All education proceeds by the participation of the individual in the social consciousness of the races."[32] It means that education has a preparatory function because it prepares the individual to participate in group life and enables him to become a participating member of his society. As education helps in the development of attitudes, ideas and behaviour patterns, educated person is expected to be possessing a higher degree of the sense of responsibility and social consciousness; and, hence, his activities and behaviours are different from the behaviours and activities of uneducated people. Consequently, from this point of view also, education plays a vital role in changing society, social system and social structure.

Dealing with the functions of education, Payne has pointed out that education performs the three functions of assimilation of traditions, development of new social order and creative and constructive role. It is obvious that the function of assimilation of tradition refers to the continuity of culture and social stability. But the remaining two functions, i.e., development of new social order and constructive and creative role refer to the significance of education in

32. Brown, F.J., 'Educational Sociology'.

bringing about social change. It is obvious that in case new social patterns develop, the social system and social structure will undergo radical change. In the same way, creative function of education and its constructive roles are also of key importance in changing and developing society. The countries having considerable advance in higher scientific education have achieved a lot in the field of scientific invention and development in the field of science and technology has revolutionised their social structure. In this way the constructive and creative roles of education are also significant in generating and facilitating the process of social change.

Analysing the concept and importance of education in human life, Stewart and Glynn have pointed out, "Education has the universal function of contributing to the perpetuation of societies, transmitting their ideas from generation to generation, and preparing the young for active roles in the culture. Education is, therefore, a reflection of the culture itself, and in complex and changing societies it displays some of the value conflicts and strains between real and ideal norms that are typical of all cultures. Since social change is an inevitable part of societies, specially modern societies, education does more than merely transmitting the accumulative wisdom of the past. It has the function of adding to the knowledge of the past, helping to select what is being retained and making critical evaluation of tradition. For this reason, education, like religion, is complementary and sometimes conflicting function—thus of preservation and innovation. Schools can be so rigid in their attempt to instil loyalty to old traditions that they become stiffling to the needs of social change; or they may virtually ignore tradition, making their cultures seem rootless and lacking in sense of identity."[33]

It is evident from the above given views that education performs the dual role of stabilisation of social order and generating, or facilitating, social dynamism. It depends upon the type and nature of education what function will it perform in the society. In case the education is sacred and authoritarian, the content of education is faith-oriented which is

33. Stewart, E.W. and Glynn, J.A , 'Introduction to Sociology', p. 323.

conservative and orthodox in nature. Consequently, this type of education does not help in favouring social change, rather it develops a trend to maintain whatever has been existing. The authoritarian system of education means that the right of education is not given to all sections of the society rather it is the privilege of a particular section occupying higher status or power in the society. Consequently, this privileged section does not favour the idea of any change in the system of social hierarchy and the patterns of social stratification, etc., to maintain and preserve whatever has been existing. Consequently, if a society has authoritarian and sacred system of education, the change is either absent or very slow. Here the education performs the task of assimilation of tradition and transmission of culture. It maintains the continuity of culture. But in case education is secular and democratic, functions of education are quite different. A secular system of education is that in which the content of education is reason-oriented and concerned with the problems about the man and around the man. In the same way the democratic system of education means that education is not a monopoly or an exclusive privilege of the upper stratum of the society, rather educational institutions are open to all. It is obvious that under a democratic and secular system of education youths from lower strata are also encouraged and motivated to receive education. Moreover the content of education helps in developing rational outlook and modernism resulting in the break-away from orthodox and irrational traditionalism. Consequently, this type of education is highly significant in bringing about changes in social structure, social system, modes of behaviour and patterns of social relationship.

With the advent of democracy and uprooting of the authoritarianism, both developed and developing nations have adopted secular and democratic system of education. In the pre-British days the system of education prevalent in India was authoritarian and sacred. The Britishers introduced secular and democratic system of education and provided opportunities for low caste and low class people to receive education. The democratic system of education helps in the rationalisation of attitude and outlook through recognition of broader ideas and views about humanity and human survival, and rejecting the conservative norms, value and ideas. After achievement of independence, specific steps were taken to promote the condition of literacy and education among weaker section of the society. Besides adopting a policy of mass literacy for children up to the age of 14, the Central and the State Governments have had taken different measures to help the socially and economically handicapped children and youths to receive school and college education. Facilities of free education have been provided for scheduled castes and scheduled tribes and seats have been reserved for them in educational institutions. Stipends and scholarships are also being awarded to promising youths as well as to the youths belonging to weaker sections or lower classes of the Indian society. Moreover a large number of schools, colleges and universities have been set up in the country for meeting the demands of expanding education. The expansion in higher education may be realised from this simple fact that at the time of achievement of independence there were only 21 universities in the country, but today there are about 160 universities in the country. The number of colleges and, consequently, the number of youth receiving college and university education has also increased proportionately. Though of late, the necessity of girls schools and colleges has also been felt to attract the tradition-oriented women youth towards formal education. The role of women being pivotal in the well-being of society as well as of nation, the national government could not turn a deaf ear to the educational requirements of the fairer sex. Hence, under a sophisticated programme of all-round development of this section of the society, special arrangements have been made for women education. Women being part and parcel of the human society and commanding nearly half of their population, the national government could hardly afford their seclusion within the four walls of homesteads and destroy nearly half of the national human resource or manpower. It was also obligatory on the part of national government under the Constitution to make every possible effort for the development of the conditions of women. Separate schools and colleges for women is not a part of state policy, as a developing economy can ill afford such a heavy burden on one hand and it cannot encourage a distance between national brothers and sisters in the making of the nation. Hence co-education is the social as well as economic need of the nation.

Census reports present an encouraging result and a positive impact of the efforts of national government on the attitude of the Indian women. This impact is evident from the presenee of women in almost all walks of life and faculties of teaching and learning. This impact is quite visible and large in the urban communities. In the early morning one may witness long lines of girls going to schools and colleges, women youth travelling by buses to attend their duties in government, semi-government and private establishments and the housewives crowding the market places for evening marketing. This surely speaks of a drastic change in the attitude of the Indian woman. How far the urban Muslim women of Patna have modified their age-old traditional norms and values, attitudes and behaviours, life style—is the main objective of the present study. The impact of modern currents may differ from age to age, caste to caste, literacy level to literacy level, income to income and the past social background. Hence it was planned to study these facts through interviewing 300 women of Muslim community residing in Patna. The data have been tabulated and analysed on the basis of different variables to understand clearly the variation in the degree of their susceptibility to the modern currents and forces as well as to locate the forces of resistance and their extent. The results have been tabulated and presented in the following tables.

It is evident from Table 1 that, on the whole, 19.3% of the sample is illiterate, 31.6% is literate, 28.0% is high school pass, 15.0% of the women are college educated and 6.0% of them is post-graduate. On the basis of age, among post-graduate the highest population of 13.3% is up to 25 years of age, 6.6% is between 26-35 years and 2.4% of

Table 1
Age and Education of the Respondents

Age	Educational Level					Total
	Illiterate	*Literate*	*High School*	*College*	*Post-Graduate*	
Up to 25	8	13	24	22	10	75
	8 0	17.3	32.0	29.3	13.3	
26-35 yrs.	7	25	39	13	6	90
	7.7	27.7	43.3	14.4	6.6	
36-45 yrs.	16	44	13	7	2	82
	19.5	53.6	15.8	8.5	2.4	
46 +	29	13	8	3	—	53
	54.7	24.5	15 0	5.6		
Total	58	95	84	45	18	300
	19.3	31.6	28.0	15.0	6.0	

Decimal Figures are percentages.

them is in the age-group of 36-45 years. No woman respondent beyond 45 years of age has attained post-graduate level of education. There appears a consistent decline in the percentages of response declaring education up to post-graduate level with the rise in age. In the same way, among college educated women we see the same trend of response. 29.3% of the respondents having college education are in the age-group up to 25 years, 14.4% are in the age-group of 26-35 years, 8.5% are in the age-category of 36-45 years, 5.6% are in the age-group of 46 and above. Thus we see that the percentage of higher education is higher in lower age categories and lower in higher age categories, which speaks of greater consciousness of higher academic pursuit among the younger generations than among the elder generation. It shows an encouraging impact of academic consciousness on the post-independence generation of the fairer sex. 32.0% of respondents in the age-group up to 25 years, 43.3% in the age-group 26-35 years, 15.8% in 36-45 years and 15.0% in the age above 46 years have read up to high school standard. Though any consistency in the rise or fall of the percentages of response in this respect is not found, it is quite clear that the two younger categories read up to high school standard in higher percentages than the two elder age-groups. So far illiteracy is concerened, the table shows that 8% of respondents up to 25 years, 7.7% of 26-35 years, 19.5% of 36-45 years and 54.7% of the pre-independence generation of women are illiterate. A near-consistent rise in the percentages of response in respect of illiteracy is quite evident with the rise in age. It means that during pre-independence era education had little value in the eyes of Muslims and this consciousness started rising with independence of the country and ceaseless efforts of the national government for the spread of mass education as well as higher education specially for women. It may, therefore, be interpreted that age is significantly relevant to the level of education among the fairer sex. It may be due to the fact that, during British rule, social and national consciousness was very poor among Indians in general and among Indian women in particular. The presence of women in the political and economic fields was never thought of by

Table 2
Caste and Education of the Respondents

Caste	*Educational Level*					*Total*
	Illiterate	*Literate*	*High School*	*College*	*Post-Graduate*	
Saiyid	1 1.8	22 40.0	17 30.9	10 18.1	5 9.9	55
Shaikh	3 5.0	16 26.6	22 36.6	12 20.0	7 11.6	60
Pathan	4 8.1	19 38.7	14 28.5	9 18.3	3 6.1	49
Mallick	6 16.6	7 19.4	14 38.8	17 47.2	2 5.5	36
Ansari	20 36.3	16 29.0	12 21.8	6 10.9	1 1.8	55
Rayeen	9 60.0	5 33.3	1 6.6	—	—	15
Chique	12 60.0	6 30.0	2 10.0	—	—	20
Kalal	3 30.0	4 40.0	2 20.0	1 10.0	—	10
Total	58 12 3	95 31 6	84 28.0	45 15.0	18 6.0	300

Decimal Figures are percentages.

people, hence only home education backed by a little religious education was thought enough. Hence there was no question of formal education among them.

It is evident from Table 2 that, on the whole, 19.3% of the women respondents are illiterate, 31.6% are literate, 28.0% are high school pass, 15.0% are college educated and 6.0% are post-graduate. On caste basis, 11.6% of Shaikhs, 9.9% of Saiyids, 5.5% of Mallicks, 6.1% of Pathans and 1.8% of Ansari women are post-graduate. In the same way, 47.2% of Mallicks, 20.0% of Shaikhs, 18.3% of Pathans, 18.1% of Saiyids, 10.9% of Ansaris, 10.0% of Kalals and 0% each of Rayeen and Chique are graduate; whereas 38.8% of Mallick, 36.6% of Shaikhs, 30.9% of Saiyids, 28.5% of Pathans, 21.8% of Ansaris, 20.0% of Kalals, 10.0% of Chiques and 6.6% of Rayeens are high school passed. Though the response patterns do not show any marked consistency on caste basis, one thing is clear that education including the higher education is found in higher percentages among higher castes than the lower castes. On the contrary, barring Kalal respondents, a consistent rise in the percentages of illiteracy is found from the table on caste basis —i.e. the percentage of illiteracy is lower in higher castes and higher in lower castes. 1.8% of Saiyids, 5.0% of Shaikhs, 8.1% of Pathans, 16.6% of Mallicks, 36.3% of Ansaris, 60.0% each of Rayeens and Chiques and 30.0% of Kalals are illiterate. At the same time 40.0% each of Saiyids and Kalals, 38.7% of Pathans, 33.3% of Rayeens, 30.0% of Chiques, 29.0% of Ansaris, 26.6% of Shaikhs and 19.4% of Mallicks are simply literate or home-educated. In this respect caste does not appear to be relevant; but on the whole caste is significantly relevant to the response patterns. In other words, education up to matriculation and above is found in greater percentages among higher castes than among lower castes. Higher education is completely absent among Rayeens and Chiques, whereas only one respondent of Kalal caste (10.0%) is reported to have read up to college level. Among lower castes it appears to have striden fast in the pursuit of formal education which is evident from this fact that 21.8% of them are matriculate, 10.9% graduate and 1.8% post-graduate. It is perhaps because of their active leadership and

Table 3

Income and Education of Respondents

Income	*Educational Level*					*Total*
	Illiterate	*Literate*	*High School*	*Graduate*	*Post-Graduate*	
Up to Rs. 500	34	51	7	—	—	92
	36.9	55.4	7.6			
Rs. 501—1000	12	20	29	4	1	66
	18.1	30.3	43.9	6.0	1 5	
Rs. 1001—1500	6	12	36	8	3	65
	9.2	18.4	55.3	12.3	4.6	
Rs. 1501—2000	4	7	8	12	5	36
	11.1	19.4	22.2	33.3	13.8	
Rs. 2001+	2	5	4	21	9	41
	4.8	12.1	9.7	51.2	21.9	
Total	58	95	84	45	18	300
	19.3	31.6	28.0	15.0	6.0	

Decimal Figures are percentages.

educational facilities (like freeships, scholarships, books, etc.) provided to them by Government; while the other lower castes appear to be lagging behind either due to absence of good leadership among them or due to traditional orthodoxy or social backwardness of these castes.

It is apparent from Table 3 that both the amount and level of education have risen with the rise in income, though not very consistently. 36.9% of the income-group of up to Rs. 500, 18.1% of the income-group of Rs. 501-1000, 11.1% of the income-group of Rs. 1501-2000, 9.2% of the income category of Rs. 1001-1500 and 4.8% of Rs. 2001 and above are illiterate. Barring the second highest income-group of Rs. 1501-2000, the percentages of illiteracy have consistently fallen with the rise in income. It means that income is significantly relevant in removing illiteracy from the Muslim women respondents of this urban setting. It may, therefore, be interpreted that economic backwardness is the main hurdle in the way of urban women securing education, and, if this bottleneck is removed, it is expected that Muslim women would stride fast in the way of academic pursuit. In the same way, 55.4% of the women in income group up to Rs. 500, 30.3% of Rs. 501-1000, 19.4% of the income-group of Rs. 1501-2000, 18.4% of the income category of Rs. 1001-1500 and 12.1% of the highest income group of Rs. 2001 and above are simply literate or home-educated. These may be those women whose family head/family environment may be conservative in the matter of sending women to fomal schools. One thing is quite apparent from these response patterns that the grip of this conservatism is loosened with the rise in income level, because the percentages in respect of literacy have consistently fallen with the rise in income level. Literacy up to matriculation level commands second position after simple literacy, which means that the grip of traditionalism is, on the whole, loosening and the general Muslim population is getting conscious of the importance of formal education. 7.6% of the income category of up to Rs. 500, 43.9% of the income group of Rs. 501-1000, 55.3% of Rs. 1001-1500, 22 2% of the second higher income group of Rs. 1501-2000 and 9.7% of the highest income group of Rs. 2001 and above have read up to matriculation. This response pattern suggests the percentages in respect of education up to matriculation have risen consistently from lowest to middle income-group. But the same has fallen to the extent of 22.2% in case of the income-group of second highest and 9.7% of the highest income group. It is because a sizeable portion of the women in these two highest income-groups have striden further to college and university education, whereas in case of the three lower income groups women in lower percentages have attained education up to college or university level. The table shows that 0% of the income category of up to Rs. 500, 5.6% of Rs. 501-1000, 12.3% of Rs. 1001-1500, 33.3% of Rs.1501-2000 and 51.2% of the highest income group have attained education up to graduation level. In the 0% of the lowest income group, 1.5% of the second lowest income group, 4.6% of the middle income group, 13.8% of the second highest income group and 21.9% of the highest income group have read up to post-graduate level. Thus we see that the percentages of response in case of college and university education have consistently risen with the rise in income level. It means that income is significantly relevant to higher education of Muslim women of this urban setting. Thus, on the whole, it may be interpreted that income is significantly instrumental in removing illiteracy and attainment of higher levels of education.

The role of family background is very significant in evolution of the level of education. Educated families are expected in a greater percentage to allow their wards or push them to high and highest level of educational pursuit despite economic bottleneck. Hence it was desired to evaluate the impact of educational level of the respondents in the light of the educational backgrounds of their families of procreation as well as of the families of parents. Generally a sizeable part of educational age is spent by women with their parents. If their parents are educated they like their daughters too to be educated in majority of the cases, and if they are illiterate or semi-literate they are little conscious of the importance of education of women in the modern age. In the same way, if their families of procreation are educated they like their daughter-in-laws or wives too to be educated even if they have

Table 4

Educational Background of Respondents' Mother, Father and Husband

Relation	*Educational Level*					*Total*
	Illiterate	*Literate*	*High School*	*College*	*Post-Graduate*	
Mother	154	119	19	6	2	300
	51.3	39 6	6.3	2.0	0.6	
Father	64	77	111	38	10	300
	21.3	25.6	37.0	12.6	3.3	
Husband	22	80	84	78	36	300
	7.3	26.6	28.0	26.0	12.0	

Decimal Figures are percentages.

not previously been educated. In many cases it is found that a girl was married just after learning up to matriculation or passing matriculation examination and their husbands managed to push them up in acquiring college and university level education. In this way the impact of family's education is significant in the improvement of the educational status of women, also because educated families are generally less conservative and more progressive in ideas and approach and they give equal importance to women and men's education in the modern age.

It is evident from Table 4 that in case of 51.3% of the respondents their mothers are illiterate, 39.4% literate, 6.3% high school pass, 2.0% college educated and 0.6% are post-graduate. Thus in majority of the cases mothers of the respondents are illiterate, whereas in a little less than fifty per cent of the cases they are either literate or educated. In all about 9% mothers are matriculate or highly educated. This figure is, however, not very encouraging from mothers' side. So far fathers are concerned, 21.3% of them are illiterate, 25.6% are literate, 37.0% are high school pass, 12.6% are graduate and 3.3% post-graduate. Thus we see that 53.0% of the fathers are either matriculate or highly educated, whereas only 9% of the mothers are in this category. So far husbands are concerned, 7.3% of them are illiterate, 26.6% literate, 28 0% high school pass, 26.0% are college educated and 12.0% post-graduates. Thus 66.0% of them are either matriculate or highly educated. Though these figures are not very encouraging in generating impetus for higher education, but at the same time it cannot be taken as degenerating figure. It is true that the older generation of women is lagging behind the average figure of women in respect of education, but the same figure in respect of fathers and husband is matching to other communities of the country. In all 42.8% of the parents and husbands are educated or highly educated and they have generated a population of 49.0% of educated or highly educated women. This upward trend of education speaks of consciousness of the Muslim community in respect of female education.

Table 5

Difference in Education between Mother and Daughter (Respondents)

(Percentage in brackets)

Level of Education	*Mother's Education*	*Daughter's (Respondents) Education*	*Difference in percentages of their education*
Illiterate	154(51.3)	58(19.3)	—32.0
Literate	119(39.6)	95(31.6)	— 8.0
High School	19(6.3)	84(28.0)	+21.6
College	6(2.0)	45(15.0)	+13.0
Post-Graduate	2(0.6)	18(6.0)	+ 5.3
Total	300	300	100

Table 5 presents a generational gap in educational levels of mothers and daughters (i.e. respondents). It shows a marked decrease (of 32.0%) in the volume of illiteracy between the elder generation and present generation. In the elder generation 51.3% of the mothers were illiterate whereas only 19.3% of the women respondents are illiterate. In the same way 39.6% of the elder generation (women), or the mothers of the respondents, are simply literate or home-educated whereas in the present generation this percentage is 31.6, showing a decrease of 8% in the percentage of simply literate among the present generation. Likewise there appears an improvement of 21.6% in the high school education, 13.0% in college education and 5.3% in university education over the elder generation. These figures are quite encouraging and they show an increasing consciousness of the Muslims of Patna about the importance of women education.

Table 6 presents difference between the educational levels or the gap between the male and female education in the present generation. According to the table 7.3% of the

Table 6

Difference in Education between Husbands and Respondents (Wives)

(Percentage in brackets)

Level of Education	*Husband's Education*	*Wife's Education*	*Difference (Percentage)*
Illiterate	22(7.3)	58(19.3)	12
Literate	80(26.6)	95(31.6)	5
High School	84(28.0)	84(28.0)	0
College	78(26.0)	45(15.0)	11
Post-Graduate	36(12.0)	18(6.0)	6
Total	300	300	–

husbands are illiterate whereas 19.3% of wives are illiterate. It means that 12% more women are illiterate than their male counterparts. In the same way there appears a difference of 5% in the percentages of literacy of male and female of the present generation—i.e. 5% more women are simply literate than their male counterparts. At the level of High School there appears no difference in the percentages of male and female education, i.e., both are equal. In college education 11% more males are educated at this level than their female counterparts, and in university level 6% more males are educated than their female life-partners. These figures speak of a huge difference between various levels of education of male and female population of the present generation. It may, therefore, be interpreted that though a marked consciousness about female education is found among the Muslim population under study, the gap between the two sexes is considerably high which speaks of the persistence of traditional outlook among Muslims of Patna. They do not give the same importance to the education of their daughter which they give to their son's education. For a balanced development of society education both for male and female is equally important, but this feeling is lacking among the Muslims of Patna as it is evident from the table under review.

Table 7

Respondent's Education and Objective of Education

(Percentage in brackets)

Education	*To acquire knowledge*	*To improve status*	*To get a good husband*	*To get good job*	*No specific aim*	*Total*
Illiterate	20(34.4)	12(20.6)	8(13.7)	—	18(31.0)	58
Literate	20(21.0)	12(12.6)	10(10.5)	—	53(55.7)	95
High School	19(22.6)	17(20.2)	14(16.6)	2(2.3)	32(38.0)	84
College	10(10.5)	16(35.5)	3(6.6)	8(17.7)	8(17.7)	45
Post-Graduate	4(22.2)	3(16.6)	1(5.5)	10(55.5)	—	18
Total	73(24.3)	60(20.0)	36(12.0)	20(6.6)	111(37.0)	300

It is evident from the table that majority (37.0%) of the respondents have no specific aim behind their educational programme. It means that majority of the Muslim women respondents are in disillusion and they have no future programme or consciousness about their social or national responsibilities and they want to remain a simple housewife. 24.3% of them have undertook academic pursuit with a view to enlighten themselves with higher thoughts and knowledge. 20.0% feel that education is an integral part of human status and they also feel that the status of women is lower in society because of their illiteracy. Hence they want to come at par with their men counterparts through securing education. 12.0% of the respondents feel that their better academic career may fetch better match for them, and 6.6% of the women respondents have secured education with a view to get good job in teaching or service occupations. Thus we see that among these women respondents economic pursuit is of very little value. It means that social and national service occupies the least place in the mind of these Muslim women respondents, and it is an indicator that this section of the Indian population has not yet come out of the clutches of traditionalism and religious conservatism.

On literacy basis, 34.4% of illiterates, 22.6% of high school passed, 22.2% of Post-graduates, 21.0% of literates and 10.5% of college-educated women have (or are) contented themselves with acquisition of knowledge as the main aim of their education. 35.5% of college educated women, 20.6% of illiterates, 20.2% of high school pass, 16.6% of post-graduates and 12.6% of literates' main objective of education is to improve their status in society and family. This opinion of the women respondents is based on their personal experience. They see in their day-to-day life that educated women are regarded both in family and society and exploitation is rare in their cases. They occupy respectable place in society as well as in their family; and, hence, a sizeable section of the Muslim women has acquired or is acquiring higher education to improve their status and to save themselves from exploitation by their husbands, other family members and society. 16.6% of high school pass, 13.7% of illiterates, 10.5% of literates,

6.6% of college-educated women and 5.5% of post-graduate respondents have expressed their aim of getting a good husband behind their pursuit of education. It is remarkable that quite insignificant percentages of college-educated (6.6%) and post-graduate respondents (5.5%) have given this reason. It is perhaps because due to their higher academic status they have no such problem and they are sure to get good matches. But the respondents up to high school standard are anxious about a good match and hence a good percentage of them has given this reason as the objective of their academic pursuit. 0% of illiterates and literates, 2.3% of high school pass respondents, 17.7% of college-educated women and 55.5% of post-graduate respondents have declared white-collar job to be their main aim of getting education. It is quite natural hat illiterates or simple literate Muslim women cannot expect a respectable job in offices or schools or colleges and they cannot accept menial job of class category, and hence none of them has expressed this aim behind their academic pursuit; but women of matriculation standard and above do legitimately hope for a respectable job in government offices, private establishments or in academic institutions. They are optimistic about their brighter career, and hence they aim to acquire higher education in order to get a respectable job. Still it is a fact that majority of the Muslim women do not want or they do not hope that their family heads would allow them to earn money or do service and work among men; and hence they want to maintain a distance between men and women. They are not ready to break their age-old tradition and treat service as a denegrading or disrespectful profession for the fairer sex. They are not ready to mingle with men of different castes and creeds and to become target of their amusement and eve-teasing, and hence, also, they do not have any specific aim of education in their minds. They are learning as a fashion of the age, and not with any motive or aim in their mind. Such women are 31.0% among illiterates, 55.7% among literates, 38.0% among high school pass ladies, 17.7% among college-educated respondents and 0% among post-graduate women. It may, therefore, be interpreted that aimlessness is in majority of the women up to high school

Table 8

Caste and Reason of remaining Illiterate

Caste	*Reasons*					*Total*
	Parents illiteracy	*Poverty*	*Lack of facility*	*Lack of encouragament*	*Any other*	
Saiyid	—	—	—	1 100	—	1
Shaikh	1 33.3	—	—	1 33.3	1 33.3	3
Pathan	1 25.0	—	—	2 50.0	1 25.0	4
Mallick	1 16.6	—	—	2 33.3	3 50.0	6
Ansari	4 20.0	3 15.0	3 15.0	5 25.0	5 25.0	20
Rayeen	3 33.3	1 11.1	1 11.1	2 22.2	2 22.2	9
Chique	3 25.0	2 16.6	2 16.6	2 16.6	3 25.0	12
Kalal	1 33.3	—	—	1 33.3	1 33.3	3
Total	14 24.1	6 10.3	6 10.3	16 27.5	16 27.5	58

Decimal figures are percentages.

standard and 17.7% of college-educated women, whereas no post-graduate woman is aimless. On the whole no significant consistency in response patterns is found on education basis, which means that education level is not significantly relevant in rationalising the attitude of women under study and majority of them have not come out of traditional clutches despite considerable rise in educational volume and percentage among them.

It is evident from Table 8 that the illiterate respondents (58) were asked to disclose the reasons of their being illiterate. In all four specific reasons have been given by the respondents alongwith fifth reason of 'any other', like lack of interest, bad treatment of step mother, ill health, etc. A majority of 27.5% each have stated the reasons of 'lack of encouragement' and 'any other' for their remaining illiterate, whereas 24.1% of the respondents have stated parents' illiteracy to be the reason of their illiteracy. 10.3% each have stated that poverty and lack of educational facilities like time, dress, electrical facility, etc. were the main reasons for their remaining illiterate. In fact both these reasons are analogous and they resemble to each other; and, thus, we may combine both the responses and can say that 20.6% of the respondents could not prosecute on their studies due to financial bottleneck or paucity of time.

Among Saiyid respondents only one is illiterate and she has given the reason of her illiteracy to be the lack of encouragement. There was none in her family or surroundings who could adduce her to learn reading or writing or to take admission in a school. 33.3% each of Shaikh respondents have given the reasons of parents' illiteracy, lack of encouragement and 'any other' reason for their remaining illiterate; whereas 25.0% of Pathan women have stated that their parents were illiterate and hence she could not learn to read and write, 50.0% of them said 'lack of encouragement' to be the reason of their illiteracy and 25.0% could not learn to read and write because of 'any other' reason. Among the six Mallick illiterates, 1 (16.6%) stated that her parents were illiterate and hence she is illiterate, 33.3% of them said 'lack of encouragement' to be the reason and 50.0% stated unspecified reason. Among 20 Ansari illiterate women, in case of 4 (20%) parents' illiteracy was the reason, in case of 25.0% each 'lack of encouragement' and 'any other' reason was the reason of their illiteracy and 15.0% each stated poverty and the lack of facility to be the reason of their illiteracy. In case of 9 Rayeen illiterates, 3 (33.3%) stated parents' illiteracy, 22.2% each gave the reasons of 'lack of encouragement' and 'any other' reason and 11.1% each gave the reasons of poverty and lack of facility. Among 12 Chique respondents, 3 each (25.0% each) gave the reasons of parents' illiteracy and 'any other' and 16.6% each (2 respondents each) gave the reasons of poverty, lack of facility and lack of encouragement. Among 3 Kalal illiterates, one each (33.3% each) mentioned the reasons of parents' illiteracy, lack of encouragement and any other reason for their remaining illiterate. These response patterns are not consistent with caste grading and hence it may be stated that caste is not significantly relevant to the reasons of the illiteracy of the respondents. Though there is no consistency in response patterns on caste basis, one thing is clear that Ansari, Chique and Rayeen respondents have mentioned the five reasons to be responsible for their illiteracy whereas in all other castes three reasons of (1) parents' illiteracy, (2) lack of encouragement and (3) any other have been mentioned. This finding suggests that these three low-ranking castes of Ansari, Chique and Rayeen are more problem-ridden; and in their cases poverty and lack of facility is the additional problem in way of their learning and education. Despite various facilities announced by the Government (like full freeship, liberal issuance of books) for these low-ranking castes, they are unable to manage other facilities like clothing, timing, fooding and lighting due to their immense poverty and financial backwardness. In case of Kalal these problems do no exist, because their business of toddy and wine is pretty fine and as such they have no financial problem. Kalals stand at par with high castes like Saiyid, Shaikh, Pathan and Mallick so far reasons of remaining illiterate are concerned.

The respondents were also asked if they are satisfied with their present level of education, and, if not, what was the reason blocking their way to achieve their aspired goal. This question was aimed to know their ambitions with regard to higher education and to find out whether there is aspirational mobility in the respondents with regard to their academic career. The responses obtained from them have been shown in Table 9.

It is evident from the table that this question was not asked from illiterates and post-graduates because, in the former case the respondents were not expected to have any such ambition or dissatisfaction and in the case of latter because they have already attained the highest level of education and they require no more institutional coaching. The most important reasons of dissatisfaction with the present state of educational attainment, given by 31.2% of the respondents, is parents' dislike. It means that in the opinion of the majority of the respondents parents did not like them to prosecute on further studies because of one reason or the other, and hence they could not achieve their aspired goal. The next important reason stated by 27.2% of the respondents was the economic hardship of the family which did not allow to continue further studies and they had to discontinue it under pressing economic circumstances. The third important reason of not achieving the desired goal, stated by 16.9% of the respondents, was the lack of institutional facilities like boarding, library facility, lack of practical instruments, etc. The next reasons given by 16.6% cf the respondents was lack of husband's approval. They got married before achieving their aspired level of education and after marriage they were crowded by familial responsibilities like service to husband, children and other family members, or, their husbands were of conservative attitude and they did not like to send their wives to academic institutions for further studies. 13.3% of the respondents had no outward reason or compulsion for breaking their studies, but they could not find themselves in a position to continue their studies for their own reasons like their consciousness about their family responsibilities and duties. On literacy basis, there does not appear to be any

Table 9

Education and Dissatisfaction with the Present State of Education

(Percentage in brackets)

Education Level	*Reason of Dissatisfaction*					*Total*
	Lack of institutional facility	*Economic hardship*	*Lack of husband's concurrence*	*Parents did not like more*	*Personal problems*	
Literate	10(10.5)	34(35.7)	—	35(36.8)	16(16.8)	95
High School	23(27.3)	20(23.8)	12(14.2)	22(26.1)	7(8.3)	84
College	5(11.1)	7(15.5)	13(28.8)	13(28.8)	7(15.5)	45
Total	38(16.9)	61(27.2)	25(16.6)	70(31.2)	30(13.3)	224

significant relevance of educational level to the reason of dissatisfaction. Hence it may be interpreted that educational level is not relevant in this case.

Lastly, the respondents were asked to express their opinion of favour or disfavour for the system of co-education. This question was very important because according to Islamic injunctions women are ordained to maintain a distance from stranger men, and free mixing of men and women, especially of young boys and girls, is strictly forbidden. Women may assemble with men on congregational occasions, but with special arrangement of their separate seating and proper veiling. The traditional customs further tightened the conditions and put them in virtual house-arrest – forbidding even talk in loud or lucrative voice with men folk. In such a situation, it was thought to be of highly sociological value to know their attitude in this regard in the present age when they are allowed to attend schools and colleges, to do marketing and do outing with or without escort. Co-education system may be of extra-modern arrangement in the eyes of Muslim women where there is no restriction of mixing with men. The responses obtained from the Muslim women respondents have been given in Table 10 below.

Table 10
Education and Attitude towards Co-education in Higher Classes

(Percentage in brackets)

Education	*Attitude*		*Tota.*
	Favourable	*Unfavourable*	
Illiterate	9(15.5)	49(84.4)	58
Literate	22(23.4)	73(76.8)	95
High School	34(40.4)	50(59.5)	84
College	36(80.0)	9(20.0)	45
Post-Graduate	18(100)	—	18
Total	119(39.6)	181(60.3)	300

It is evident from the table that 60.3% of the women respondents have disfavoured and 39.6% have favoured co-education system. 84.4% of illiterates, 76.8% of literates, 59.5% of high school passed respondents, 20.0% of college educated respondents and 0% of post-graduates have disfavoured co-education. It shows a consistent fall in the percentages of disfavour with the rise in educational level. In the same way, 15.5% of illiterates, 23.4% of literates, 40.4% of high school pass, 80.0% of college-educated women and 100% of post-graduates have favoured co-education. Here also a consistent rise in the percentages of favour for co-education is evident with the rise in educational level. It may, therefore, squarely be interpreted that educational level is significantly relevant to the response in respect of co-education. Highly educated Muslim women do not find any harm in sitting with boys in classrooms whereas lowly educated women disfavour it and they want to maintain a clear-cut distance with men or male students. Hence it may be interpreted that education is a powerful force to rationalise the attitude in regard to unrestricted mixing of young boys and girls in educational institutions.

6

Purdah

Purdah is a Persian word, meaning 'veil' or curtain. In its general meaning it is an Islamic custom ordained by God both for men and women. As per Qur'an, as stated earlier, purdah means 'casting down of one's looks' and 'guarding of one's private parts' and 'avoiding display of women's beauty to other than her own husband or his very nears and dears'. In other words. purdah is a measure to safeguard the chaste of the fairer sex and to control the weakness of man about sex. The aim of this provision is to maintain purity of character and loftiness of man vis-a-vis other animals.

Though we have mentioned the relevant verses of Qur'an (vv. 30 and 31 of chapter 'Al-Noor') in the earlier chapter on 'Muslim Women under Islam' as a cursory reference, here we intend to use the same verses in some details to know the real mode and extent of the term 'purdah' as ordained by God and displayed by His Prophet. Let us first repeat the verses of Qur'an referred to above once again :

> "Wa qul lilmo'minate yaghzuzna min absarehinna wa yahfazna furujahunna we la yubdina zinatahunna illa ma zahara minha wal yazribna bekhumurehinna 'ala juyubehinna wa la yubdina zinatahunna illa leboula-tehinna au abaihinna au abai boulatehinna au abnai

boulatehinna au ikhwanehinna au bani ikhwanihinna au bani ikhwatehinna au nisaihinna au ma malakat aimanohunna awittabeina ghaire oolirbate minarrijale awittif-lillazina lam yazharu 'ala auratennisai wa la yazribna be-arjolehinna leyo'lama ma yokhfina min zinatehinna wa tubu ilallahe jamian ayyohalmo'minuna l'allahum tuflehun."

"And say to the believing women that they cast their look down and guard their private parts, and display not their ornaments except what appears thereof, and let them wear their head-coverings over their bosoms, and not display their ornaments except to their husbands or their fathers, or the father of their husbands or their sons, or the sons of their husbands or their brothers or their brother's son or their sister's son or their women, or those whom their right hands possess or the male servants not having need (of women) or the children who have not attained knowledge of what is hidden of women; and let them not strike their feet so that what they hide of their ornaments may be known, and turn to Allah all of you, O believers ! so that you may be successful."

The above verses relate only to women's purdah. It is multi-dimensional—1. casting down of looks, 2. guarding of private parts, 3. display not their ornaments except what appears thereof, 4. wearing their head-coverings over their bosoms, and 5. prohibition against 'striking their feet' while passing through streets, with the clear intention of attracting the passersby towards their beauty, which is the natural ego of a feminine.

The first provision of casting down one's gaze is a safeguard against pilferage or instigation of the natural human disease of sexual emotions. One can ask, if the main aim of purdah is the safety of chaste of the womanfolk, why ban on her gaze ? One must know that it is not only man who is diseased, rather women also have germs of sexual lust. This fact is corroborated by the action of Zolaikha with regard to

Joseph mentioned in Qur'an. Joseph, the son of Hazrat Yaqub (Israil), was very beautiful. Though being a simple slave of Zolaikha (Queen of Egypt), she could not restrain herself after having a gaze at Joseph. When the elite women of Egypt started murmuring about the unexpected behaviour of the Queen, Zolaikha arranged for them a meet and gave an apple and a knife in the hands of each woman asking them to cut the apple in two pieces as soon as Joseph passes by them. As soon as Joseph stepped in all the women were absorbed in his beautiful look and cut their fingers out of unconsciousness. This story corroborates the fact that it is not only man who has the weakness of sexual passion, rather women are equally diseased. And hence a ban on their gaze also.

The second provision regarding 'guarding of private parts' is the object of purdah. The word 'absar' or gaze denotes deep look at anything, and it is different from a cursory look. A gaze is intentional and it has a particular aim. The gaze at a beauty attracts the looker, enraging love and passion at the first instance and to obtain and possess the object as its resultant or natural move in the second instance. And hence necessity to guard the object, i.e. chastity or person of the lady, so that one may not dare to steel way to usurp other's property. Woman is ordained not to have a gaze at *ghair-mahram* male nor to allow anybody's gaze at her by resorting to what is provided in the third clause—i.e., 'display not their ornaments' (beauties).

In the matter of displaying of ornaments the nears and dears have been declared *mahram*, i.e. entitled to have a look as listed in the *ayats*. But in the matter of 'guarding of private parts', nobody except the husband is allowed to have a look.

The fourth clause, i.e. 'wearing of head-coverings over their bosoms', ordains to put up veil on the bosom over and above the normal clothing. It is this veil which is questiond in the modern societies. Originally the Muslim women used a plain piece of cloth known as 'maqna' or mantle to cover their heirs and bosoms. We may name it as small *chadar* of some one-and-half metres in length. And this much piece of cloth suffices the *shara'i* need of veil. This fact is corroborated by the words of Hazrat A'isha which she spoke in praise of the ladies of Ansar (Medinian followers of the Prophet): "Excellence for the ladies of Ansar that no sooner than the ayats of surah Noor were revealed, no one of them was seen out of her house in her previous manner. All the ladies covered their heads with black maqna's as if crows were sitting on their heads." In another report appearing in Sunan-e-Abu Daood, Hazrat Umme Salma, another wife of Prophet Muhammad said, "After the revelation of verse 59 of Sura Ahzab 'Udnina A'laihinna mın jalabibehinna' the ladies of Ansar adopted this way (wearing of maqna over their heads)." Though these two reports do not mention covering of the bosom, many other reports show that the maqna' was also used to cover the bosom alongwith head. This much is *shara'i purdah*.

Women, nowhere in Qur'an or Hadith, have been forbidden of going out or meeting the requirements of social etiquettes or national and religious exigencies. The practical concept of purdah has been given, or displayed by, the households of the Holy Prophet—i.e., Ahl-e-Bait and Harem-e-Rasool. Prophet's own daughter, 'The lady of Paradise' Hazrat Fatima, once went to the battle-field of Badr when she heard of the injury of her Holy father Muhammad. She also accompanied her father, her husband and the two sons to the field of '*mubahila*' against Bani Najran. She also addressed a large gathering of Sahaba-e-Keram while pleading her case of *Fidak* in the court of first Caliph, Abu Bakr. These three instances, at least remove the controversy of the confinement of women within the four walls. There are also reports about meeting of Harem-e-Rasool (wives of the Holy Prophet) with Ashab-e-Keram from behind the curtain and talking with them on explanations of Qur'an and Hadith. Hundreds of such explanations have been recorded from the Holy Ladies of the Prophet's household. The information, further, removes the controversy over the verbal intercourse between men and women.

Those excluded from the commandment of purdah are:

1.	*leboulatehinna*	own husband,
2.	*au abnaihinna*	father and grand-father.
3.	*au aabai boulatehinna*	father and grand-father of husband,
4.	*au abnaihinna*	own sons,
5.	*au abnai boulatehinna*	sons of own husband,
6.	*au ikhwanehinna*	own brothers,
7.	*au bani ikhwanehinna*	sons of own brothers,
8.	*au bani akhawatehinna*	sons of own sisters,
9.	*au nisaihinna*	own women,
10.	*au ma malakat aimana-hunna*	own slaves (male or female),
11.	*awittabeina ghairo oolil irbate*	those males who have no need of women,
12.	*awittifl-il-lazina lam yazharu auratin nisai*	and those children who are unconscious about sexuality.

This arrangement is aimad at providing convenience in the family life.

While own husband is allowed to see even most private parts, all the rest are restrained from it. The rest are entitled to see adornments like ornaments, *bindya, sringar*. They cannot, however, enter private rooms of ladies without prior permission and intimation.

The Over-garment (*Jilbab*)

Jilbab or over-garment is meant for outing. It is not necessary to put on a *chadar, maqna'* or *burqa'* while engaged in indoor activities. The provision of 'Jilbab' or veil is itself a proof of the fact that Islam does not forbid women taking up outdoor activities.

Now the question is, what is 'Jilbab'?, what is its extent? and what its purpose?

With regard to the first question—what is jilbab?, the commentators have different opinions, and it is very difficult to pinpoint the actual shape and length of the cloth used as jilbab during early Islam.

According to *Al-Munjid* (an encyclopaedia of Arabic) 'jilbab' is '*al-qamis awis-saub-al-was'e*', i.e., an open clothing or cloak.

According to '*Mufradat-e-Raghib*', which is a very reliable book of explanation to Qur'anic terms, 'jilbab' is a gawn or veil.

Qamus says that 'jilbab' is an over-garment, a big and open cloth smaller than a quilt, or a thin quilt with which a woman covers her clothings, or a veil.

The writer of '*Lisan-al-Arab*' says, "*Al-jilbabo saubun aus'a minal khumare dunar ridla t'azzu behil miratu rasiha wa sadriha*", i.e. 'jilbab' is an over-garment longer than a *dopatta* but shorter than an, *eba* (cloak) with which women cover their heads and bosoms.

'*Kashaf*' : "*Al-jilbabo khumar-al-miratu-al-lazi yoghatti rasiha wa wajhiha iza kharajta lihajatin*", meaning, 'jilbab' connotes the head-covering with which women cover their heads and faces when they go out.

In short, 'jilbab' is neither a full *chadar* nor a cloak rather it is an open piece of cloth longer than a *dopatta* but shorter than a cloak which the Christian priests and Popes, or Muslim Ulema use as '*eba* or over-garment.

The purpose of 'jilbab' is apparent from Qur'an itself: Sura '*Ahzaab*', verses 59-60:

> "Ya ayyuhan Nabi ! qul li-azwajika wa banatika wa nisail mo'mineena yudnina 'alaihinna min jalabibehinna; zalika adna an-yo'rafna fala yu'zaina; wa kana Allaho Ghafuran Rahima. Lain-lam yantahil munafequna wallazina fi qulubehim marazun wal murjefuna fil madinate lanughreyannaka behim summa la yujawiru-naka fiha illa qalila."

O Prophet ! tell thy wives, thy daughters and the women of the believers to cover themselves with over-garments;

this is for their identity and safety from appeasement; and Allah is Great Forgiver and Merciful.

If the hypocrites and those having disease in their hearts and the terrorists would not cease their activities, We shall give thy power over them and then they cannot live in thy neighbour but for a little time.

The purpuse of covering heads and bosoms with 'jilbab' was to separate the identity of Muslim and non-Muslim women. In an Islamic state it was very necessary to introduce such a system, so that the offenders may not have any excuse that they did not know as to who the woman was. If a non-Muslim attacked the chastity of a Muslim woman covering a 'jilbab', he was liable for punishment under Islamic laws; and if she was not a Muslim woman, the offender would incur punishment as per law of the lady offended against. In short the intention of over-garment is 'identification' of Muslim woman from a non-Muslim woman, and to ascertain the law under which an offender has to be treated. In other words, it is a measure to uphold justice and fairplay in the society and to safeguard the chastity of women.

Face

The most controversial point among the Muslim juries has been the opening of face and hands by women while outing. A *hadith* from Sahih Bukhari reads, "Ibn Abbas said that during the Farewell Pilgrimage (Hajjatul Wid'a) a woman belonging to the tribe of Khasam came to see the Holy Prophet. Ibn Abbas's brother, Fazal, was riding behind the Prophet on the same camel. The woman sought the Prophet's permission to perform the Haj in place of her aged father. The Prophet permitted her. She was very beautiful young lady. Fazal began to look at her. Thereupon the Holy Prophet turned his face away and said, 'a young male and a young female, I am afraid the Devil might jump between them'." (Sahih Bukhari: Vol. 8, p. 62).

From this *hadith* it is apparent that the lady's face was open and Fazal gazed at her face, and the Holy Prophet turned Fazal's face but did not ask the lady to cover her face. As per Qur'an (Sura Noor) both men and women have ordained to lower down their gaze, which Fazal did not do. This shows that opening of face while outside the house is not necessary. Had it been so, the Prophet (PUH) must have asked the lady to hide her face.

The other evidences of uncovering of face by women outside their houses are :

(a) A bridegroom is allowed to see the face and physique of the bride before marriage with the pure intention of selection of life partner. There are many instances in *hadith* when the Holy Prophet advised his followers to see the proposed bride well before marrying her. If opening and seeing of a woman's face would not have been permissible under Islam, the Holy Prophet would have never advised men to see women—rather he would have advised to their female relatives to see the would-be bride and report to the groom, as in vogue today. (This can be found from Sahih Muslim, Vol. 4, page 142).

(b) During Hajj pilgrimage, where lacs of men and women perform hajj together under the open sky, the opening of face, hands and feet is allowed for women. If uncovering of face in general gatherings would have been prohibited, the Prophet of Islam would have ordained to do so while performing Hajj. But there is no *hadith* or Qur'anic injunction against uncovering of face by women during Hajj.

(c) There are a lot of reports of women participating in congregational prayers in mosques in the time of Muhammad (PUH). The garment prescribed for women during nemaz is such that keeps the face, hands and feets open. No lady is allowed to cover her face during nemaz. This proves that Muslim ladies can participate in congregational prayers with their faces open or uncovered.

With regard to participation of women in congregational prayers, Syed Murtuda Mutahhari writes, "Islam permits women to participate in congregational prayers in mosques, but not mingling with men. It provides them a separate place. It is said that during the life-time of Hazrat Muhammad (PUH) the Prophet himself earmarked a particular gate (for entrance and exit) for women in Masjid-e Nabawi. One day he, pointing out towards a gate, said: '*Lau tarakna hazal babu linnisai*', meaning, it is better to reserve that gate for women."[1]

Mutahhari further says that Hazrat Omar clearly prohibited men to enter that gate.[2] It is also said that the Holy Prophet had ordered that women should be allowed exit before men after performing the 'night prayers'. The Prophet did not like exit of men and women together because mischiefs generally find way through the very free mixing of the two sexes. The Prophet advised women to walk through the side-corner of the lane or road, whereas he ordered males to walk leaving the side for women.

All these hadiths and reports indicate that while women were allowed to keep their faces open while outing, the free mixing of men and women was hated. That's why the Islamic Jurisprudents have given *fatwah* (decree) of '*karahit*' (abhorrence) about the free-mixing of the two sexes in outdoor social gatherings. And it is this legal state of affair that in all social gatherings seating arrangements for male and female are kept separate in almost all Eastern societies, in general, and in Islamic societies in particular. Islam has liked to keep a distance between men and women in their educational, economic and political gatherings; and it is hundred per cent cogent taking the emotional and psychological facts into account. One can easily reconcile with the Islamic stand if he peeps through the case files of immoral turpitudes of the free western societies.

1. Mutahbari, Shahid Murtuda, "Islam men Masla-e-Hijab" (Urdu), Islamic Culture House of Iran, New Delhi, p. 214.
2. Sunan-Ibn Daood, V. I, p. 109.

Outing

The colonial powers' propaganda about seclusion of women in Islam is baseless and unfounded, a political stunt and a religious bigotry. See their cunningness—they blame Islam and produce evidences from kingships, dictatorships and wayladen people, and never from Islamic law books, i.e. Qur'an and Sunnah. Excepting the Holy Life-partners of the Holy Prophet, nobody can produce a single *ayat* (verse) from Qur'an or the Holy Prophet's injunction restricting women's outing. The prohibitionary ayats about the wives of the Holy Prophet, too, are not for the life period of the Prophet—rather they relate to post-demise period. After the death of Prophet no wife could go out of Prophet's house till her life, and that is a provision to safeguard the chastity of Harem-e-Rasool (PUH).

During life-time of the Prophet, his wives used to go out even without the Prophet. We find one *hadith* in Sahih Bukhari reporting that one night Prophet's wife Sooda went out with his permission. In the way Hazrat Omar saw her and said, "Do you think that I did not recognize you in this night ? Verily I did. Never try to come out in future." Janab Sooda returned back in a feat of anger and narrated the whole story to the Prophet. At that time the Holy Prophet was at supper with a bone of meat in his hands. Just after a while the condition of revelation set at the Prophet; and when he was free, he said: "*Innahu qad azina lakunna an takhrijanna lihawaijikunna*," meaning, "You womenfolk are permitted to go out of your houses as per your requirements." (Sahih Bukhari: Vol. 7, p. 49; Vol. 8, p. 66 and Sahih Muslim, Vol. 7, p. 6).

About Hazrat Omar, it is reported that he was very strict in the matter of women's outing. He disliked it—rather abhorred it at times, especially in case of Prophet's wives. Oftenly he used to say to the wives of the Prophet, "If I would have power, no eye could have seen you." One day Hazrat Omar came to his daughter Hafsa (one of the wives of the Holy Prophet) and lovingly said to her, "You life-partners of the Holy Prophet are different from the general women, as your husband is different from the general men. It is befitting your loftier position that you remain under purdah." Hazrat Zainab, another wife of the Holy Prophet, retorting Omar's advice said, "O son of Khattab ! Qur'an has been revealed in our house and thy art teaching us the manner and suggesting restrictions for us ?" (Jahiz's 'Al-Bayan wat-Tibyeen', Vol. 2, p. 90 and Vol. 3, p. 155).

The above *hadiths* (traditions) prove that women were allowed to go out, without men, as and when they required. It also proves that women of Prophet's time had enough freedom of speech, and at times women had bravely stood even before the Caliphs in defence of their right to freedom and the Caliphs had to bow down before their reason-based arguments.

The second point evident from the foregoing *hadiths* is that women of early Islamic days quite conscious of their rights and duties and they never tolerated any suppression of or infringement upon their social, economic and political rights. In this matter they were so daring that they retorted any attempt on the part of their Caliphs to abrogate or infringe upon their rights even in fullfledged Majlis (Council), and the rulers had to take back their unjust proposals.

But, unfortunately, this tempo could not continue beyond the period of Khilafat-e-Rashida (40 A.H.). The Umayyad and Abbasid caliphs superseded many of the freedom rights of women and confined them to the four walls branding them as 'harem'. They snatched away their right to freedom of outing, freedom of speech and freedom of choice for a life-partner. Outing was banned and eunuchs were imposed upon them. Discussing this point, Mazharul Haque Khan writes,

> "Purdah, as a ystem of female exclusion from social life, first appeared among the ruling aristocracies of the later Umayyads. The causes were their increasing profligacy, unrestricted polygamy and concubinage and the inevitable male jealousy and prudery to conceal his innumerable wives and concubines from public eyes. This was the genesis of the medieval Purdah institution of *harim*:

> "The *harim* system was first adopted during the reign of the Umayyad Caliph, Walid II (743-44 A.D.), who was also the first of the Umayyads to adopt the Byzantine custom of employment of eunuchs. They were castrated slaves employed by their masters to guard the honour of their harims, that is, of their secluded wives, concubines and other women.
>
> "As a matter of fact, the word *harim* meant both the women and the female quarters of the house or palace..."
> "With the advent of the Abbasid Caliphate the institutions of the Purdah began to diffuse among the middle classes in the feudal villages and rural communities and in the commercial towns and cities of the Caliphate. It spread even among the lower sections of the Abbasid society. The Abbasid Caliphs of the ninth and tenth centuries A.D. took decisive steps to turn Purdah system into a regular social institution. Al-Mutawakkil (847-861 A.D.), the last of the greater Abbasids, during whose reign their Caliphate first began to disintegrate, decreed the segregation of the sexes at feasts and public ceremonies. Final steps were taken by the Abbasid Caliph Qadir b'Illah (991-1030 A.D.), who proclaimed female seclusion as an Islamic institution by his royal edicts."[3]

Thus we see a clear difference between the 'Shara'i Purdah', i.e. purdah to the extent of 'hejab' or veil ; and 'Muharraf Purdah', i.e. purdah to the abhorrent extent of seclusion or house-arrest. For these changes, Islam or the Divine Philosophy of Life cannot be blamed. The onus of restrictions or encroachments on the freedom of women goes to the illegitimate or un-Islamic rulers.

Here it must be noted that Islam is not a mere ideological vision. It is on the other hand a practical system of life that fully appreciates all the genuine needs of mankind and tries to realize them. In trying to meet the genuine requirements

3. Khan, Mazharul Haque, "Pathology of the Muslim Society" Amar Prakashan, Delhi, 1978, pp. 32-33.

of man Islam effects a perfect balance so far as the limitations of human nature would allow. It starts with the individual maintaining a balance between his requirements of body and soul, reason and spirit and in no case allows one side to predominate the other. It does not suppress the animal instincts in order to make the soul ascend the higher planes, nor does it in hankering after the bodily desires and comforts, make man stoop down to the low level of mere materialism or animalism. Islam makes them both meet on a single higher plane doing away with all the internal psychological conflicts that threaten the entity of human soul or set a part of it against the other parts. Thence it proceeds to achieve an equilibrium between the needs of the individual and those of the community. It allows not an individual to transgress against other individuals, or the community. Nor does it allow the community to commit transgression against the individual. It also does not approve of one class or people to enslave another class or people. Islam exercises a beneficent constraint on all these mutually opposed forces, prevents them from coming into collision with one another, calling upon them all to join hands, and co-operate for the general good of mankind as a whole.

With regard to women, Islam has effected a reasonable balance between 'morality' and their 'requirements' of life. Women are human beings like men, having alike feelings, ambitions and emotions. As a human being they have been bestowed upon equitable social, economic and spiritual rights. The restriction of 'hijab' or gaze is not due to any difference in nature of woman, but because of the both sexes with regard to sexual instinct. This instinct is so powerful that Islam has employed three forces—of 'piety', hijab' and 'punishment'—to contain it and keep it within a certain limit of permissibility. In order to satisfy this instinct, 'nikah' or marriage has been encouraged, whereas the 'craze for sex' has been abhorred. While the former is aimed at satisfying the need and thereby maintaining a civilized human generation, the latter is aimed to avoid the chances of disruption of family and social life.

Hence we see that Islam is not against outing of women, rather it has permitted them as per their requirements. This conditional permission is, no doubt, a bit different from 'full freedom'. There are two conditions for outing of women—(1) veiling of their person, and (2) outing under necessity. This 'necessity' has neither been defined nor confined. In general the term 'necessity' under Islam connotes the obligations of life, prestige and service to the Almighty Allah. And, under the obligations of life, so far women are concerned, they are allowed to go out for acquisition of knowledge, procurement of food and cloth if there is no male in her house, and even procurement of livelihood if she has no male member to earn bread for the family. If necessary, she can also take to arms to defend herself, her family, and even her nation. But in case she has male members to manage outdoor duties, she is not required to go out merely to make merry. This does not mean that she is cut out from social obligations. She can attend marriage ceremonies, religious congregations and other social and economic meets with proper regard for 'hijab'. She can deliver lectures, she can plead her case before juries and she can serve the injured in battle-fields. Islamic history has such instances. Hazrat Fatima Zahra (PUH) pleaded her case before Khalifa Abu Bakr and argued her title over Fidak for many hours. She also went to the Maidan-e-Mubahela to defend the divinity of Islam vis-a-vis Christianity. She went to the Battle-field of Badr to serve her injured Holy father, Muhammad (PUH).

As already said, procurement of bread is not an obligation of woman where male members are available to fulfil this obligation. Unless procurement of livelihood becomes necessary, she is not troubled for that. Thus the freedom of outing under Islam is different from the freedom allowed under modernity.

So far the history of purdah is concerned, we do not have a compact knowledge of the subject. Stray references are, however, available in writings of different scholars. These references suggest that purdah. in variant degrees, was observed by ancient Persians, Jews and, perhaps, by Indians too; and their laws were much more harder than the Islamic laws of purdah. The Arabs had no concept of purdah, and this system was adopted by them after the advent of the Prophet of Islam.

Will Durant, in his 'History of Civilization', writes about the Jews and their laws of purdah: "If a woman defied the Jewish laws regarding purdah, for example, if she came out in the gathering of males or was seen spinning in thoroughfare or expressing her grievances before strangers or if she talked in loud voice which her neighbours could hear, her husband had got a right to divorce her without paying *mehr*."[4]

About Persians during Zoarastrian period, Will Durant writes, "The status of women during Zoarastrian era was very high and they moved among people with open faces freely."

Just after it, he writes, "After Dariush, especially among capitalists, the position of women fell down. The position of economically backward classes of women, however, remained intact, and they continued to move out for petty manual work; but among the affluent class, because the women obliged to take refuge during menses, the period was by and by enlarged to engulf their entire life. . . . Women of the high stratum could not dare to go out without palanquin. They were never allowed to mix with men. Married women had no right to see any man except their husband. They could not even see their father and own brother after marriage."[5]

Thus we see that in ancient Iran, purdah system was much tougher than under Islam. Women were not allowed to see even their father and own brother after marriage.

According to the opinion of Will Durant, the ancient laws of Parsis under which a woman had to seclude herself in a room during menses, formed the basis of purdah in ancient Iran.

4. Will Durant, 'History of Civilization' (Persian), Vol. 12, p. 30.
5. Ibid.

According to him, the Jewish laws were similar to that of Parsis.

Will Durant opines that Islam also carried similar laws, which is incorrect. Everyone knows that during menses, a Muslim woman has been forbidden to perform *namaz*, *roza* (fasting) and touch Qur'an and man is forbidden to make sexual intercourse; but she has never been ordained to go in seclusion or to perform her day-to-day routine duties.

Will Durant has also written that the tough laws of ancient Iranians crept into Arabs (Muslims) when they came in contact with Persians after conquering Iran. This contention of Will Durant, also, is baseless because the ayats with regard to purdah had been revealed well before the Arabs conquered Iran. Thus the further contention of Will Durant that the ancient laws regarding seclusion of Persian women continued among them even after accepting Islam and it was these laws of ancient Persians which became instrumental in having a distance with women during menses period under Islam, is also baseless. Rather the fact is that Islam removed the toughness of the Zoarastatian and Parsian laws of seclusion of women during that particular period and allowed them to perform their routine business, barring prayers.

About Arabs Will Durant writes:

"The contact of Arabs with Iranians became instrumental in the system of purdah and sodomy in the Islamic world. Arabs always doubted the feminine charms and they were also fond of them. Yet under their natural ego of superiority they denied the due status and natural charms of women. Hazrat Omar used to say to his tribesmen: 'Consult your women and act against it'; but during the first century A.H. the Muslims did not impose purdah laws on their women. Men and women met each other freely, they walked in thoroughfares side by side and prayed together in mosques."[6]

He further writes that the systems of purdah and eunuchism was invented during the Caliphate of Walid II (126-127 A.H.). According to him, the seclusion of women

5. Ibid., Vol. I, p. 552.

was because they were unlawful for men during the period of menstruation. This point has already been dealt with and proved to be baseless.

While it is correct that the system of eunuchism started during later period of Umayyads, but it is incorrect to say that purdah system started during Umayyad period and it was non-existent in the first century A.D. The claim of Will Durant that men and women of first century A.D. met each other freely, is also wrong. Islam ordained a distance between the two sexes in social and religious gatherings and made arrangements for its maintenance by either providing a distance or laying a curtain between them, besides the normal veil or 'hijab'. Will Durant talks in such a way as if there was no law with regard to purdah in Islam during the life-time of the Prophet of Islam. Through this claim of his, he presumably intends to give a notion to the Muslims in general and the western society in particular that the Islamic injunctions about purdah were not given practical shape by the Prophet of Islam in his life-time; and thereby he wants to say that whatever was non-existent during the life-time of the Prophet of Islam, it cannot be obligatory for Muslims after his death, thus paving the way for abrogation of the purdah system from Muslim society. This claim of Will Durant is quite contrary to the established historical facts. No doubt the women of the period of ignorance were of the type Will Durant has claimed for, but Islam brought a revolution in this regard too; and, as we have already quoted from Hazrat Aisha, as soon as the injunction of 'hijab' was revealed the entire female population of Medina adopted veil in all sincerity and in true words and spirit of 'hijab' (veil).

Kent Gubino in his book 'Three Years in Iran' asserts that the tough purdah system of Sasanis continued among Iranians even during the period of Islam. He says that purdah was not the only problem during Sasan dynasty, rather they kept women in full secrecy. He further states that the princes and religious leaders of that period were so unbridled during that period that people kept their beautiful girls in strict secrecy did not disclose their existence in their houses to anyone, because any leakage of this secret could lead to deprivation from life and property.

Relying on these and such other writings of Western Scholars, Pandit Jawahar Lal Nehru also opines that the purdah system crept into the Islamic world from Roman and Persian civilizations of non-Muslims. In his book 'A Glance at the World History', while admiring the Islamic civiliza ion for effecting reforms in the tough laws of Roman and Persian civilizations, he says: "One mote big and deplorable change took shape gradually, and that was about women. Among Arabs purdah system was not in vogue. They (women) did not live under veil or separate from men, rather they participated in social gatherings like 'wa'az' prayers, etc. and at times they also delivered lectures; but the Arabs during their victories beyond the Arab Peninsula, gradually adopted the rites and customs prevalent in their two neighbouring Great Civilizations of Rome and Persia. They conquered the dynastics of Rome and Persia, but became prey of the social and habitual evils of those people; and, as already stated, it was the impact of those two Great Civilizations that gave rise to seclusion and veiling among Arabs and the system of 'harem' came into existence and men and women fell apart."[7]

This contention of Pandit Nehru is contrary to the historical fact. The fact is that the contact of Arabs with non-Arabs hardened the purdah system. It is not a fact that the present tough system of purdah is the outcome of Arabs' contact with non-Arabs.

One thing which comes to light from the writings of Mr. Nehru is that (perhaps under the influence of Jews) purdah was in vogue among Romans too alongwith eunuchism, which found its way into the Muslim world during Umayyad Caliphate. The other writers too have supported this contention.

Expressing his undesirability at another place, Mr. Nehru writes, "This undesirable custom formed a characteristic of the

7. Nehru, Pt. Jawahar Lal, 'A Glance at the World History', Vol. I, p. 328.

Muslim society by and by and India also imitated the Muslims on their advent here."[8]

The above opinion of Mr. Nehru, too, is not corroborated by historical fact. Whatever be the shape and extent of purdah, it existed in the later Vedic period and the Medieval period in the Indian society. One of the Rig Veda's hymn says, "The wife is the home", the apparent meaning of which is that the universe of activities of a married lady must be the boundaries of her home. In other words, ladies were not expected to indulge in outdoor activities of life. Commenting on the relevant Vedic hymns, Max Muller observes, "The hymn throws a curious light on the social character of Vedic times, as it presupposes two classes of wives—not necessarily simultaneous, however—a housewife who stays at home and is not much seen, and a wife who appears in public and takes part in society and conversation of the Sabha, the assembly room, and the Vedathas, the meetings."[9]

Deliberating on the subject, P. Thomas writes, "All told, the position of women, in the Grihya Sutra period (6th century B.C. to 4th century B.C.) deteriorated still further from the later Vedic period."[10] This means that from the later Vedic period till the advent of Buddhism, the fate of female folk in India further deteriorated and Grihya Sutras were unable to mend their fate.

S. Das in his book 'Purdah—The Status of Indian Women' writes under the caption 'Women in the Zenana', "In the previous chapters we have indicated the cause, extent, and reasons for stricter imposition of purdah. No doubt it would have been absolished as soon as the Mohammedan aggression and with it the protective value of purdah ceased, were it not that it found powerful support in the general age-long Hindu belief in the advisability of restricting women's freedom.

8. Mutahhari, 'Islam men Masla-e-Hijab' (Urdu), Iranian Art Printers, Delhi, 1984, p. 15.

9. Thomas, P., Quoted in Indian Women Through the Ages', Asia Publishing House, Bombay, 1964, p. 53.

10. Ibid., p. 68.

Classical and later Hindu literature gives further proof of this attitude, it teems with slighting references to women's character. One may trust deadly poison, a river, a hurricane, the beautiful, large and fierce elephant, the tiger roaming for prey, the angel of death, a thief, a savage, a murderer; but if a man trusts a woman, he will surely be reduced to wander through the streets in desolation."[11]

S. Das's findings are mainly based on archaeological facts revealed through excavations of the later Vedic and Sutra periods which prove that the houses and castles of those periods provided for 'zenana' and 'mardana' apartments. In his book S. Das sketches the deplorable conditions of the 'zenana' apartments which lacked ventilation and access of sun rays. In his own words, "The fact that purdah turned the zenana into the exclusive dwelling-place of women had far-reaching effects. It soon inculcated in their minds the deep conviction that freedom of movement outside the house would lower their standing and place them on a common level with low-castes. Not only this, but even within the house itself it made for a sharp division of family life into two sections, zenana and men's quarters. The outer rooms and verandahs became closed territory for the women. They never visited them except on rare and furtive excursions, and when fully assured that no men were about."[12]

Even the woman of Medieval India was not better than her Muslim counterpart. The punishment suggested for moral turpitude and allied offences of women in Kautilya's Artha Shastra (Mauryan period—4th century B.C.) speak of the fact. The laws regarding adultery and allied offences may be quoted in some detail as it will give us an idea of the nature and extent of restrictions imposed on the fairer sex in pre-Buddhism period:

> "If a woman engages herself in amorous sports or drinking, in the face of an order to the contrary, she

11. Das, S., 'Purdah—The Status of Indian Women', Ess Ess Publications, New Delhi, 1979, p. 93.
12. Ibid, pp. 93-94.

shall be fined three panas. She shall pay a fine of six panas for going out at daytime for sports to see a woman or spectacular show. For the same offence committed at night, the fines shall be double. If a woman goes out while her husband is asleep or under intoxication, or if she shuts the door of her house against her husband, she shall be fined 12 panas. If a woman keeps him out of her house at night, she shall pay double the above amount. If a man and a woman signs to each other with a view to sensuous enjoyment, or carry on secret conversation with the same purpose, the woman shall pay a fine of twenty-four panas and the man double the amount; a woman holding out her hair; the tie of her dress round her loins, her teeth or her nails, shall pay the first amercement, and a man doing the same, twice the first amercement. For holding conversation in suspicious places, whips may be substituted for fines. In the centre of the village a Chandala (outcaste) may whip the adulteress five times on each side of her body. She may get rid of being whipped by paying a pana for each lash."[13]

The above Hindu laws speak of a much more tougher restrictive legislation for Hindu women than their Muslim counterparts in veil or *burqa*. The medieval Hindu woman was not allowed to drink, whereas there was no such restriction for men. Their outing, even to see a woman, during day or night hours was prohibited. In case of Muslim women, as we have shown earlier, there is no such restriction on their movement. Hindu laws did not tolerate even talks between opposite sexes. In Islam a woman can well have conversational intercourse with the opposite sex from behind the curtain or under *sharai* veil or *hijab*. Under Islamic laws, hands, feet and face are excluded from the injunction of 'hijab', whereas under the medieval Hindu laws a woman could not expose even her teeth or nails.

13. Thomas, P., Ibid., p. 75.

Shortly after Mauryan period, Buddhism came to rescue this poor creature—woman—from the apalling yoke of Hindu laws. But under the forceful patronage of King Asoka, Buddhism reformed many a social laws to make it lenient for women. It allowed them freedom of speech. outing and social intercourse with the opposite sex. Buddhism was dominant till the eighth century A.D.(4th century B.C. to 8th century A.D.) when it received a serious setback by the rising tide of Hindu revival. Shortly after, it disappeared from the land of its birth. However, it left an indelible mark on Hindu religion and society. The Brahmins who were, during the Vedic period, great sacrificers, Soma-drinkers and meat-eaters, emerged in the Buddhist period as vegetarians and teetotallers.

The institution of purdah being one of the hottest topics of the time, we would like to remove some doubts about it before concluding this discussion. The objective of purdah, as apparent from various laws quoted hereunto, is decidedly safety of the chastity of women. The critics of purdah system, at the outset, attack on the very objective of this institution. It is true that purdah alone cannot be enough to guarantee the safety of feminine modesty—it can at best serve as an evidence of the 'chaste motive' of the woman observing it. Then there is Islamic law to deal heavily with the offender. The modesty of women has, however, been guaranteed in any law—whether Islamic or non-Islamic—whatever weightage may it carry in different systems in vogue today. Purdah is at least a proof of the fact that the lady observing it has due regard for her modesty, where an offender stands a 'wanton aggressor'. This legal privilege is doubtful to go in favour of a lady not observing purdah, and in whose case there is every likelihood of the offender getting the benefit of doubt, or the offended earning a blame of enticement. Thus, purdah provides a legal privilege to the woman against sexual crimes.

The next objection laid against it is that purdah system restricts the movement of women. This objection can, to a certain extent, be true in case of the traditional purdah—and not in case of the '*sharai purdah*' as in vogue in Iran, Turkey, Egypt, etc. The true Islamic purdah is not much different from what the monks, nuns, judges, fathers' (priests) dress.

The cloaks and gawns used by them is similar to '*maqna*' or '*chadar*' (*jilbab* or overgarment) used by Muslim women. If popes and judges do not feel inconvenience, due to their official dress, in the discharge of their normal duties or functions, a purdah-observing woman also is not faced with any difficulty in the discharge of her outdoor activities in 'hijab'. Had the Muslim authorities restricted purdah to the true Islamic spirit, there would have been no question or comment on it. There is, therefore, the need for revival of the 'sharai purdah' in place of the orthodox conventional Indian purdah.

The third pertinent point of objection is that purdah has diminished the status of woman in society. It is, to the researcher, just a fallacy. An impartial observer peeping through the present deplorable condition of the unmarried mothers and the divorced wives in the western world, can best judge the real status of woman in the human society. It is unrestricted freedom of women in the western society which has become a curse for them now. Millions of unclaimed children and women-without-shield have posed great problems before the respective governments and societies.

The fourth criticism advanced against the institution of purdah by the modernists is that a pardahnashin lady is deprived of the conditions necessary for health. To prove this, they advance the example of zenana structures of homestead lacking in ventilation and sunlets, restrictions on feminine outings, etc., and thereby they try to demonstrate a very pitiable condition of women full of health hazards. They claim that Muslim women, due to the Islamic injunction of purdah, are forced to remain in suffocative conditions throughout their life.

No doubt the rural structure of Muslim homesteads normally provides for zenana and mardana apartment, the former for the use of family members and the latter for the use of the male members of the family and the strangers or guests. The zenana apartments invariably contain 'roshandans', 'khirki', 'jangla', verandahs, rooms, halls and courtyards. This picture of a purdah-observing family's house is much different from what many sociologists depict about.

The low-caste families, not observing purdah, do not require such a spacious and fancy design of homesteads as their female members remain most of the day time out in search of bread or agricultural activities. Hence a picture of their homestead cannot legitimately be advanced to prove the contention of modernism and abhorrence against purdah. Ill health and poor sanitary conditions are generally found among the ignorant and poor families.

The modernists present a very gloomy picture of purdahnashin ladies, as if they are kept bound in a golden chain and are not allowed to move or do anything. The reality is that purdahnashin ladies are never kept idle, rather they perform all the indoor activities—rough and fancy. They clean, dry and preserve their agricultural produce; grind wheat, split pulses, wash clothes and utensils, cook foods, besides stitching, knitting, weaving, rearing of children, service to the husband and other family members. These indoor activities provide no lesser opportunity to them for physical exercise than the ladies of any other class.

On the other hand, the modern ladies after acquiring education and getting a job generally consider the hard manual household works degrading and against their position. No doubt, they also do cooking, washing, knitting, decorating, but dislike the works like grinding, sweeping, cleaning utensils and houses. The items of work requiring extra labour are seldom done by modern ladies. Thus they loose the chance of optimum physical exercise so necessary for health. They may have their own excuses for it, such as, tiredness due to official work and lack of time. The modern ladies, thus, compare feebly on the count of physical exercise vis-a-vis those purdahnashin ladies managing the entire household works.

Likewise, the traditional ladies also visit their relatives, participate in social and religious gatherings, go for recreation, marketing, etc., sometime alongwith a male member or a female companion and sometime alone. Such outings have both entertaining and health value.

Purdah, thus, does not stand in the way of movement of women and it is not correct to say that purdah institution is detrimental to the requirements of health, rather it is ignorance and under-nourishment, unhygienic conditions, etc, responsible for ill health.

The fifth comment on the purdah institution is that it diminishes the status of women. It is apparent from the foregoing discussions that purdah does not stand in the way of a woman as an obstacle, provided it is restricted to the *sharai* limit, as is in vogue in many Islamic countries. Sharai purdah is never a seclusion or house-arrest. It is customary Indian purdah which certainly carries demerits affecting the creative worth of the fairer sex. While the avenues of female activities are somewhat different from that of males, women have never been deprived of the use of their genius under proper 'hijab'. A Muslim woman can well join teaching, nursing, medicinal, cottage industrial jobs and can earn livelihood for the betterment of their own and family life. Purdah-observing does not necessarily mean strictly purdah-nashini, or seclusion. As per hadith of the Holy Prophet, already quoted, women are allowed to participate in outdoor activities and help their male counterparts even during battle. Wise and sincere women in most of the cases have been seen dominating their family affairs, irrespective of their being modern or purdah-observing. At the same time, an extra-modern lady is at times found low in family and society for her disrespect for others and non-cooperating attitude. Hence, in short it is the quality of a lady which determines her weight and prestige in society. Chastity, beauty and good manners are the three basic factors which determine the status of a woman. Purdah is, in fact, a co-ordinating factor to the former two qualities of women, and not a degenerating factor.

Purdah is, therefore, virtue for women than vice if observed in the real spirit of Islamic injunction.

The Islamic traditions were more of less adhered to by the Indian women during Moghal period. During this period too there were two distinct classes of Muslim women, viz., (1) the aristocrat class including the middle class (Ashraf), and (2) the labour class (Atraf). So far purdah is concerned, the aristocracy not only maintained the Islamic 'hijab' but showed an exuberant tendency to the extent of 'seclusion' or house arrest of the fairer sex; while the latter one tried to maintain the true Islamic character of 'hijab' by narrowing down their veil over their faces and using loose garments while at work in the field. Even today one can easily witness this tradition even among the non-Muslim women of Marwar (Rajasthan) and the western parts of Uttar Pradesh. With the advent of British rule and introduction of western culture and secular form of education in Indian schools and colleges, the aristocrat class hastened to adopt the western culture and secular norms and values; whereas the middle class under the anti-western propaganda of the clergy preferred to remain loyal to the Islamic injunctions, norms and values. The labour class, however, maintained the *status quo*. In later part of the British rule a group of enlightened Muslim leaders like Sir Syed Ahmad Khan, foreseeing a pathetic future of the Muslim community as a whole, started persistent efforts to link the community with the fast moving age of modernity and opened a few Anglo-Oriental or Anglo-Arabic schools and colleges both for gents and women, which gradually loosened the impact of clergical propaganda and consequently the middle class started allowing its wards to the newly established Anglo-Oriental schools. This marked shift in the attitude and outlook of the middle class facilitated modern education of the younger generation. Various cities and towns of India followed the example of Aligarh and opened Anglo-Arabic or Anglo-Oriental schools and colleges which was welcome by Muslim masses. The efforts of these leaders emerged in the shape of three Muslim Universities, viz., Muslim University (Aligarh), Jamia Millia (Delhi) and Usmania University (Deccan). Patna also followed the suit and established two high schools, namely, Anglo-Arabic Mohammad High School, Guzri (Patna City) and the Muslim School at Muradpur. Then with the emergence of national government and introduction of democratic system of education in the Indian perspective, the propensity of modern education further grew among Muslims in general and among Muslim women in particular. In the present age almost every urban Muslim has realised the importance of modern education and the demand of the time and is sending his sons and daughters to schools and colleges. And, thus, the modern education has been instrumental in rationalising the attitude and outlook of the Muslim masses in almost all spheres of life. Under the impact of modern education the institution of purdah is loosing its tenacity and seclusion of women has become a story of the past. The Muslim women youth are attending schools and colleges, doing marketing and outing for entertainment. They are no longer secluded creatures. This trend is now general and the Muslim women all over India are enjoying comparatively a good deal of freedom of outing, education and profession than ever in past. It was in this perspective that a few questions were put to the women respondents to understand their degree of liberty and change in their attitude and outlook under the influence of various currents of modernity and rationality.

The data collected from the field were classified and tabulated in the following tables on different variables like caste, age, literacy level, income, etc. Table 1 presents the picture of observance of purdah in the families of respondents of different castes on age basis. The age-groups shown in the table present the age of a girl when she starts adherence to the injunction regarding purdah.

Before analysing the figures it is important to mention that the vertical totals show the total number of respondents in whose families purdah is observed in a particular age-group and the horizontal totals indicate the population of respondents of different castes in the sample. It is evident from the table that, on the whole, 60% of the entire sample has favoured the age-group of 10-13 years to be the most reasonable age at which girls should or normally start observance of purdah in their families, whereas the least favoured age-group is 18-21 years (2.0%). The second majority of 23.0% has favoured the age-group of 6-9 years and the third majority has favoured the age-group of 14-17 years to be the reasonable age for observance of purdah; whereas a very insignificant percentage of 3.0 has reported that their families do not observe purdah at all. In this connection it is important to note that according to the Islamic injunction the puberty age

Table 1

Caste and age at which a girl starts observance of purdah in the families of the respondents

(Percentage in brackets)

Caste Category	*Age at which the girls start observance of purdah*					*Total*
	6-9 yrs.	*10-13 yrs.*	*14-17 yrs.*	*18-21 yrs.*	*Never observe*	
Saiyid	11(20.0	33(60.0)	8(14.5)	1(1.8)	2(3.6)	55(18 3)
Shaikh	14(23.3)	34(56.6)	8(13.3)	3(5 0)	1(1.6)	60(20.0)
Pathan	9(18.3)	31(79.4)	9(18.3)	—	—	49(16.3)
Mallick	7(19.4)	24(66.6)	5(13.8)	—	—	36(12.0)
Ansari	18(32.7)	31(56.4)	3(5.4)	—	3(5.4)	55(18.3)
Rayeen	1(6.6)	6(40.0)	3(20.0)	2(13.3)	3(20.0)	15(5.0)
Chique	6(30.0)	14(40.0)	—	—	—	20(6.7)
Kalal	3(30.0)	7(70.0)	—	—	—	10(3.4)
Total	69(23.0)	180(60.0)	36(12.0)	6(2.0)	9(3.0)	300(100)

begins, in case of women, from the 10th year; but due to variations in biological, climatic and food habits of different regions and socio-economic categories of the people this age of puberty) differs from place to place and from family to family. In the same society in some quarters of well-to-do people the puberty age commences at the 10th year, while in other families it rises by a few years (say 2 or 3 years). Generally in cold countries puberty starts at a higher age while in hot climates it starts at an earlier age. In India, in general, the puberty age starts after 13 years of age in case of women and after 18 years of age in case of males. In the light of this fact it may be said that majority of the families of Muslims under review confine their girls' outdoor activities at an age earlier than the exact puberty age. 60.0% of the samples favours the age of purdah observance for their girls a bit earlier than the standard puberty age in the Indian conditions and 23.0% of them favours the conservative age of 6-9 years and this pattern of response suggests that a sizeable section of the respondents is heavily influenced by religious orthodoxy, whereas a very insignificant percentage (3.0%) of the respondents has no regard for religious sanctions in this respect.

On caste basis we do not see any significant relevance of the response pattern to the age at which a girl should observe purdah. In all the caste categories the highest percentages of response have gone in favour of the age-group of 10-13 years and the next highest percentages in favour of 6-9 years, then to 14-17 years. Very insignificant percentages of Saiyids (1.8%), Shaikhs (5.0%) and Rayeen biradari (13.3%) have favoured the age-group of 18-21 years to be the age at which their daughters go in purdah. A very low percentage (6.6%) of Rayeens favour 6-9 years to be the age of observance of purdah, whereas 13.3% of them have favoured the age-group of 18-21 years. Thus we see that there is no significant relevance of caste to the age of observance of purdah by their girls.

Table 2 represents freedom of outing of girls or women respondents on the basis of age. This question was aimed to find out the extent and degree of the impact of religious sanction in this urban population of the Muslim community of Patna as also the extent of the impact of urbanism and modernism on the actual behaviour of respondents in respect of observance of purdah. Whether they still stick strictly to the traditional system of complete seclusion from the male or they have developed consciousness about the need of the hour and co-operate with their male counterparts in day-to-day outdoor affairs of the family and society is the main aim of this question. The responses given by the respondents in this regard are given in Table 2.

It is evident from the above table that the highest (34.3%) percentage of response has gone in favour of freedom of visit to close relatives, the next highest percentage (27.0%) has gone in favour of freedom to visit neighbours and friends, the third highest percentage in favour of freedom to visit friends on special occasions, the second lowest percentage (13.3%) has gone in favour of freedom of visit wherever necessary and the least (3.3%) favour has gone to complete freedom of going anywhere according to choice or need. This response pattern suggests neither complete freedom nor complete seclusion as found in the past among Muslims. The first two columns of the table consists of 'complete' and 'near complete' degrees of feminine freedom, the third column presents moderate or reserved freedom whereas the fourth and the fifth columns stand for traditionalism or conservatism. The table shows that among 300 respondents 40 have shown 'near complete' freedom, 10 have shown 'complete freedom', 103 are on the moderate line (i.e. neither freedom nor conservatism), 81 and 66 show either an edge towards conservatism or complete conservatism and orthodoxy in the matter of outing.

The table further shows 4.0% of the age-group of up to 25, 4.4% of the age-group of 26-35 years, 2.4% of the age-group of 36-45 years and 1.9% of the age category of 46 and above have shown complete freedom of outing. Though these percentages of favour for complete freedom are very low, it shows an encouraging development towards modernity because even in low strata of the Muslim society women of young age are never allowed this much of freedom. Hence

Table 2

Age and Freedom of Outing

(Percentage in brackets)

Age Category (Yrs.)	*Extent of Freedom*					*Total*
	Free to go anywhere I like	*Free to go where necessary*	*Free to visit only close relatives*	*Free to visit neighbours/friends*	*Free to go on spl. occasions to friends*	
Up to 25	3(4.0)	12(16.0)	27(36.0)	18(24.0)	15(20.0)	75
26-35	4(4.4)	12(13.3)	30(33.3)	24(26.6)	20(20.2)	90
36-45	2(2.4)	11(13.4)	36(43.9)	21(25.6)	12(14.6)	82
46+	1(1.9)	5(9.4)	10(18.8)	18(34.0)	19(35.8)	53
Total	10(3.3)	40(13.3)	103(34.3)	81(7.0)	66(22.0)	300

this shows a marked impact of urbanism on the Muslim women. 16% of up to 25, 13.3% of the age between 26-35 years, 13.4% of the age-group of 36-45 years and 9.4% of women of the age of 46 and above have shown 'near complete freedom' of going where it was necessary. Here a consistent rise in the percentage of response is found with the fall in age of the respondents. Women of younger age are more free than women of older age. It shows that the degree of freedom of outing has risen with the fall in age. The highest percentages of response, excepting that of the age-group of 46 and above, show a restricted freedom of outing within the circumference of relationships. 36% of the age-group of up to 25, 33.3% of 26-35 years, 43.9% of 36-45 years and 18.8% of the eldest age-group of 46 and above have shown a restricted freedom of outing within the circumference of relationship; whereas 24.0% of up to 25, 26.6% of 26-35 years, 25.6% of 36-45 years and 34.0% of the eldest age-group of 46 and above have shown movement within the circle of neighbourhood and friends while 20.0% of the youngest age-group of up to 25, 20.2% of the second youngest age-group of 26-35 years, 14.6% of 36-45 years and 35.8% of the eldest age-group of 46 and above have shown extra conservatism in movement within the circle of friends and that too only on special occasions like marriage, festivals, etc. It is important to note that the percentages of favour for this extra-conservative type of outing have risen with the rise in age, which shows that women of elder age-groups carry a higher degree of conservatism than those of younger age. It shows a positive impact of urbanism and rationalism among the women of younger age than among the elder age-groups. It may, therefore, be interpreted that age is relevant in modernizing the attitude in respect of observance of purdah and outing.

Table 3 presents the manner of outing—i.e., alone, escorted and according to the situation—on age basis. In Muslim societies of the past adult women or underteen girls were never allowed to go out without escort and proper veil, but now-a-days even girls of underteen age are seen in schools, colleges and market place with or without escort. It was in this perspective that the Muslim women respondents were put such a question to disclose the fact whether they go out alone or with some escort in order to know whether they are still fearful of their male counterparts and like to maintain a distance from them or they have developed an intimacy with them and need not any such fear these days. The responses obtained from them are given in Table 3.

Table 3

Age and Outing

(Percentage in brackets)

Age Category	*Manner of Outing*			*Total*
	Alone	*Escorted*	*Depending on situation*	
Up to 25	8(10.6)	36(48.0)	31(41.3)	75
26-35	10(11.1)	43(47.7)	37(41.1)	90
36-45	10(12.2)	44(53.6)	28(34.1)	82
46+	7(13.2)	30(56.6)	16(30.1)	53
Total	35(11.6)	153(51.0)	112(37.3)	300

It is evident from the table that, on the whole, 51.0% of the respondents go for outing under escort of some male or female member of their family whereas 37.3% of them move out sometimes under escort and sometimes without escort according to the demand of the situation or length of duration of outing. 11.6% of the respondents have declared that they do not need any escort while going out, which means that this section of the women respondents do not have any fear of males and hence they do not feel any necessity to have an escort for going out. The table thus suggests that still the majority of the Muslim women is fearful of male folk or wants to maintain its age-old tradition of moving under escort. A sizeable population of them (37.3%) are half-way between the two ends of traditionalism and modernism, as they sometimes move without escort and sometimes under escort, which shows a bent towards rationality. 11.6% of the respondents have adopted the path of rationality and they do not feel any necessity of having escort while moving out. They are, perhaps, those women who are either attached to some educational institution in the pursuit of learning or teaching or are related to modern families of Muslim society. It may, therefore, be interpreted that a phase of tradition-modernity-continuum has set in the Muslim society in the present day, and women are conceiving the reality of life and participating with their male folk without fear in their outdoor activities.

The table further shows that 10.6% of the respondents in the age-group up to 25 years, 11.1% in the age-group of 26-35 years, 12.2% of 36-45 years and 13.2% of 46 years and above move out without any escort and without any care for situation; whereas 41.3% of the youngest age-group, 41.1% of the second youngest age-group, 34.1% of the second highest age-group and 30.1% of the highest age-group have declared that they move out both ways. Perhaps they are those who take escort only when moving out of station or for attending a strange gathering, and in normal course they move freely without escort. Thus they are midway traditionalism and modernity having an edge towards modernity. This response pattern also suggests a consistent rise in the degree of modernity with the rise in age in the first column and an inverse relation of age with the rise in moderacy of attitude in this respect. Relatively women of younger age move alone in comparatively lesser percentage whereas women of older age move alone in a higher percentage. The mid-way situation is found in higher percentage in case of women of younger age and in comparatively lesser percentage in case of women of older age. It shows that younger women are more free in in-station outing than the older ones, and they find the necessity of an escort only when they go out-station. On the contrary, the younger population of women goes out alone in a lesser percentage whereas elder population moves alone in a higher percentage.

On the other hand 48.0% of the age-group of up to 25 years, 47.7% of the age-group of 26-35 years, 53.8% of 36-45 years and 56.8% of respondents of 46 and above move out strictly under escort. These are the women who are clearly under the sole impact of traditionalism and they are not ready to break through the clutches of traditional norms and values. This response pattern also shows a consistent rise in the percentages of response in favour of movement under escort with the rise in age It may, therefore, by said that age is directly related to the degree of conservatism and orthodoxy. The younger population of women is less conservative than the older ones.

Table 4

Education and Types of Purdah Observed

Type of Purdah Observed	*Educational Level of Respondents*					*Total*
	Illiterate	*Literate*	*High School*	*College*	*Post-Graduate*	
Strictly traditional	23 21.2	54 50.0	29 26.8	2 1.8	0	108
Sharai	17 20.7	23 28.0	21 25.6	15 18.2	6 7.3	82
Liberal	18 17.8	18 17.8	34 33.6	21 20.7	10 9.9	101
Total	58 19.9	95 32.6	84 28.8	38 13.0	16 5.4	291

Decimal figures are percentages.

The above table aimed to evaluate the impact of education on the choice for the type of purdah observed by the respondents, i.e., whether education has been instrumental in liberalising the attitude of the Muslim women and has been able to soften the traditional rigidity in this respect. It is evident from the table that out of 291 women (who observe purdah), 108 (37.1%) observe the strictly traditional purdah, 82 (28.1%) observe Sharai purdah and 101 (34.7%) observe liberal purdah. It means that 37.1% of the respondents wear burqa and cover their faces while outing, 28.1% wear burqa but they do not cover their faces and 34.7% are those who neither wear burqa nor cover their faces rather they use loose garments and wear a chadar over their breast and/or head. It may, therefore, be interpreted that though in the present days majority of the Muslim women like to observe strictly traditional purdah, a shift from the conservative standpoint to the liberal standpoint is quite apparent. Observance of Sharai purdah is also a reform in the traditional system of purdah whereas the liberal type of purdah is quite rational and modern approach towards emancipation of women from the clutches of traditional sanctions and customary rigidity. Thus if we combine the percentages of women observing Sharai and liberal purdah, we can say that 62.7% of the Muslim women are against the rigidity and conservatism of the traditional system and they are either completely abandoned by them or are in the process of reform in the light of Islamic Shariah.

On literacy basis we see that the highest percentage of literate women (50.0%), the second highest percentage of high school educated women and the third highest percentage (21.2%) of illiterates have expressed that they observe strict type of traditional purdah, while a quite insignificant percentage (1.8%) of college educated and 0% of post-graduate respondents have shown favour for this type of purdah; whereas significant percegtages of college educated (18.2%) and post-graduate (7.3%) have said that they observe Sharai purdah. 28.0% of literates, 25.6% of high school pass and 20.7% of illiterate respondents observe this type of purdah. The total strength of reformists is 28.1% of the entire population observing purdah, which shows a marked shift from traditionalism to reformism in which the share of highly educated women is quite significant. It shows impact of education on the attitude of Muslim women towards observance of purdah. It is further evident from the table that 9.9% of post-graduates, 20.7% of college educated respondents have come out the clutches of traditionalism and religious orthodoxy, whereas 33.6% of high school pass, 17.8% of literates and illiterate respondents have reported that they observe liberal type of purdah—i.e., they neither wear burqa nor cover their faces while outing. These response patterns show encouraging response from literate section of women, which shows the impact of education on rationalisation of the attitude of these Muslim women in respect of observance of purdah. Hence education is quite relevant to the response patterns.

Table 5

Age and Type of Purdah Observed

(Percentage in brackets)

Age	*Type of Purdah*			*Total*
	Strictly Traditional	*Sharai*	*Liberal*	
Up to 25	6(9 0)	26(39.3)	34(51.5)	66(22.7)
26-35	23(25.5)	20(22.2)	47(52 2)	90(30.9)
36-45	41(53.6)	25(30.4)	13(15.8)	82(28.2)
46 +	35(66.0)	11(20.7)	7(13.2)	53(18.2)
Total	108(37.1)	82(28.1)	101(34.7)	291(100)

It is not necessary to discuss the total because we have already discussed it in the preceding Table 4. Here we intend to explore whether age has any bearing on the choice for different types of purdah in vogue in the present days. We have, however, seen in the previous table that the second majority (34.7%) of the sample under study observes liberal type of purdah. Of them 52.2% in the age-group of 26-35 years, 51.5% in the age-group up to 25 years, 15.8% in the age-group of 36-45 years and 13.2% in the age-group of 46 years and above have declared to be observing liberal type of purdah. It is quite evident that the former two early age-groups have declared observance of this modern or rational type of purdah in over fifty per cent of their total strength, whereas 15.8% of the age-group of 36-45 years and 13.2% of 46 and above have favoured this type of so-called purdah. It shows popularity of this type of (liberal) purdah in majorities of the younger generation. Hence it can be interpreted that age is greatly significant in the choice for liberalism in respect of observance of purdah. So far sharai purdah is concerned, here also we see that the highest percentage (39.3%) of the youngest age-group of up to 25 observes this reformed type of purdah, whereas a very small percentage of them (9.0%) observes the strict traditional type. 30.4% of the age-group of 36-45, 22.2% of 26-35 and 20.7% of the eldest age-group of 46 and above have declared to be observing sharai purdah. Though any consistency is not reflected from the response in favour of sharai purdah, one thing is apparent that the eldest age-group observes this reformed type of purdah in the least (20.7%) percentage while the youngest age-group of up to 25 years observes this type of purdah in the highest percentage. Thus it can be said that age is relevant to rationalisation of attitude in this respect. On the other hand we see that 66.0% of women in the highest age-group, 53.6% of 36-45 years, 25.5% of the age-group of 26-35 years and only 9.0% of up to 25 years observe the strict type of traditional purdah. This response pattern reflects a consistent rise in the percentages of response in favour of strictly traditional purdah with rise in age of the respondents. This clearly shows relevance of age to the adherence of conservatism and traditionalism. Higher the age of the respondent, higher is the degree of her traditionalism and vice-versa.

Table 6 was framed with an intention to understand whether there is difference in the attitudes of the respondents on the basis of caste; or, in other words, whether caste has any bearing on the choice for various types of purdah in vogue in the Muslim society. In the traditional society of the past it was seen that the lower classes of the Muslim women, called Atraf, had the least care for purdah in the sense the Ashraf took it. But with the passage of time many conditions of life have changed or are changing very fast. For instance the then Ashraf have now lost the very basis of their sharafat (nobility)—the wealth and zamindari. In the present age of democracy the wealth is moving towards the labour class and the down-trodden, whereas the so-called Ashraf of the foregoing centuries are only counting their days of nobility or groaning under duress caused by active and

Table 6

Caste and Type of Purdah Observance

(Percentage in brackets)

Caste	Type of Purdah			Total
	Strictly Traditional	Sharai	Liberal	
Saiyid	10(20.0)	10(20 0)	30(60.0)	50(17.3)
Shaikh	14(25.0)	22(39.2)	20(35.7)	56(19.4)
Pathan	14(28.5)	17(34.6)	18(36.7)	49(16.8)
Mallick	10(27.7)	14(38.8)	12(33.3)	36(12.3)
Ansari	25(45.4)	12(21.8)	18(32.7)	55(18.9)
Rayeen	10(66.6)	2(13.3)	3(20.0)	15(5.1)
Chique	15(75.0)	5(25.0)	—	20(6.8)
Kalal	10(100)	—	—	10(3.4)
Total	108(37.1)	82(28.1)	101(34.7)	291(100)

competitive norms of social appreciation, which they were never in habit of or they ever thought of such a change in social norms. With the mobility of wealth and riches towards the industrious section of the society, the concept of sharafat (nobility) is also moving in favour of the then Atraf. Under the economic pressure the so-called Ashraf families have choosen to come out the fortification of sharafat (nobility) in search of livelihood and to save the name and fame of their forefathers. These facts must have their own impact on the attitude and appreciation of different castes in different degrees, which forms a valuable aspect of sociological probe.

It is evident from the table that 20% of Saiyids, 25% of Shaikhs, 28.5% of Pathans, 27.7% of Mallicks, 45.5% of Ansaris, 66.6% of Rayeens, 75.0% of Chiques and 100% of Kalals observe strict type of traditional purdah. This response pattern clearly shows a consistent rise in the percentages of response in favour of this rigid type of purdah with the fall in status of castes. It means that higher classes of the Muslim society have lesser degree of favour for this rigid type of purdah, and this degree of favour has been increasing with the fall in the status of caste. Lower caste women in majority have shown favour for this outdated type of purdah, whereas higher classes have rationalised their attitudes in higher degrees, and have switched over either to the reformed type of Sharai purdah or complete liberal type of purdah. As evident from the table 39.2% of Shaikhs, 38.8% of Mallicks, 34.6% of Pathans, 21.8% of Ansaris, 20.0% of Saiyids, 13.3% of Rayeens, 25.0% of Chiques and 0% of Kalals have declared to have been observing Sharai purdah. On the other hand, 60.0% of Saiyids, 36.7% of Pathans, 35.7% of Shaikhs 33.3% of Mallicks 32.7% of Ansaris 20.0% of Rayeens and 0% each of Chiques and Kalals have informed that they observe liberal type of purdah, i.e., they wear only chadar in place of burqa and do not cover their faces while out. A marked change is thus witnessed in the behaviour of upper classes of the Muslim women. Saiyids, who once stood on the first ladder of conservatism and orthodoxy in this respect, are now seen at its lowest ladder (20.0% each of strict type and sharai purdah) whereas 60.0% of them have choosen to divorce both types of restrictive purdahs. The other upper classes have followed the suit. In the nutshell, the higher classes of Muslims are experiencing very fast movement from traditionalism to moderacy and from moderacy to rationalism, whereas the lower classes are gradually taking the place of higher classes of the past. It is because of the natural push and pull of economy of the respective classes. Thus caste does not seem to be relevant in this respect.

Literacy and education is accepted to be a powerful force rationalising the attitude, norms and values of a society. But the impact of education varies from condition to condition and from caste to caste depending upon the susceptibility and sensitivity of respective individuals or groups or classes to the call of rationality. Hence it was thought to probe the reasons for fall in favour of purdah observance among various levels of education of the respondents. The responses obtained in this respect have been given in Table 7.

Table 7

Education and Reason of Diminishing Purdah Observance

Reasons	Education					Total
	Illiterate	Literate	High School	College	Post-Graduate	
Personal dislike	8 13.7	16 16.8	12 14.2	6 13.3	4 22.2	46 15.4
Elders' disinterestedness	7 12.0	28 29.4	21 25.0	12 26.6	4 22.2	72 24.0
Circumstance/Social requirements	27 46.5	22 23.1	25 29.7	14 31.1	6 33.3	94 31.3
Fashion/Modern attitude	10 17.2	17 17.8	18 21.4	12 26.6	4 22.2	61 20.3
Any other	6 10.3	12 12.6	8 9.5	1 2.2	—	27 9.0
Total	58 19.3	95 31.6	84 28.0	45 15.0	18 6.0	300 100

Decimal figures are percentages.

It is evident from the table that the majority (31.3%) of the respondents have given own circumstances or social requirements of the respondents themselves to be the main reason of diminishing purdah observance. It means that the economic and social needs of individuals concerned are the main reason for liberalising or bidding fare to the observance of purdah by the Muslim women under study. The second important reason mentioned by 24.0% of the respondents is elders' disinterestedness in the practice of purdah observance. The elders, especially of the Ashraf class, who were very particular about the purdah of their women in past, are now liberal enough inasmuch as they do not insist on observance of purdah by their women and have left this topic entirely to the choice of the female itself. In many cases the male themselves allow their female wards to go to school/college or for marketing with or without burqa or escort as per their own choice. This liberalism has got second position in the ladder of reasons for diminishing purdah among the Muslim women. The third reason given by 20.3% of the respondents is fashion and a competition for modernity so rampant in the Muslim society. This fashion and competition has relaxed the tenacity of purdah observance, as it eats away the very objective of fashion and display of modernity. Fashion and modernity demand freedom of show, purdah restricts it to the limit of husband and kith and kins and it goes against the very objective of fashion and modernism. Personal dislike has been given as the fourth reason by 15.3% of the respondents, which means that this percentage of respondents has an aversion for purdah and does not like to observe it. A very marginal percentage of 9.0 has suggested reasons other than the above four, to be instrumental in diminishing the observance of purdah.

So far educational level is concerned, majorities of all educational categories, excepting the category of literates, have ranked 'Own Circumstance and Social Requirements' to be the first reason or the most important reason for diminishing purdah observance in the Muslim society. The second majorities of the respondents, excepting the illiterates, have given 'elders' disinterestedness' to be the second important reason for diminishing purdah observance in the Muslim society, fashion being the third and personal dislike of the respondents' fourth reason. Thus we see that the most important reason for diminishing purdah observance is the economic reason, and the second most important reason is the softening of the attitude of elders in the families, the third important reason being fashion and fond of modernity. Thus it is seen that education has no significant relevance with the reasoning for diminishing purdah observance.

In Table 8 the reasons for diminishing purdah observance are evaluated on the basis of age of the respondents. Age is an important factor influencing the attitude towards a social problem. At times we see a marked division between the youth and the elders on the same problem. They are different both in meaning and manner, time and approach. Hence it was expected that women respondents of different age-groups may have different reasons for diminishing purdah observance. The responses obtained from the respondents are given in Table 8.

It is evident from the table that 50.0% of the respondents of age-group 26-35 years, 26.0% of the age up to 25 years, 15.2% of the age-group of 36-45 years and 7.5% of the age-group above 46 years have shown favour for personal dislike being the reason for diminishing purdah in the Muslim society; whereas 44.4% of 26-35 years, 23.6% of up to 25 years, 22.2% of the age-group 36-45 years and 9.7% of the respondents of 46 and above have given 'elders' disinterestedness' to be the reason for diminishing purdah. 29.8% of up to 25 years, 24.4% of 46 and above, 23.4% of 36-45 years and 22.3% of 26-35 years have mentioned personal circumstance and social obligations to be the reason for diminishing purdah observance in the society. Fashion and/or modern attitude has been mentioned by 40.9%of the age-group of 36-45years, 22.9% of the youngest age-group of up to 25, 21.3% of the eldest age-group of 46 and above have given fashion and modern attitude to be the reasons for diminishing purdah observance in the Muslim women. 44.4% of the age-group of 36-45 years, 22.2% of 46 and above, 18.5% of 26-35 years and 14.8% of up to 25 years have mentioned reasons other than the

Table 8

Age and Reason of Diminishing Purdah Observance

(Percentage in brackets)

Reasons	*Age of Respondents*				*Total*
	Up to 25	*26-35*	*36-45*	*46+*	
Personal dislike	12(26.0)	23(50.0)	7(15.2)	4(7.5)	46(15.4)
Elders' disinterestedness	17(23.6)	32(44.4)	16(22.2)	7(9.7)	72(24.0)
Social Requirements/ Circumstances	28(29.8)	21(22.3)	22(23.4)	23(24.4)	94(31.3)
Fashion/Modern attitude	14(22.9)	10(14.7)	25(40.9)	13(21.3)	61(20.3)
Any other	4(14.8)	5(18.5)	12(44.4),	6(22.2)	27(9.0
Total	75(25.0)	90(30.0)	82(27.3)	53(17.6)	300(100)

former four to be the reason for diminishing purdah observance. Though these response patterns do not suggest any significant relevance of age to the response patterns, this much is clear that the younger age-groups attribute personal dislike and social/personal circumstances to be the most important reasons affecting observance of purdah among the Muslim women whereas the elder age-groups in majorities have attributed fashion/modernity, other reasons and social/personal circumstances to be the most important reasons for diminishing purdah observance. It may, therefore, be interpreted that the younger generation has personal reasons for aversion to purdah observance, which are genuine and in consonance of the demand of the time; whereas the elder generation attributes impersonal or outward reasons for diminishing purdah observance. In other words, it can be said that the younger generation has broken through the traditional sanctions under personal or social pressure or on their own volition; whereas the elder generation has accused the modern currents and fashion of the age to be the main reasons for diminishing purdah observance. It may, thus, be interpreted that the younger generation is conscious of the reality of life in adapting the liberal way of living and outing, but the older generation wants to stick to the traditional way of living but it has least control over the younger generation in keeping it within their own fold, and hence they accuse the modern currents and fashion of the younger generation. They have not yet conceived the demand of the time and they want to stick to the traditional way of living.

Table 9 presents the reasoning of diminishing purdah observance on the basis of monthly income of their families. It is a well-established fact that economic condition of an individual or of a family has a direct bearing on one's attitude, norms and values and its impact on the life style, thinking and social behaviour is quite significant as evidenced by various studies made by social scientists in different societies.

On the whole, as per the table, the most important reason mentioned by the majority (31.3%) of the respondents for diminishing purdah observance is social requirement or

Table 9
Income and Reason of Diminishing Purdah Observance

Reasons	Income Level					Total
	Up to Rs. 500	*501 to Rs. 1000*	*1001 to Rs. 1500*	*1501 to 2000*	*2000 and above*	
Personal dislike	3 6.5	5 10 8	14 30.4	20 43.4	4 8 6	46 15.3
Elder's disinterestedness	7 9.7	12 16.6	28 38.8	17 23.6	8 11.1	72 24.0
Social Requirement/ Circumstances	14 14.8	27 28.7	24 25.5	16 17.0	13 13.8	94 31.3
Fashion/Modern attitude	2 3.2	5 8.1	19 31.1	27 44.2	8 13.1	61 20.4
Any other	4 14.8	6 22.2	7 25.9	10 37.0	—	27 9.0
Total	30 10.0	55 18.3	92 30.6	90 30.0	33 11.0	300 100

Decimal figures are percentages.

personal circumstances followed by elders' disinterestedness (24.0%) and fashion/modern attitude (20.3%). A very small percentage of the respondents (9.0%) has mentioned reasons other than the afore-mentioned four reasons to be instrumental in diminishing purdah observance among the Muslim women.

Personal disliking has been mentioned by the second highest majority (43 4%) of the income-group of Rs. 1501-2000 and third highest majority (30.4%) of the middle income-group of Rs.1001-1500, besides very small percentages of 10.8% (Rs.501-1000), 8 6% (Rs.2000 & above) and 6.5% of the lowest income categories. The highest percentage (38.8%) of the middle income-group, the third highest percentage (23.6%) of the second highest income-group (1501-2000) have mentioned elders' disinterestedness to be the most important reason for bidding farewell to the purdah observance or diminishing its use. The highest percentage of the second lowest income-group (501-1000) and the fourth highest percentage (25.5%) of the middle income-group has mentioned social requirement or personal circumstances to be the most important reason for diminishing purdah observance; whereas the highest percentage (44.2%) of the next highest income group (1501-2000) and the second highest percentage (31.1%) of the middle income group has mentioned fashion and modern currents to be responsible for diminishing purdah observance among the Muslim society. 37.0% of the next highest income category, 25.9% of the middle income category and 22.2% of the second lowest income category have mentioned other reasons to be responsible for diminishing purdah. Besides them, very small percentage have favoured the afore-mentioned reasons. Any consistent variation with rise in income level is not found. Though income does not appear to be significantly relevant to the response patterns, this much is clear from the table that the higher income-groups have attributed more importance to personal disliking, elder's disinterestedness and fashion to be the most important reasons affecting purdah observance; whereas the lower income-groups have attached greater importance to social requirement and personal circumstances to be instrumental in breaking through the sanctions of purdah. It means that higher the income, lesser the liking for purdah; and lower the income, higher the necessity to break through the traditional sanctions regarding purdah. Thus both affluence and poverty appear to be instrumental in breaking through the traditional rigidity with regard to purdah—in the former case with personal inclination and in the latter case under duress of economic and educational pursuits.

In the following three tables (10, 11 and 12) the responses of the 291 purdah observing respondents with regard to reasons for their purdah observance on the bases of educational level, monthly family income and age have been analysed to understand the relevance of the three variables to education, income and age to the norms and values attached by them with purdah, and the degree of their religiosity, traditionalism and rationality. Table 10 presents the responses on the basis of education. Education is supposed to be one of the most powerful force in rationalising the attitude and behaviour, norms and values of human beings. Now-a-days almost every society has conceived the importance of education and is sending its wards to schools and colleges for acquiring knowledge as well as for enabling themselves to earn their livelihood, raise prestige in society and become respectable citizen of the nation.

The table has been framed with a view to understand the impact of education on the attitude of respondents with regard to the reasons of observance of purdah by them, and thereby to know the degree of their attachment with traditional norms and values and/or their mobility towards rationales of the present-day human life. It is evident from the table that 38.8% of the post-graduate, 37.7% of college-educated, 34.5% of high school educated, 20.4% of illiterates and 18.9% of literates attach safeguard to modesty to the observance of purdah. On the average 27.8% of the respondents observe purdah with a view to safeguard their modesty. In other words, this percentage (27.8%) of the respondents feels the necessity of a distance from the male section of the society in order to safeguard its chastity. On the other hand, 30.6% of illiterates, 28.4% of literates, 22.2% of college

Table 10

Education and Reason of Observing Purdah

(Percentage in brackets)

Education	*Reasons for Observance of Purdah*				*Total*
	Safeguards modesty	*Family tradition*	*Social compulsion*	*Religious sanction*	
Illiterate	10(20.4)	15(30.6)	11(22.4)	17(34.6)	49(16.8)
Literate	18(18.9)	27(28.4)	18(18.9)	28(29.4)	95(32.7)
High School	29(34.5)	8(9.5)	24(28.5)	23(27.3)	84(28.8)
College	17(37.7)	20(22.2)	5(11.1)	13(28.8)	45(15.4)
Post-Graduate	7(38.8)	3(16.6)	2(11.1)	6(33.3)	18(6.3)
Total	81(27.8)	63(21.6)	60(20.6)	87(29.8)	291(100)

educated respondents, 16.6% of post-graduates and 9.5% of high school pass respondents observe purdah as family tradition; whereas 28.5% of high school educated, 22.4% of illiterates, 18.9% of literates and 11.1% each of college-educated and post-graduate respondents observe purdah under social compulsion. It means that these percentages of respondents are afraid of society, that if they abandon purdah, the society will boycott it or shall degrade them in social status and hence they are bound to observe purdah. On the other hand, this response pattern shows that these respondents are not willing to observe purdah but for the fear of the society. 34.6% of illiterates, 33.3% of post-graduates, 29.4% of literates, 28.8% of college-educated respondents and 27.3% of high school educated respondents observe purdah because of the respect for religious sanction. On an average, the highest percentage of 29.8 observes purdah due to religious sanction, the second highest percentage (27.8%) observes purdah in order to safeguard the modesty, 21.6% observes it because of family tradition and 20.6% because of social compulsion. It is important to point out that the first and the last reasons show reverence for the religious sanctions, whereas the intermediary two reasons of family tradition and social compulsion are void of such respect. It is quite evident from the table that the first and second highest majorities of the respondents have given religious sanction and safeguards to modesty being the most important reasons for their observing purdah. It may, therefore, be interpreted that majority of the respondents observe purdah due to religious reverence. But, at the same time, the table also suggests that sizeable section of the respondents (21.6% and 20.6%) observes purdah either as family tradition or for the fear of society, otherwise, this section of women is not willing to observe it. It shows mobility of a sizeable section of the Muslim society towards rationality. This response pattern suggests persistence of a tradition-modernity-continuum among the Muslim women under study. The table does not, however, suggest any consistent variation in the response pattern on the basis of education; and, hence, education does not appear to be relevant to response patterns.

Table 11

Income and Reason of Observing Purdah

(Percentage in brackets)

Income	*Reasons*				*Total*
	Safeguards modesty	*Family tradition*	*Social compulsion*	*Religious sanction*	
Up to 500	12(20.6)	8(13 7)	14(24.1)	24(41.3)	58(19.9)
501-1000	25(26.3)	17(17.8)	22(23.1)	31(32.6)	95(32.6)
1001-1500	23(27.3)	23(27.3)	15(17.8)	23(27.3)	84(28.6)
1501-2000	15(38.4)	1 (28.2)	7(17.9)	6(15.3)	39(13.6)
2001+	6(40.0)	4(26.6)	2(13.3)	3(20.0)	15(5.3)
Total	81(27.8)	63(21.6)	60(20.6)	87(29.8)	291(100)

It is evident from the table that the highest percentage (40%) of the highest income-group of Rs. 2001 and above has expressed safeguard to modesty being the most important reason for their observing purdah. 38.4% of the second highest income group, 27.3% of the middle income-group, 26.3% of the second lowest income-group and 20.6% of the income-group up to Rs. 500 have given this reason. It shows a consistency of response on income basis. The percentage of response in favour of safeguard to modesty as reason for observance of purdah has risen consistently with the rise in income; and, hence, it may be said that income is relevant to the consciousness about modesty. In the same way, an adverse relation of income is found in the response in respect of 'social compulsion'. The degree of fear of society has risen with the fall in income level. 13.3% of the income group of Rs. 2001 and above, 17.9% of the income-group of Rs.1501-2000, 17.8% of Rs. 1001-1500, 23.1% of Rs. 501-1000 and 24.1% of the income group of up to Rs. 500 have this fear. It means that income is instrumental in removing the fear of society in respect of observance of purdah or other such religious or traditional sanctions. Poorer section fears more than the richer section, and this fear plays a positive role in adherence to religious or traditional practices by a sizeable section of 20.6% of the whole sample. Such a consistency is not found with regard to religious sanction or family tradition. 41.3% of the income category of up to Rs. 500, 32.6% of 501-1000, 27.3% of 1001-1500, 15.3% of 1501-2000 and 20.0% of the income category of 2001 and above have shown respect of religious sanction in the observance of purdah. Barring the highest income-group (i.e. 20% of respondents), the percentages of response in respect of religious sanction have fallen with the rise in income. It means that, though majorities of almost all sections of the respondents have shown a bent towards religiosity, the degree of reverence for religious sanction in respect of purdah has consistently fallen with the rise in income. It shows a positive role of income level in decreasing the degree of religiosity and traditionality. 28.2% of the

Table 12

Age and Reason of Observing Purdah

(Percentage in brackets)

Age	*Reasons*				*Total*
	Safeguards modesty	*Family tradition*	*Social compulsion*	*Religious sanction*	
Up to 25	14(18.6)	11(14.6)	25(33.3)	25(33.3)	75(25.8)
26-35	23(26.4)	18(20.6)	20(22.9)	26(29.8)	87(29.9)
36-45	24(30.3)	24(30.3)	11(13.9)	20(25.3)	79(27.2)
46+	20(40.0)	10(20.0)	4(8.0)	16(32.0)	50(17.1)
Total	81(27.8)	63(21.6)	60(20.6)	87(29.8)	291(100)

second highest income-group, 27.3% of the middle income-group, 26.6% of the highest income-group, 17.8% of the second lowest income-group and 13.7% of the lowest income-group have given the reason of family tradition for observance of purdah. It means that these percentages of respondents observe purdah as a fashion and they are neither afraid of society or religious sanction. These women are, in fact, on the brink of switching over to liberlism or modernity the moment they like. It may therefore, be interpreted that income is significantly relevant to the response pattern, though it is not very significant in removing the reverence for religious sanction or consciousness for modesty.

This table too presents almost the same picture as seen in Table 11. A consistent rise in response pattern with regard of safeguard to modesty is seen with rise in age. It means that the degree of consciousness about modesty has risen with the rise in age. This consistency speaks of the relevance of age to the response pattern in respect of conscious about modesty. The same trend is found in adverse shape in respect of the reason of social compulsion being the reason for observance of purdah. The fear of society has risen consistently with the fall in income. Barring the highest age-group of 46 and above, similar consistency in response pattern in respect of the reason of 'religious sanction' is found from the table. The reverence for religious sanction has risen with the fall in age level, which means that the younger generation is more enthusiastic about religious sanctions with regard to purdah than the elder generation with the exception of the eldest age-group which coparts with the younger population in this respect. Almost similar picture is witnessed in respect of family tradition. Barring the highest age-group, a consistent rise in adherence to family tradition is witnessed with the rise in age. It means that age is significantly relevant to response patterns.

To sum up: Purdah observance is found in 100% of the cases of Pathans, Mallicks, Chiques and Kalals and 98.3% of Shaikhs, 96.3% of Saiyids, 94.5% of Ansaris and 80.0% of Rayeens observe purdah. The data analysed in this chapter show that 3.3% of the population is quite free to visit any place as it likes, 13.3% are semi-free to visit wherever necessary whereas 83.3% of the respondents have restricted outings and they cannot move outside according to their own choice. It shows that the female section of the Muslim community of Patna is still in majority of the cases, under the grip of traditionalism and religious orthodoxy and only 16.6% of them have a freedom of outing in the real sense. The tables further reveal that 11.6% of the respondents have a freedom to move out alone, 37.3% have a liberty to move either with escort or alone as per demands of the situation; but a majority of 51.0% of them cannot move without escort. The tables further show that 34.7% of the purdah observing ladies observe liberal type of purdah, i.e., they use only a chader in place of burqa and do not cover their faces while outing; 28.1% are those who observe shari purdah, i.e., they wear burqa but do not cover their faces; and 37.1% are those who observe strict type of traditional purdah with burqa and face-covering. The data further reveal that 60.0% of Saiyids, 36.7% of Pathans, 35.7% of Shaikhs, 33.3% of Mallicks, 32.7% of Ansaris and 20.0% of Rayeens observe liberal type of purdah whereas not a single respondent of Chique and Kalal has reported to be observing this type of purdah. It is because the downtrodden classes of the Muslim society have in general found refuge in Jammat-e-Islami, an organization of Muslim fundamentalists, and it is under the influence of that Jamaat that no respondent of Chiques and Kalals observes liberal type of purdah rather 100% of them observe either sharai purdah or strictly traditional type of purdah. It is important to note here that 15.3% of the purdah observing respondents have an aversion to it and in cases of 24.0% of the respondents' elders are disinterested with this topic whether their women should not observe purdah. 31.3% of the respondents feel social or personal reasons for diminishing purdah observance and 20.3% of them feel fashion and modern attitudes of the younger generation responsible for diminishing purdah observance. When asked reasons for observance of purdah, 27.8% of the respondents expressed the reason of 'safeguard to modesty',

21.6% 'family tradition', 20.6% gave the reason of 'social compulsion' and 29.8% of them said that they observe purdah only because God wants to do so. These responses reveal that the intermediate (42.2%) sections do not carry any religious sentiment with purdah observance, whereas the first and the last sections of 'safeguard to modesty' and 'religious sanction' carry religious sentiments with purdah practices.

7

Family Planning

India is facing a serious problem of over-population and it is stated that the stage of population explosion has reached in this country. China has the largest population of the world and the second largest population resides in India. But it is important to point out that the density of population in India is much higher than the density of population in China. It means that the per-head space for an Indian is much lesser in India than in China and this higher population density means that there is a huge concentration of population in this country. The data in respect of population densities in various countries of the world show that India is one of the most thickly populated countries of the world. The density of population in Canada and Australia is 3 per square mile, in USSR 10 per square mile, in Egypt 27 per square mile, in USA 30 per square mile, in China 123 per square mile, in UK 215 per square mile, in Netherland 348 per square mile and in India 410 per square mile. These figures show that the density of population in India is 3.3 times the density in China. This situation is quite alarming and it is justified to say that India has reached the stage of population explosion.

The data with regard to the density of population in the country suggest that there has been a continuous rise in population density in the country. In 1921 the density of population in India was 81 per square kilometre which rose to 90 per square kilometre in 1931, 103 per square kilometre in 1941, 117 per square kilometre in 1951, 142 per square kilometre in 1961, 177 per square kilometre in 1971 and 215 per square kilometre in 1981. In the last decade, i.e., between 1971-81, there was an increase of 20% in the country's density of population. The data showing density of population in the country suggest that there has been not only an increase in the density rather there has been an increase in the rate of density growth too. It is due to the fact that the country's population has been increasing alongwith the increase in the rate of population growth. The Census Reports reveal that during the decade 1901-1911 the population increased from 238.4 million to 252.1 million. The percentage of increase in population growth was 5.75. In 1921, the country's population was 251.1 million which rose to 279.0 million in 1931 and during this decade the percentage increase in population was 11.01. In 1941, the population of the country was 317.7 million showing 13.51% increase in population size of the country. In the following decade of 1941-51, the population increased from 317.7 million to 361.1 million showing an increase of 14.02 per cent. In 1961, the population of the country was recorded as 439.3 million and the increase in population during this decade was 21.63 per cent. The population of the country rose to 546.95 million showing an increase of 24.57 per cent in the size of the population in the preceding decade (i.e. 1971-80). In 1981, the population of the country was recorded as 683.8 million and the increase in population during 1971-81 was 24.75 per cent. The percentage increase in the size of population from 192: onwards reveals that there has been not only continuous increase in the size of the population rather the rate of growth of population has also been increasing at a higher rate. It is obvious that in case the population size is getting enlarged at such an alarming rate, the density of population is also bound to increase rapidly resulting in the crisis of serious over-population.

It is also important to note here that the continuous rise in the density of population and continuous enlargement in the size of population is not due to increase in birth rate or fertility only. In fact the fertility, or birth rate, in India has been declining right from the year 1911 to 1971, except in the year 1961. According to the available data the birth rate in the country was 51.3 per thousand in 1911, 49.2 per thousand in 1921, 46.4 per thousand in 1931, 45.2 per thousand in 1941, 39.9 per thousand in 1951, 41.7 per thousand in 1961 and 38.6 per thousand in 1971. Thus there has been a continuous decline in the fertility and birth rate and it came down from 51.3 per thousand to 38.6 per thousand in a period of 60 years (1911-1971). But in spite of this fall in birth rate, population growth has been taking place continuously with an increase in the percentage of growth. It is not due to the rise in birth rate but to the fact that death rate has declined more rapidly than birth rate in the country. In 1911 the death rate in the country was 41.1 per thousand which rose to 48.6 per thousand in 1921, again declined to 36.3 per thousand in 1931, 31.2 per thousand in 1941, 27.4 per thousand in 1951, 22.8 per thousand in 1961 and 14.0 per thousand in 1971. It means that the death rate declined from 48.6 per thousand to 14.0 per thousand in a period of 50 years (1921-1971), whereas the birth rate declined from 49.2 per thousand to 38.6 per thousand during the same period. In other words, there was a fall of 10.6 per thousand in birth rate in a period of 50 years whereas the death rate decreased by 34.6 per thousand during this period. This difference between the decline in birth rate and death rate has resulted in an increase in population size as well as in the rate of population growth.

In the light of above facts it appears that the real cause of over-population crisis in India lies in the slow decline in birth rate. The fertility is still on the high side in comparison to many developed countries of the world. In Japan the birth rate is comparatively much lower than in India and there was a time when the Government of Japan had to propagate for increasing fertility and announced incentives and awards for women giving birth to twins or more than two issues at a time. In USA the birth rate in 1971 was 21.0 per thousand which is much lower than the birth rate in India in 1971, i.e. 41.1 per thousand. In the same way in USSR the birth rate was recorded as 17.6 per thousand in 1972. Even in developing countries like Ceylon the birth rate is lower than that in India, because, in 1961, the birth rate in India was 41.7 per thousand whereas in Ceylon it was 36.6 per thousand in the same year. Hence it appears that in comparison to many developing and developed nations of the world the fertility rate is much higher in India and it is the main reason for the rapid growth in Indian population. Hence the way to check the population growth in the country is to regulate fertility and to reduce birth rate. It is important to point out that temperamentally and traditionally Indian population is faith oriented and religion minded. The entirety of social life is governed, to some extent, by religious sanctions and any measure which goes against faith or religious sanction is vehemently opposed by majority of the people. In many developing countries today abortion has also been adopted as a measure for reducing fertility and limiting live-birth. In some of the countries abortion has been legalised and married women are allowed to adopt this measure for stopping the birth of unwanted child. But in a country like India where religion still plays a dominant role and ethics and morality are of greater importance, abortion cannot be approved as a measure for regulating fertility behaviour. It is considered to be an act of genocide or homicide and is openly condemned in society. Hence the only way to resolve the crisis of over-population is to check conception, and thus to limit the birth of child. The family planning, or family welfare programme launched in India aims at regulating fertility behaviour not only through stopping birth but also through providing spacing between births. These programmes are regularly transmitted through radio, television, movies films, news-papers, magazines, family planning workshops and periodical literatures and people residing even in the remote rural areas are now acquainted with this national programme. But in spite of all these efforts and provision of all medical facilities at the doorstep of the people throughout India the birth rate in the country is still much higher and reflects an alarming situation. The persistence of high fertility is a reality and the relevant data provide ample evidence to this fact that the decline in birth rate is far less than the satisfactory.

The persistence of high fertility in the country cannot be explained in term of a single factor. There are a number of factors which contribute to high fertility in the country. Educational backwardness, dominance of faith and religious sanctions, superstitions, notion of children being divine blessing, lack of adequate knowledge about the methods and measures of birth control, non-availability of effective measures of birth control to the needy people, carelessness and lack of sense of responsibility or duty on the part of the personnel associated with family planning programme, poor economic condition not permitting to spend any amount over the adoption of family planning measures, traditional and conventional norms and practices and non-realisation of the responsibility in respect of country and nation are the factors responsible for persistence of high fertility in the country. A loyal and conscious citizen is expected to ward off all such bottlenecks which are responsible for retarding the rate of national growth and well-being of the human race in general and of countrymen in particular. A small family provides better opportunities and amenities for the growth of the existing generation. It also provides security against natural calamities and hazards of health and mind. A care-ridden and unhappy family cannot produce a healthy environment congenial to a prosperous future.

In the light of the above facts it was thought necessary to probe the feelings, attitudes and actual practice of the Muslim women of this urban setting. How far they are acknowledged about this global and national problem, how far they feel it and how far they practise its regulating measures ? What are the reasons behind the persistence of high fertility and to what extent the sample under study is conscious of it ? These were the questions in mind of the investigator when she was interviewing her respondents and recording their responses. The responses obtained from them are classified in Table 1.

Table 1

Education and Attitude towards Limiting Family Size

(Percentage in brackets)

Educational level	*Attitude*		*Total*
	Favourable	*Unfavourable*	
Illiterate	36(62.0)	22(37.9)	58
Up to Middle	72(75.7)	23(24.2)	95
Up to Matric	79(94.0)	5(5 9)	84
College	43(95.5)	2(4.4)	45
Post-Graduate	18(100)	—	18
Total	248(82.6)	52(17.3)	300

It is evident from the above table that the majority of 82.6% of the respondents is in favour of limiting family size and only 17.3% of them are opposed to it. It means that the Muslim women of Patna are fully conscious of this national problem and they want to limit the size of their families. 62.0% of illiterates, 75.7% of respondents read up to middle stage, 94.0% of up to matric, 95.5% of college-educated and 100% of post-graduates have favoured the programme of family planning; whereas 37.9% of illiterates, 24.2% of up to middle, 5.9% of up to matric, 4.4% of college-educated and 0% of post-graduates have opposed to this programme. This pattern of response suggests a consistent rise in the percentages of favour for family planning programme with the rise in educational level and a consistent fall in the percentages of disfavour with the rise in educational level. We find 100% favour in case of post-graduate women. This is quite encouraging and shows a positive change in the attitude of Muslim women of this urban setting. It also shows that education is significantly relevant in rationalising the attitude in respect of limiting family size.

Table 2

Income and Attitude towards Limiting Family Size

(Percentage in brackets)

Income Level	*Attitude*		*Total*
	Favourable	*Unfavourable*	
Up to Rs. 500	22(73.3)	8(15.3)	30
Rs. 501—1000	42(76.3)	13(26.6)	55
Rs. 1001—1500	76(82.6)	16(17.3)	92
Rs. 1501—2000	78(86.6)	12(13.3)	90
Rs. 2001+	30(90.9)	3(9.0)	33
Total	248(82.6)	52(17.3)	300

It is evident from the table that 73.3% of the respondents having income up to Rs. 500%, 76.3% having income of Rs. 501-1000, 82.6% of the income-group of Rs. 1001-1500, 86.6% of the income category of Rs. 1501-2000 and 90.9% of the highest income group of Rs. 2001 and above have favoured family planning and limiting the size of family. On the other hand 15.3% of up to 500, 26.6% of the income-group of 501-1000, 17.3% of 1001-1500, 13.3% of Rs. 1501-2000 and 9.0% of the highest income category of Rs. 2001 and above have opposed to limit the family size. These response patterns show a consistent rise in the percentages of response in favour with the rise in income and, on the other hand, a consistent fall in the percentages of response of disfavour. It may therefore be interpreted that income is significantly relevant to the response pattern with regard to limiting of family size.

It is evident from Table 3 that 89.3% of the age-group of up to 25 years, 85.5% of 26-35 years, 79.2% of 36-45 years and 73.5% of the highest age category of 46 years and above have favoured the idea of limiting the size of family; whereas 10.6% of up to 25 years, 14.4% of 26-35 years, 20.7% of the

Table 3

Age and Attitude towards Limiting the Size of Family

(Percentage in brackets)

Age category	*Attitude*		*Total*
	Favourable	*Unfavourable*	
Up to 25 years	67(89.3)	8(10.6)	75
26-35 years	77(85.5)	13(4.4)	90
36-45 years	65(79.2)	17(20.7)	82
46 +	39(73.5)	14(26.4)	53
Total	248(82.6)	52(17.3)	300

age-group of 36-45 years and 26.4% of 46 years and above have opposed this idea. It means that younger generation is more in favour and less in opposition of the idea of limiting family size than the elder generation. This shows a marked relevance of age on rationalisation of attitude towards regulation of fertility behaviour and limiting the family size.

Table 4

Education and Practice of Birth Control

(Percentage in brackets)

Educational level	*Yes*	*No*	*Total*
Illiterate	31(53.4)	27(46.5)	58
Literate	59(62.1)	36(37.8)	95
Up to Matric	66(78.5)	18(21.4)	84
Graduate	42(93.3)	3(6.6)	45
Post-Graduate	18(100)	—	18
Total	216(72.0)	84(28.0)	300

It is apparent from the table that 72.0% of the respondents practise family planning measures and 28.0% of them does not practise it. When we compare this figure with that of Table 2, we find a difference of 10.6% in favourable response and 10.7% in negative response. It means that there is a gap between ideology and practice and 10.6% of the women favouring family planning at ideological level do not confirm it at practical level. It may be because of their lethargy, poverty, ignorance or disapproval by the husband. It is further evident from the table that 53.4% of illiterates, 62.1% of literates (middle pass), 78.5% of matriculates, 93.3% of graduates and 100% of post-graduate respondents practise family planning measures, but 46.5% of illiterates, 37.8% of literates (middle), 21.4% of matriculates, 6.6% of graduates and 0% of post-graduates do not practise family planning or birth control measures. These response patterns show a consistent rise in the percentages of affirmative response in respect of practising family planning or birth control measures with the rise in educational level; and, on the other hand, a similar trend is found in negative response where the percentage of negative response has consistently fallen with the rise in literacy level. It may, therefore, be interpreted that literacy level is significantly relevant to the response patterns in regard to the practice of birth control measures.

Table 5 shows that 56.6% of the respondents in income-group up to Rs. 500, 56.3% of Rs. 501-1000, 63.0% of Rs. 1001-1500, 88.8% of Rs. 1501-2000 and 90.9% of the highest income category of Rs. 2001 and above practise birth control measures; whereas 43.3% of up to Rs. 500, 43.6% of Rs. 501-1000, 36.9% of Rs. 1001-1500, 11.1% of Rs. 1501-2000 and 9.0% of the highest income category of Rs. 2001 and above do not practise birth control measures. These response patterns show consistent rise in affirmative response with the rise in income level and a consistent fall in negative response with the rise in income level. It means that income level is relevant to the response patterns. This finding corroborates the theoretical stand that like education, income

Table 5

Income and Practice of Birth Control

(Percentage in brackets)

Income level	*Yes*	*No*	*Total*
Up to Rs. 500	17(56.6)	13(43.3)	30
Rs. 501—1000	31(56.3)	24(43.6)	55
Rs, 1001—1500	58(63.0)	34(36.9)	92
Rs. 1501—2000	80(88.8)	10(11.1)	90
Rs. 2001+	30(90.9)	3(9.0)	33
Total	216(72.0)	84(28.0)	300

also is instrumental in rationalising the attitude of people and breaking the traditional ties.

Table 6

Age and Practice of Birth Control Measures

(Percentage in brackets)

Age group	*Yes*	*No*	*Total*
Up to 25	65(86.6)	10(13.3)	75
26-35 years	72(80.0)	18(20.0)	90
36-45 years	51(62.1)	31(37.8)	82
46+	28(52.8)	25(47.1)	53
Total	216(72.0)	84(28.0)	300

Table 6 shows that 86.6% of up to 25 years, 80.0% of 26-35 years, 62.1% of 36-45 years and 52.8% of 46 years and above practise birth control measures, whereas 13.3% of up to 25 years, 20.0% of 26-35 years, 37.8% of 36-45 years and

47.1% of the age-group of 46 years and above do not practise birth control measures. Here also we see that the percentages of affirmative response have consistently fallen with the rise in age and, on the other hand, it has consistently risen with the rise in age. It shows relevance of age with response patterns. In other words, respondents of younger age practise family planning or birth control measures in higher percentages than the respondents of elder age. It may, therefore, be interpreted that age is significantly relevant to the practice of birth control measures.

In the following set of three tables the reasons given by the respondents for practising birth control measures by them have been analysed on literacy, income and age basis. Their responses on literacy variable basis are given in Table 7.

It is evident from the table that, on the whole, 50.9% of the respondents practise birth control measures because of their poor economic condition, 17.2% practise it in order to lessen the problem of child care and their bringing up problems, 16.2% of them practise birth control in order to keep their own health intact, 12.9% of the respondents practise it for unspecified reasons and 2.7% for maintaining health of the children themselves. Thus the most important reason weighing before the respondents in practising birth control measures is their economic hardship and poverty. A greater number of children means a greater burden on the economy of the family. Every child requires food, cloth, medical care, education, supervision and a greater number of children demands greater income and greater amount of ways and means for their proper bringing up and development. The Muslim women in majority are poor and they are unable to shoulder heavy burden of children. and hence they practise birth control measures so that they could keep a control on fertility and birth within their means. The next important reason for practising birth control measures by these Muslim women is the child-rearing problem. Bringing up of each child takes a lot of time and energy and brings a lot of problems. The respondents have no stamina to confront a bogey of problems and hence they practise family planning

Table 7

Education and Reason of Practising Family Planning Measures

(Percentage in brackets)

Educational level	*Economic hardship*	*Child rearing problems*	*Personal health*	*Child's health*	*Any other*	*Total*
Illiterate	19(61.2)	2(5.4)	5(16 1)	—	5(16.1)	31
Middle	38(64.4)	6(10.1)	6(10.1)	—	9(15.2)	59
Matric	33(50.0)	11(16.6)	15(22.7)	—	7(0.6)	66
Graduate	15(35.7)	10(23.8)	6(14.2)	4(9.5)	7(16.6)	42
Post-Graduate	5(27.7)	8(44.4)	3(16.6)	2(11.1)	—	18
Total	110(50.9)	37(17.2)	35(16.2)	6(2.7)	28(12.9)	216

measures to check birth and to keep it within the limit of their worth. The third important reason for practising birth control, as stated by the Muslim women respondents, is their personal health. Every child takes a lot of their blood and taxes a lot on their physical health, which they do not find to be proper for their own existence. They want to maintain a good health, to bear healthy children and to rear the existing ones in proper manner; and, hence they practise birth control measures. The fourth reason stated by the respondents was unspecified and the fifth reason quite insignificant (2.7%). Hence it may be stated that economic hardship, child rearing problems and personal health of the respondents are the three main reasons for which they practise birth control measures.

It is apparent from Table 8 that the highest percentage (76.9%) of respondents in the lowest income group, the second highest percentage (70.9%) in the second lowest income group, the third highest percentage (62.9%) in the middle income group of Rs. 1001-1500, the second lowest percentage of 38.7 in the second highest income group and the lowest percentage (26.6%) in the highest income group have stated economic hardship to be the most important reason for practising birth control measures by them. The percentages of response in favour of this reason of poverty have consistently declined with the increase in income level, which is quite natural. In case of other reasons no consistency in response patterns is found on income basis. Hence it may be interperted that income level is not relevant to the response patterns in respect of any reasons other than the reason of economic hardship. But one thing is noteworthy that the two lowest income groups have mentioned only three reasons of economic hardship, child rearing problem and personal health while the rest three higher income groups have mentioned all the five reasons in varying frequencies to be instrumental for practising family planning measures. It is, perhaps, because of the fact that the poor families' ambitions are limited and hence their problems are also limited. But, on the other hand, the well-to-do families have comparatively a longer list of ambitions and hence they are encountered with comparatively more

Table 8

Income and Reason of Practising Family Planning Measures

(Percentage in brackets)

Income	*Economic hardship*	*Child rearing problem*	*Personal health*	*Child's health*	*Any other*	*Total*
Up to Rs. 500	10(76.9)	2(15.3)	1(7.6)	—	—	13
501—1000	22(70.9)	8(21.6)	1(3.2)	—	—	31
1001—1500	39(62.9)	12(19.3)	7(11.2)	2(1.6)	3(4.8)	62
1501—2000	31(38.7)	9(11.2)	20(25.0)	2(3.5)	18(22.5)	80
2001+	8(26.6)	6(20.0)	6(20.0)	3(10.0)	7(23.3)	30
Total	110(50 9)	37(17.1)	35(16.2)	6(2.7)	28(12.9)	216

Table 9

Education and Reason of not Practising Birth Control

(Percentage in brackets)

Literacy level	*Against the will of God*	*Children are source of additional income*	*Harmful for health*	*Any other*	*Total*
Illiterate	20(74.0)	3(11.1)	—	4(14.8)	27
Middle	16(44.4)	7(19.4)	5(13.8)	8(22.2)	36
Matric	8(44.4)	4(22.2)	3(16.6)	3(16.6)	18
Graduate	2(66.6)	—	1(33.3)	—	3
Total	46(54.7)	14(16.6)	9(10.7)	15(17.8)	84

problems, to ward off which they plan to adopt remedial measures.

It is apparent from Table 9 that only 84 respondents out of 300 do not practise family. Out of these 84, 46 (54.7%) do not practise birth control measures because, according to them, it is against the will of God, 17.8% have given unspecified reasons, 16.6% want more and more children because in their opinion children are source of additional income. 10.7% of the respondents feel that the birth control measures are injurious for health and cause complications and hence they do not practise it. It means that the most important reason for not practising birth control measures by the women respondents is the fear of God. The majority of them think that control on fertility behaviour means genocide of the future generation, which is forbidden by God. This concept of the respondents is based on the well-known tradition of the Prophet, "*Tanakahu wa tanasalu*" (do nikah and expand generation), and "*An-Nikahu sunnati fa-man raghiba sunnati laisa minni*" (i.e., nikah is my tradition, and whoever desists from it is not from me). This emphasis on *nikah* and the objective of nikah being procreation is not so simple to be overlooked by a faithful Muslim. It is true that Islam does not permit stoppage of birth for any reason other than danger to life of the mother. But, at the same time, certain temporary measures for spacing between births with the objective of health of the mother and children is allowed. In this connection, it would not be out of place, to record a 'Fatwah' given by Maulana Mujahidul Islam Quasemi, Chief Qazi (Muslim Jury) of Imarat-e-Sharia, Bihar and Orissa, Phulwarishariff, Patna (India) in the shape of an interview with a delegation of South African Muslim Doctors at Durban in 1979 arranged by the Muslim Students Association of South Africa and the Islamic Medical Association (South Africa) when the Maulana had visited that country to address an International Meet of the Jamiat-ul-Ulema. The interview having been conducted between the two real partners of the problem, i.e. medical practitioners and a theological jury, covers a vast variety of relevant questions on the subject, which the present researcher feels expedient to quote here in toto.

The Interview

Family planning is a new problem. A concise essay expounding the basic Islamic principles to various questions with regard to this problem is not available. Thanks to the Muslim Students Association of South Africa and the Islamic Medical Association (South Africa) whose combined effort led to an interview with Maulana Mujahidul Islam Quasemi, Chief Qazi (Muslim Jury) of Imarat-e-Sharia, Bihar and Orissa, Phulwarishariff, Patna (India) and the local doctors believing in Islam at Durban in 1979 when the Maulana had visited that country to address an International Meet of Jamiat-ul-Ulema. The interview having been conducted between the two real partners of the problem, covers a vast variety of relevant questions on the subject, which the researcher feels expedient to quote here in toto.

"I wish to express from the bottom of my heart, my joy in meeting you doctors. I am happy not because you are successful doctors or knowledgeable students of medicine but that, in this age, when religion is considered an obsolete tradition, you have not forsaken your trust in Islam. In fact you are keen in asking guidance from the teachings of the Qur'an and Sunnah. Before I answer your questions, I want to elaborate on what a Muslim doctor's role in society must be.

"Firstly, medical practice serves the whole of humanity and it should not be considered merely as new and exclusive scientific knowledge. If a doctor sincerely, honestly and conscientiously uses it to serve mankind, then it becomes an act of worship. Medical practice then is elevated to the position of worship. Our Prophet said, "Knowledge has two aspects—one aspect is concerned with the knowledge of religion and the other is the knowledge of the body." God has given you knowledge of the body and through it you can bring relief and comfort to suffering humanity. This in itself is one of the many favours of God upon you.

"As Muslim doctors you are destined to render sterling service to humanity in this world. According to Islam, all mankind is the family of God. A person who deals in the best possible way with any member of this family becomes nearer and dearer to God. As doctors you can render the best service to humanity and thus achieve a noble position in becoming the worthiest servants of God.

"In society, doctors generally command great respect and authority. There are different kinds of professions but no professional enjoys as much love and respect of the people he serves as much as a doctor. The doctor-patient relationship is unique in that the patient considers the doctor as a healer and a kind person—someone with whom he can share his suffering, who can relieve him of his misery and in whom he or she can confide.

"The great tragedy of present day Muslim is that we have receded farthest from the field of knowledge and, in fact, have even begun to dislike pursuit of it. Faith has left our hearts and knowledge our minds. The new generation of Muslims is under the misconception that all new branches of knowledge originated and flourished in Europe. As students of medicine you know that medicine had its foundation from Greek medicine. It was the Muslims who preserved this knowledge and saved it from perishing. It was this heritage that was transferred from one Muslim generation to the next at a time when Europe was languishing in darkness. Not only did Muslims preserve this knowledge, but they also improyed upon it, made research in many branches of knowledge, proposed new theories and developed them to the best of their abilities. All Europe did was to take this improved base of scientific knowledge and to develop it further. Therefore, knowledge and research in fact are the heritage of Muslims, not of Europe. To shy away from the acquisition of knowledge and to dislike it does not befit a Muslim.

"I dearly wish that every Muslim student of medicine, engineering or any branch of science should not only study his field as a professional but should also be actively involved in research and thereby serve mankind in alleviating its misery. When new principles derived therefrom, then this will also serve to produce a profound beneficial effect on the general condition of the Muslims. I hope all of you pay serious attention to this matter and try to regain the lost position of being leaders in the field of research and knowledge.

"Lastly, I hope by our character, moral recitude and deep knowledge, you will remain true and ideal Muslims—that you will use your noble profession to serve mankind, and be an effective means for the progress and propagation of Islam. You will surely be rewarded by God.

Family planning, i.e., limiting the number of children to specific number and population control, i.e., the regulation of growth of population in such a way that it exceeds not a certain limit. The concept of birth control is based on the Malthusian theory which states that while the harvest reaped from the available land is limited, the rate of growth of human population is not; consequently, it will continue to increase and will eventually reach an explosive proportion whereby the available land will not be able to support the vastly expanded population. Malthus stated that to control the growth of population, the husband and wife should exercise self-restraint for curbing population growth. Owing to mass propaganda, the phobia of 'population explosion' reached such proportions that any and all methods, including abortion to control population growth were advocated and accepted. However, at present, the situation is such that abortion even of well formed fetuses is considered justified and has been legalized in many countries. This is despite the fact that Malthusian and Neo-Malthusian theories over the past two centuries have been disproved, and the myth of 'population explosion' laid bare.

The Islamic Viewpoint

In order to understand whether Islam permits or prohibits birth control, certain basic and essential concepts need to be clearly understood. . These are based on the Holy Qur'an and the Sunnah of the Prophet. Their validity cannot be questioned by our limited knowledge of Islam, preconceived notions, selfish motives and apologetic attitudes.

Consider the answers to the following questions: As Muslims, what is our belief ? What is our concept of God ? What is our position in the universe ? What is the basic economic principle in Islam ?

As Muslims, it is our belief that God the Almighty is Lord of the Universe. The quality of Lordship belongs to God. He is the Creator, Nourisher, Sustainer, Protector and Master of all that is in the Universe.

We believe that God has created us and the universe and made all the necessary and complete arrangements for our sustenance before our creation. It is God who has taken upon Himself the responsibility to sustain all the creatures on earth. God states in the Qur'an, "*There is no creature on earth but whose sustenance is on God.*" (9.6)

God the Most High has also undertaken to maintain a balance in the production of crops and the supply of all our essential needs in proportion to our requirements. Nothing has been created in an unbalanced disproportionate manner. The source of all potential forces and energies being with God, it is inexhaustible and unlimited. God states in the Qur'an, "*And there is not a thing but its treasures are with Us, but We only send down thereof in due and ascertainable measure.*" (15 : 21) "*All things have We created in proportion and measure.*" (54 : 9)

At another place, it is stated that if man were given all things beforehand, then man would destroy it or be extravagant in its use. Thus everything has been created in a balanced way. Such a situation will never arise on a universal scale, when there will be people but no food to eat. Shortage of food in the world is not real but apparent and based on artificial premises. Scarcity of food is a man-made situation created by manipulation of the laws of supply and demand by business interests for the sake of excess profiteering. In order to increase the price of grain, shiploads thereof are sunk.

It is an accepted and recognized fact that the potential of a piece of ground to bear fruit, crops and vegetation is not limited by God to a specific amount. Modern methods of irrigation and cultivation have been responsible for a tremendous increase in the output of the same piece of ground which used to bear a limited percentage of crop or was altogether barren, desert land.

To think that God has forsaken the world and that population explosion would occur so that man would starve to death is the view of a person who does not believe in God. God is an Ingenious Power, the best of Planners and can accomplish anything. As Muslim, we firmly believe in this concept and therefore cannot accept the economic reason for family planning.

That the increase in population should be curbed for economic reasons is not a new proposition. This concept was not exclusive to the Malthusian theory. The same concept was prevalent during the pre-Islamic period.

The Qur'an should be read and understood in the proper perspective. In Sura Bani Israel from verses 23-31, the Qur'an teaches us the following: To worship not but God; to be kind and fulfil one's duties to one's parents; to help the poor, weak and needy; not to be extravagant nor practise niggardliness; God provides sustenance for whom He pleases; not to kill children for fear of want.

God has ordered man to maintain a balance between his income and expenditure. The word 'iqtisad' used in Arabic conveys the meaning that the Islamic law of economics is based upon following a middle and balanced course in expenditure. Islam demands that one should neither be miserly (to the extent of not even spending on essential requirements), nor should one be a spendthrift indulging in extravagance. Not to spend on necessary requirements is niggardliness and to spend lavishly is extravagance. Both are extreme courses. Therefore a balanced way in expenditure should be adopted.

God knows best the true needs of every person and cares for them. To some He gives in abundance and others receive less, but in all cases He gives in just measure. "Verily your Lord does provide sustenance in abundance for whom He pleases, and He provides in a just measure, for He does know and regard all His servants." (17 : 30) In the next verse, God wants: "Kill not your children for fear of want; We shall provide for them as well as for you; verily the killing of them is a great sin." (17 : 31)

The purpose of the sequential teaching is to show that this is not simply a question of killing. If it were so then there would be no need for such a verse since murder whether of child or of an adult remains a crime which has been prohibited by the Qur'an. Therefore there was no need to mention it in the above verse (if the intention was only limited to prescribing a crime). But by mentioning in the above verse, God analyses the mentality of the person who kills his children and the reason for his doing so. (The Arabs, according to the present researcher, did not kill their male children. They killed only their daughters, and that too not for the fear of poverty rather because they did not like to become one's father-in-law and regarded it against their dignity).

Some of the Arab tribes practised female infanticide. Even now, infanticide is practised in many countries for economic reasons. The key words are 'for the fear of poverty' and thereby try to curb the population is an abhorrent idea which the Qur'an cannot tolerate and does not propagate.

The protagonists of birth control have exploited the similar mentality of present day man to the maximum. They declared that if no attempts were made to curb the rate of population growth, then there would soon be insufficient food for people to eat. Millions who accepted the assertion without questioning its validity were misled and eventually started practising birth control without paying any attention to what the consequences might be.

Such thinking is totally repugnant to the spirit of Islam. It is diametrically opposed to the teachinge of the Qur'an. The Qur'an makes it clear, in no uncertain terms, that it is God and God alone who provides mankind with sustenance. A person can only give to another person what he himself has received from God.

God created both man and woman and assigned different roles, responsibilities and functions to them. Procreation and reproduction of mankind is a basic object of marriage in Islam, and therefore any action which has an effect of curbing or stopping altogether this process cannot be acceptable from the Islamic point of view.

In man's quest for bodily comforts and luxuries many expenses have to be borne to maintain a high standard of living and in this process life becomes intolerable. In his selfishness and greed, he wants numerous items on his dining table at any meal time. He is not content with one food item only. There is no need for one to have so many courses at a particular meal with the resultant left-overs being thrown away. At lunch and dinner parties, thousands of rands are squandered and instead of making provision for the future generation, one would rather see them killed (through birth control). Such thinking is unacceptable in Islam. The desire to have a small family is not validated by the notion that one has to undergo many difficulties. This is the result of non-Islamic thinking. There is no justification to encourage this kind of thinking.

Islam has taken into consideration the real needs of man at all times and the changing circumstances and problems. It has a solution to all problems but it cannot change its laid down rules to suit the condition of a society which is materialistically inclined and devotes itself to the attainment of evil desires.

Birth control should be viewed in the light of the above facts. Nevertheless, Islam being a perfect code of life, permits certain methods of contraception for particular cases and for specific reasons. This is explained in the next section.

Questions and Answers

Contraception

Q. Is the practice of contraception allowed in Islam ?

A. Islam allows the practice of contraception only under certain circumstances. These are discussed in the questions that follow.

Q. What methods of contraception are allowed ?

A. Basically there are two forms of contraception: the reversible methods and the irreversible methods. The reversible methods include physical—coitus interruptus, rhythm method; mechanical includes intra-uterine devices and condom or diaphragm; chemical methods include oral contraceptive pill and locally acting spermicidal jellies.

The irreversible methods include the sterilization operations of vasectomy in the man and tubal ligation in the woman.

As far as the reversible methods are concerned, Islam allows the physical methods, viz., coitus interruptus and the rhythm method. The husband must however seek the consent of his wife when practising coitus interruptus. During the period in which the Qur'an was revealed, coitus interruptus was practised by the Arabs but it was not prohibited by any verse. However, it seems that the Prophet did not approve of it entirely. Once a Sahabi told the Prophet that he practised coitus interruptus. The Prophet thrice commented: 'Oh so you practise that ?" in such a manner that it was evident that he did not approve of it entirely. Moreover, that which is destined to happen will take place. In this case it so happened that the Sahabi concerned did have a child despite his practising coitus interruptus.

The mechanical and chemical methods are permissible only under special circumstances (to be mentioned later) provided that they do not transgress any fundamental Islamic laws, i.e., they should not be harmful to the user. Therefore it would seem that the use of condoms and spermicidal jellies is permissible. As far as the intra-uterine device and the oral contraceptive pill are concerned, the physician must ensure that there is a proper indication for their use and that they would be safe for the user. Only then would their use be permissible.

The ruling of the Shari'ah on sterilisation operations is as follows:

Vasectomy in the man: This is totally prohibited in Islam.

It cannot be sanctioned by the Shari'ah under any circumstances. Islamic law also prohibits castration. A common factor between vasectomy and castration is that both destroy the power of reproduction in man although the ability to cohabit is still present. It is a cause of the murder of the future generation.

Tubal ligation in the woman: This cannot be declared permissible as a general rule because it renders a woman incapable of conceiving. There is a possibility that the factor on account of which she is being counselled for tubal ligation might change thereafter. However, there would then be little hope of her becoming pregnant again.

However, if an honest and experienced doctor fears that the life of permanent mental health of a woman would be seriously affected by a pregnancy and there is no other cure for her sickness, in such a case only would tubal ligation be permissible.

Conclusion: It must be made clear that while certain methods of contraception are permissible in Islam, they can only be used under the circumstances sanctioned by the Shari'ah. These specific circumstances are dealt with in the following lines.

Q. Does Islam allow family planning for social reasons, i.e., it is fashionable to have small families. Having a large family may curtail the social activities of the wife. Having many children may spoil her figure ?

A. Islam does not sanction family planning to meet the demands of present day fashion or social reasons. Although Islam encourages a woman to look well and to beautify herself for the sake of her husband, it does not sanction the same for the sake of public approbation which is the present trend. The Holy Qur'an says, "And tell the believing women to lower their gaze and guard their modesty. That they should not display their beauty and ornaments except what (must ordinarily) appear thereof. That they should draw their veils over their bosoms and not display their beauty except to their husbands." (24 : 31)

Q. Is family planning for professional reasons permitted in Islam, so that the wife can pursue a career ?

A. Islam places no burden on the shoulders of a woman or any responsibility for her to earn a living. Her maintenance before marriage is the responsibility of her father, after marriage of her husband, and in old age of her children. Islam does not want that a woman work like a labourer in the markets or be exploited economically. The general rule, therefore, is that it is not permissible to control the birth of children on account of professional reasons.

Nevertheless it cannot be denied that there are cases where a woman is forced to seek employment to maintain her children or family on account of desperate circumstances. Under such circumstances it would be permissible for the couple to adopt reversible methods of birth control.

This relaxation, however, does not apply to those women who merely try to maintain a very high standard of living or who try to earn and accumulate as much wealth as possible in order to keep in step with the current fashionable trends. This would defeat the object of the creation of woman and destroy the family unit which is the foundation of any society.

Q. Is family planning for spacing children permissible in Islam ?

A. The concept of spacing children means the practice of contraception in order to allow a reasonable time period between the birth of any two children; the purpose being that each child receives adequate attention of the mother in its upbringing. In the difficult task of nourishing, training and educating a child, the full attention of a mother is required. If a baby is born every year, then it is extremely difficult to provide the necessary care and attention for each child. From the discussion in Raddul Mohtar and other books of Islamic jurisprudence (on the question of abortion), it can be deduced that if another pregnancy it would seriously affect the care and upbringing of the existing child, then reversible methods of birth control may be practised.

Thus family planning towards the spacing of children so that each child receives adequate attention would be permissible in Islam. However, it must be emphasized that even this concession should be treated with respect. It must be made clear that spacing of children should not be used as a pretext for continuing family planning for an indefinite period for this will be contrary to the injunction of our Holy Prophet who said, "*Marry and procreate.*"

Family Planning for Medical Reasons

Q. Is family planning allowed if having children endangers a mother's physical health, mental health or even her life ?

A. If an experienced doctor, in all honesty and sincerity is of the opinion that having children would endanger a mother's physical health, i.e., if she is suffering from cardiac disease, renal disease or her life would be threatened, then it is permissible for the couple concerned to practise reversible methods of contraception. The same ruling applies if a mother is physically crippled and therefore unable to care for a child or if she is suffering from a psychiatric illness. It must be stressed that the decision to practise family planning under such circumstances does not rest upon the couple concerned. The decision must be taken by a physician and must be based on medical grounds.

Q. There is a risk of a baby being born with a genetic, i.e., mongolism, haemophilia. Is birth control allowed under such a situation ?

A. If it is the option of a responsible and an experienced physician that there is a high risk—not just a vague suspicion—of a baby being born with a serious genetic disease then it is permissible to adopt reversible methods of birth control.

From this it is apparent that there is a role for the Muslim doctor in genetic counselling. The risk of a baby inheriting a serious genetic disease should be carefully determined and any advice given should not be based on mere suspicion. Reversible methods of contraception should be advocated in those cases where the risk of a baby being born with a serious genetic disease is high.

Q. **What role must a Muslim doctor play with regard to contraception and sterilization for his non-Muslim patients—whether married or unmarried ? Should a different standard be adopted for them ?**

A. The attitude of a Muslim doctor at all times must be in consonance with the teachings of Islam for all his patients. Therefore, a different standard with regard to contraception and sterilization for non-Muslim patients cannot be adopted.

Abortion

Q. **Is abortion allowed in Islam ?**

A. In Islam, abortion is primarily a prohibited sphere. The general rule is that abortion is forbidden. Under certain circumstances, however, an abortion may be permissible. According to Shariah, the sin of abortion, once the limbs have formed, is the same as murder. An abortion prior to the limbs being formed would not carry the sin of murder but still is a major sin.

Q. **What is the period of gestation before an abortion can be allowed ?**

A. In a hadith related by Bukhari and Muslim, our beloved Prophet said, "Verily the creation of each one of you is brought together in his mother's womb for forty days in the form of a seed, then it is a clot of blood for a like period, then there is sent to it the angel who blows the breath of life into him.

The Qur'an described the various stages of man's primordial development but it does not specify the exact duration of each stage. In Sura Mu'minun, the Qur'an states, "Man We did create from a quintessence (of clay) ; then We placed him as (a drop of) sperm in a place of rest, firmly fixed. Then We made the sperm into a clot of congealed blood. Then of that blood We made a (fetus) lump. Then We made out of that lump, bones and clothed the bones with flesh. Then We developed out of it another creature so blessed be God, the best of creators." (23 : 12-14)

Based on this, Muslim jurists have deduced that the first four months of gestation is the critical time period. After this the fetus is regarded as being alive and an abortion is not permissible for any reason whatsoever and if performed would constitute murder. Thus an abortion may be performed when a very valid and legitimate reason exists and certain stringent criteria are fulfilled only prior to the first 4 months of gestation period.

However, if the pregnancy constitutes a serious threat to the life of the mother, then an abortion is permissible irrespective of the period of gestation.

Control of Menstruation

Q. Does Islam allow the control of menstruation with the aid of drugs to suit certain occasions, i.e., honeymoon, hajj, etc. ?

A. God says in the Qur'an, "They ask you concerning women's courses. Say, they are hurt and a pollution so keep away from women in their courses and do not approach them until they are clean. But when they have purified themselves, you may approach them in a manner, time and place ordained for you by God for God loves those who keep themselves pure and clean." (2 : 222)

From this verse it is apparent that menstruation is an impurity harmful to the body and should therefore be released and is undesirable to retain within the body. Therefore undue prolongation of the inter-menstrual period is undesirable. According to the Shariah, there is no valid reason to take drugs to control menstruation for occasions such as honeymoon and hajj. Nevertheless, there is nothing in Islamic law to declare it as prohibited, provided that the woman does not suffer any serious side effects of such drugs or any harmful effects on account of retaining the menstrual flow.

To sum up:

(1) Islam does not permit permanent stoppage of birth at any stage.

(2) It allows stoppage of birth only on the ground of danger to life of the mother or chronic disease.

(3) Islam allows spacing for better child care and mother's health.

(4) Birth control for the fear of poverty or in lust for merry making is strictly forbidden.

A 'Fatwah' is a religious decree, compulsory for the entire Muslim world. This being the position no faithful Muslim can deny the decree. The responses given by the Muslim women may be seen in this perspective. At the same time, it is not necessary that each and every Muslim man or woman is fully aware of the real position of jurisprudence in a given situation. Many of the respondents may not be aware of the permission given by Islam for spacing with a view to proper upbringing and health of both children and the mother. The women infested with chronic diseases can adopt permanent measures of birth control too if the medical expert advises them to do so. They may not be, in general, aware of these permissibilities and out of ignorance majority of them might have made up their minds that family planning measures (all) are against Islam. It is not so. Islam is not an orthodox philosophy, and at the same time it does not permit lavishness and debauchery.

The second important reason of not practising birth control by the women respondents (17.8%) is 'any other' reason. It may be their shyness. They may not like to go to hospitals for operations by male doctors, and this reason may not clearly be mentioned by them to all. It may also be because of their poverty. 10.7% of the respondents have mentioned that they do not practise family planning for the fear of it being harmful for health. Due to negligence or ill-expertise of the medical practitioners in many cases complications have been reported, and even some deaths have occurred. It is because of this fear that sizeable section of the Muslim women is not ready to adopt birth control measures. There does not appear any consistency in response patterns on literacy basis. Hence it may be interpreted that literacy level is not relevant in this case.

Table 10

Income and Reason of Not Practising Birth Control

(Percentage in brackets)

Income level	*Against the Will of God*	*Children are source of additional income*	*Harmful to health*	*Any other*	*Total*
Up to Rs. 500	8(61.5)	3(23.0)	1(7.6)	1(7.6)	13
501-1000	14(58.3)	5(20.8)	2(8.3)	3(12.5)	24
1001-1500	18(52.9)	4(11.7)	5(14.7)	7(20.5)	34
1501-2000	4(40.0)	2(20.0)	1(10.0)	3(30.0)	10
Rs. 2001+	2(66.6)	—	—	1(33.3)	3
Total	46(54.7)	14(16.6)	9(10.7)	15(17.8)	84

The table shows that the highest percentage (54.7%) of respondents desist from practising birth control measures because they think that it is a form of genocide or homicide, which is abhorred by God. The second highest percentage (17.8%) has given unspecified reason, the third majority of 16.6% have said that they do not practise birth control measures because children are the source of additional income or future hope of the family. The lowest percentage of 10.7 have mentioned that birth control measures are injurious to the health of the mother, and hence they do not like it. On income basis we do not find any significant consistency in the response patterns. Hence income does not appear to be relevant in this case.

Table 11

Age and Reason of Not Practising Birth Control

(Percentage in brackets)

Age Group	*Against the Will of God*	*Children are source of additional income*	*Harmful to health*	*Any other*	*Total*
Up to 25 yrs.	4(40.0)	1(10.0)	2(20.0)	3(30.0)	10
26-35 yrs.	8(44.4)	2(11.1)	2(11.1)	6(33.3)	18
36-45 yrs.	18(58.0)	6(19.3)	1(11.1)	6(19.3)	31
46 +	16(64.0)	5(35.7)	4(16.0)	—	25
Total	46(54.7)	14(16.6)	9(10.7)	15(17.8)	84

This table shows a consistent rise in the percentages of response in favour of the first two reasons with the rise in age. 40.0% of respondents up to 25 years, 44.4% of 26-35 years, 58.0% of 36-45 years and 64.0% of 46 years and above have given fear of God to be the reason of not practising birth control measures; whereas 10.0% of the age-group up to 25 years, 11.1% of 26-35 years, 11.1% of 36-45 years and 16.0% of 46 years and above have said that children are the additional source of income for the family and hence they do not want to check their birth. So far the other two reasons are concerned, we find no consistency in response pattern on age basis. Hence in case of these two reasons age does not appear to be relevant. This response pattern shows that religiosity as well as wordly ambitions have grown with the rise in age. It means that the younger generation is more conscious of the bad effects of having large families and the elder generation is less conscious of it. This is because of participation of the younger generation in higher percentage in modern social activities as well as their education on modern lines. The younger generation feels the hard facts of life more than the elder generation and the impact of modern forces of rationality is higher on the younger generation than on the elder generation.

Table 12

Spacing of Children

Method	*Number*	*Percentage*
Natural	16	7.4
Artificial	62	28.7
Both	138	63.8
Total	216	100

This table indicates that the respondents in favour of practising birth control, or those actually practising birth control, also practise spacing between births. Spacing or putting a larger gap between two births is also a sort of birth control device which limits the number of births in a family. Generally in case of females the age of procreation extends up to 45 years, and if the average age at marriage is taken to be 20 in Muslim women, the span of procreation available for each Muslim woman is 25 years. It has been seen that the families which do not practise birth control measures give birth to 8 or 9 children and those conscious of the bad effect of large number of children in a family have limited the size of children to 4 or 5 through spacing devices. Hence spacing between births is also a sort of birth control or limiting the size of family. It is apparent from the table that the highest majority of 63.8% of the Muslim women under study practise both natural and artificial methods of spacing, whereas 28.7% of them practise only artificial method and 7.4% only natural method. Natural method is no sure short method, whereas artificial methods are sure and easy to practise. One must be ever cautious and restrainuant for practising natural method, otherwise it may fail; but the artificial methods do not require caution and these are near guaranteed in effect. Hence an overwhelming majority of 92.6% practises artificial method of spacing or artificial and natural both. Only an insignificant percentage of 7.4 practises natural method, and they may be from the highly educated class who are supposed to be more disciplined and highly informed. Generally this method (natural method) is not possible for less qualified people as they are not expected to know the period of menstruation, period of conception and period of gestation, etc. They are also not expected to be so restrainuant or disciplined in sexual behaviour as their counterparts in highly qualified families. Less educated and poor families have lesser patience and inadequate knowledge, and hence it is very difficult for them to practise natural method of spacing and to avoid the period of conception by delineating the pre and post conception periods. Practice of spacing methods by overwhelming majority of the respondents denoted their eagerness for a limited size of family. They do not only want to practise spacing rather an overwhelming majority of them wants to be sure about it and hence it practises the surer method, or both the methods. This shows a fair attitude of the majority of respondents towards spacing between births and thus birth control.

Table 13

Ideal Number of Children

Ideal No. of Children	*Response*	*Percentage*
2	22	7.3
3	128	42.6
4	111	37 0
Undecided	39	13.0
Total	300	100

This table shows that it includes both birth control practising and non-practising multitude of the sample. Those 84 respondents who are against family planning, have also been included among the respondents to this question, because it is expected that they also being in the present-day society and feeling the brunts of large-size family must have a particular size of family in mind though not practically ready to maintain that size for one reason or the other. The highest percentage (42.6%) of respondents, according to the tables have favoured three children in a family to be the ideal number of children, the second highest percentage (37.0%) have favoured 4 children, 13.0% of them have no idea or have not thought about it and 7.3% of the respondents favour 2 children in a family to be the ideal number of children. According to the previous declaration by Government three children were announced to be proper and adequate for a couple, but as per present programme only 2 children are approved for a couple. Thus it can be interpreted that majority of the Muslim women is in favour of the early family programme of the State and the lowest percentage of 7.3 is in favour of the present programme; whereas 50% of the respondents are either in favour of 4 children or are undecided about it. Thus it can be interpreted that 50% of the Muslim women or this urban setting is in favour of the State policy about family welfare and 50% are either unconcerned or against the State policy. Thus 50% of the Muslim women's population may be regarded as rational, and the rest as irrational.

The data analysed in this chapter show that 82.6% of the Muslim women are in favour of family planning or family welfare programme of the State and only 17.4% of them are against it. This figure of acceptance is quite encouraging and at par with other sections of the society. And, hence, it is not true to say that Muslim community is against family planning. It is also evident from the data that education and age are fairly significant in rationalising the attitude of Muslim women for acceptance of the State policy in regard to family welfare. Lowly educated and elder generation is comparatively less favourable to this programme than the educated respondents and younger generation. Income level does not, however, appear to be relevant in this case. Religiosity is the main hurdle in the way of respondents not practising family planning or spacing methods, next reason being of economic benefit in having more children. The rest two reasons—i.e., health and 'any other' are of less importance. The highest majority of 42.6% is in favour of the earlier programme of the State and the lowest (7.4%) in favour of the existing ideal number of children. Thus 50% of the population of the Muslim women of Patna are in favour of State's programme and 50% are either ignorant or against the same, so far the ideal size of family is concerned. The lowest response in favour of 'health reason' for not practising family planning measures denotes that this apprehension is little or very rare among them because injury cases are not more, rather seldom or rare. On the whole, family welfare programme is quite popular among Muslim society of this urban population and disfavour is only by 17.4%. Thus it may be interpreted that urban women are no less conscious of the necessity of smaller size of family than any other section of the society.

8

Future Prospects

The report of the Committee on the Status of Women in India noted the 'paucity of data' on important socio-economic aspects related to women. This lack of full and accurate statistics on women is found not only in India but also in Pakistan, Bangladesh and Afghanistan. The dearth of research oriented literature, especially on Muslims in India, by both sociologists and social anthropologists has created great confusion about Muslims. Since Islam has been a neglected field in sociology and hardly any deep and detailed sociological study of Islam and Islamic society is available, the present researcher has tried her best to go into the socio-cultural life of the Muslim women living in the city of Patna. Patna, as the centre of administration, has a long history. People of different origins and of different socio-cultural links have come here as invaders and settled in this city as conquerers and made this city the centre of administration. Thus the city of Patna constitutes an admixture of different races, tribes and cultures. Very few cities in India possess this quality. Being the seat of administration for thousands of years, Patna developed in all aspects of life. Here one can find people of different shades, different races, different cultures and of different linguistic attachments. Thus it provided a good field for a sociological researcher.

The above-said special feature of Patna attracted the present researcher to plan and make a unique study on the socio-cultural and economic life of the Muslim women—unique in the sense that the different aspects of the life of Muslim women have been analysed in the light of Islamic ideologies and Qur'anic concepts of life, which has seldom been touched by sociological researchers. Muslim women being half of the Muslim community and a part and parcel of the Great Indian Culture, they cannot remain unaffected of the fast changes and all-round development experienced under the impact of urbanism, secularism, democracy and industrialism. Hence the main objective of the present research was to understand how far the Muslim women have acquired the modern norms and values, how far they are attached to their past traditional patterns of life and where do they stand vis-a-vis Islam and Modernism; what is the gap between their ideology and practice; how do they feel about modern concepts and currents and their mode and extent of adaptation under the modern current and cross-currents. This psycho-social approach may be useful in understanding the actual life of the Muslim women in an urban setting and the gap between the theory and practice, the degree and extent of the impact of urbanization, secularization, modernization, and Islamization on the life of Muslim women. All these facts were analysed on five different variables of age, education, income level, occupation and caste.

The entire study has been spread over four aspects of marriage and family life, educational status, institution of purdah and the problem of family planning as the main issues of research. The responses collected in respect of these items were analysed on the basis of different variables in order to find out the current patterns of beliefs and behaviours prevalent among the Muslim women of Patna, and finally the hypotheses were tested in the light of findings of the research.

Analysis of data revealed that in every major institutional sphere there have been changes from traditionalism to modernity or from conservatism to rationality. Moreover deviations from Islamic Shariah were also found, but not to the extent that one could brand the Muslim women's actions and beliefs to be un-Islamic or anti-Islamic. It is also to note that these deviations did not occur in the 20th century itself, rather it has been a continuous and long process since the death of the Prophet of Islam. An impartial evaluation of the attitudes, beliefs and practices of the respondents would show that mainly due to the ignorance of religious doctrines and certain constraints and external pressures, deviations have occurred. It does not mean that the Muslim women have abandoned their original faith or have a liking for modern concepts and practices in exchange for their belief in Islam. Lack of proper education and paucity of proper sources of information have greatly been instrumental in their adherence to conservative norms and values, attitude and opinion and shirk in participation to outdoor activities of life. Islam ordains to social service, national service and participation in all spheres of worldly life within the permissible limit and in the manners laid down in Qur'an and Sunnah. Their misconception about the very concepts of Islam leaves them far behind the main theme of Islam with regard to the practical life, and seeing their shortcomings many of the non-Muslims think that there must be some fault or shortcomings in the religion itself.

The efforts made in this work should only be deemed to be a just beginning on the topic and an humble attempt to lighten my fellow workers of the burden of misgivings and misconceptions about Islam and the Muslim. There are many a fields which require thorough study and deep insight, to which the kind attention of our fellow researchers is cordially invited. With this request, the present researcher would like to present her findings of the study as under.

Marriage and Family

The data obtained from the field and analysed in Chapter IV of this work reveal that 19.0 per cent of the married respondents were engaged in wedlock at ages below 15 and majority of 55.0 per cent of them were married between 16-20 years of age, whereas the majority of their spouses (male) were married between 21-25 years (64.0%) or at the age of 26 or above (25.3%), which is rational excepting those 19.0 per cent who were married below 15 years. The tables also show that the marriage age of both men and women has risen inasmuch as 67.6 per cent of their boys were married after 26 and no girl was married below 15 years of age. Majority of the girls of respondents have been reported to be married between 16-20 years, which is quite rational in view of the current yardstick fixing marriage age of boys between 21-25 and of girls between 16-20 years. Thus the tables show no gap between the practice and the ideal age suggested for marriage of boys and girls, by government. The shift in the age of marriage has been attributed to the poor economy, engagement in educational pursuit (both of boys and girls) and non-availability of service or suitable match. According to the respondents' education, employment of the boy and his economic status are the three essential qualities which one should see in the proposed groom for one's daughter. The traditional norms of lineage, physical soundness, character and outlook (or creed) of the boy have fetched meagre support Hence it can be said that the attitude and normative behaviour of the Muslim society has begun to experience drastic shifts from traditionalism to rationality. In selected fields, like the choice for life-partner, the Muslim women seem to be ready to allow their girls to select their spouse either directly, or indirectly, according to the demand of the situation which signifies a drastic change from traditional conservatism to modernism. In the past, virgins were not allowed even to raise their voice or to talk to a stranger or express their opinion in the matter of settlement of their marriage, whereas Islam allows the boy to see, to talk and to put searching questions to know the subjective qualities of the girl proposed to be given to his wedlock. In the light of this fact, the attitude of the present generation can't be said to be 'a deviation' or an anti-Islamic or un-Islamic approach. This stand of Islam also finds corroboration from modernity, thus there being no clash between Islam and Modernism. There are many such fields where such homogeneity has been underlined by the modern Islamic researchers between Islamic stand and the stand of the Modernism. Another marked change in the attitude of Muslim patriarchs has been reflected from the response in respect of consulation in matters of family and outward affairs. The patriarchs, in majority of the cases, are reported to be consulting their female members of family either occasionally (38.6%) or frequently (31.3%) or invariably (18.3%); whereas in the traditional Muslim society women were rarely consulted in important family affairs as they were supposed to be 'naqis-ul-aql' (of weak wisdom). In the past *mahr* (dower) was just a symbolic term and heavy dowers were fixed merely to show status and personality, but, now, the Muslim women are realising (39.3%) that *mahr* is an important right of Muslim women and an effective security against hazards of life or divorce. Dowry system has been rejected by 89.0% of the women respondents and a majority of 58.0% of them has suggested legal recourse to check this evil. At the same time the responses reveal that 11 per cent of the respondents favour dowry system. Through informal chat it was disclosed that these supporters of dowry system include both rich and poor families. It was also reported that this system has become so rampant in even the Muslim society that if a poor does not afford to meet the demands of the groom party his daughter cannot be married for long. Many women respondents also complained that the rich people have started a sort of competition in offering dowries to catch the desired match for their daughters and it has made a hell for the poor. Majority of the women respondents are in favour of widow re-marriage, especially of childless young widows and the widows having children. Re-marriage of middle-aged widows has been favoured by a very nominal percentage of 10.3, whereas 8.0 per cent of the respondents are deadly against re-marriage of any widow. Consciousness with regard to maintenance being the right of women has aroused and a sizeable section (17.0%) of the respondents are even ready to adopt legal recourse to realise it if not paid amicably, and 35.6 per cent of them have showed the courage to take up some earning job in order to mitigate their miseries in case their husbands desert them and refuse to pay maintenance to them. This is a marked shift in the attitude of Muslim women because, in the traditional Muslim society, no woman could think to take up her grievance to a court of law or to take a job outside her home. Chronic diseases, permanent disablement, refusal to sex union and quarrelsome nature of the wife have been said to be some of the important reasons compelling a husband to decide polygyny. The table also reflects that the Indian males, in general, do not like to have another wife and are submissive and tolerant in nature unlike their Western or Arabian counterparts. It is in very exceptional and distressing circumstances when a male decides to adopt polygyny, e.g., having another wife. Thus, in totality of the case, we have found the urban Muslim women coming out fast from traditionalism and stepping towards rationality, if not towards modernism in all cases. Thus it can safely be interpreted that the urban Muslim society is passing through a transitional phase of tradition-modernity-continuum with a resolve to maintain the real Islamic tilt.

Education

The data on this aspect have been analysed under Chapter V. The tables show that illiteracy is found to the extent of 8 per cent among the youngest generation of up to 25 years, 7.7 per cent among the second youngest generation and 54.7 per cent among the respondents of the age of 46 and above. On the other end, among the youngest generation 13.3% are post-graduates, 29.3% are graduates/undergraduates and 32.0% matriculates whereas among the eldest generation (46+) the figure of post-graduates is nil, graduation 5.6% and matriculation 15.8%. This comparative analysis shows a remarkable improvement in the educational level and quantum of the younger generation. In all 66% of the younger generation is either matriculate or graduate or post-graduate, whereas only 20% and odd among the eldest generation is either matriculate or college-educated. These figures suggest an improvement in educational quantum to the extent of more than 30% over the eldest generation. The analysis of data on caste basis suggests illiteracy to the extent of 34.4% among Ansaris, 20.6% among Chique women, 15.5% among Rayeen women, 10.3% among Mallicks, 6.8% among

Pathans, 5.1% among Shaikh ladies and 1.7% among Saiyid ladies. This consistency of fall in the percentage of illiteracy with the rise in the stratificational status of castes shows a remarkable relevance of caste in this aspect of life. 26.1% of Shaikh women, 20.2% of Saiyids, 16.6% of Pathan and Mallick respondents, 14.2% of Ansaris, 2.3% each of Chiques and Kalals and 1.1% of Rayeens are matriculate; whereas 22.2% of Saiyids, 20% of Pathans, 13.3% of Ansaris, 12 6% of Shaikhs and 3.1% of Mallick respondents are graduate and 38.8% of Shaikhs, 27.7% of Saiyids, 16.6% of Pathans and 11.1% of Mallick respondents are Post-Graduate. These figures speak of dominance of higher castes in the field of education. A glimpse of the educational condition of the parental generation of the respondents can be had from Table 4 of this Chapter. According to the table 51.3% of mothers and 21.3% of fathers of the respondents were illiterate; whereas 6.3% of mothers and 37.0% of fathers of the respondents were matriculates. Only 2.0% of mothers and 12.6% of fathers of the respondants are graduate and 0.6% of mothers and 3.3% of fathers of respondents were post-graduates. It would, perhaps, not be out of interest to compare the various educational levels of respondents' mothers, respondents themselves and respondents' daughters.

Generation	*Illiterate*	*High School*	*Graduate*	*P.G.*
Resp.'s Mothers	51.3%	6.3%	2.0%	0.6%
Resp. themselves	19.3%	28.0%	15.0%	6.0%
Resp.'s daughters	8.0%	32.0%	29.3%	10.0%

The above figures indicate the encouraging rate of improvement in the educational level of the three generations.

24.3% of the respondents have received education with a view merely to acquire knowledge, 20.0% of them have received education with a view to improve their status in family and/or in society, 12.% of them have received education in order to get a good husband and 6.6% have received education with a view to get job or employment. These figures show that majority of the respondents have non-economic reasons for receiving education. Only 6.6% of them want jobs. It shows that the Muslim women, in overwhelming majority, have no professional idea behind their educational pursuit, and they want to maintain a distance between male and female even after receiving higher education.

The reasons of illiteracy of the respondents were also analysed. 27.5% each gave lack of encouragement, 24.1% parent's illiteracy and 10.3% each mentioned poverty and lack of facilities to be the reason of their remaining illiterate. It shows that the two major causes of illiteracy of the respondents are 'lack of encouragement' and 'parents' illiteracy'.

39.6% of the respondents are in favour of co-education and this favour has consistently risen with the rise in educational level of the respondents. It means that the formal education has lessened the distance between male and female, or boys and girls. But, at the same time, it is a hard fact that more than 60% of the Muslim women do not favour co-education, for which only individuals cannot be blamed. Our social order is not matured enough to provide full security to the feminine chaste and dignity, and hence many of the respondents' guardians do not allow their daughters to attend co-education classes.

On the whole, it may be concluded that the educational status of Muslim women is improving at a fast rate, if not satisfactorily. Unless illiteracy is completely eradicated from society and the education takes its meaningful shape, it cannot be said to be satisfactory. Education carries two aspects: (1) enlightening the mass, and (2) solving the economic problem of the society. The first aspect of the Muslim women's education appears to be satisfactory to a greater extent, but the second aspect depicts a gloomy picture and it demands proper attention of government.

Purdah

Before giving findings it will not, perhaps, be out of

place to mention that from the word 'purdah' we mean Islamic *hijab*, and not traditional 'burqa' and seclusion. Islam is liberal enough to allow women folk to work in the field, in offices, in the battle-fields, and in schools and colleges shoulder to shoulder with their brothers and fathers, but only with a care for not exposing or displaying their parts of beauty to anybody other than their own husbands and near relations. We must not under-estimate the genius and worth of this section of our society and should plan how beautifully the nation could utilise the worth of women in the development of the nation and society. One must not forget that it is woman who gives birth to man, it is woman who feeds and rears them, it is woman who is either mother or sister of men—and hence they should be treated accordingly. In this sense of purdah, overwhelming majority of the Muslim women observe it. 3.3% of the respondents do not observe purdah at all, and they are quite free as a non-Muslim women anywhere. 83.4% of the Muslim women have restricted outings and only 16.6% of them are free to move without escort. 28.1% of the respondents observe Sharai purdah of the type mentioned hereinabove, i.e., they keep face open and cover their hair and other parts of the body except hands and feet; 34.7% observe liberal purdah, i.e., they put on a chadar to cover their breast and hair only, and 37.1% observe the strict type of traditional purdah, i.e., they cover their face also.

Family Planning

The data collected from the field and analysed in Chapter VII of this thesis show that 82.6% of the Muslim women are in favour of family planning or family welfare programme of the State and only 17.4% of them are against it. This figure of acceptance is quite encouraging and at par with other sections of the society. And, hence, it is not true to say that Muslim community is against family planning. It is also evident from the data that education and age are fairly significant in rationalising the attitude of Muslim women for acceptance of the State policy in regard to family planning. Lowly educated and elder generation is comparatively less favourable and more tradition-oriented, whereas the younger generation and educated respondents more rational in approach and outlook. Income level does not appear to be relevant in this case. Religiosity is the main hurdle in the way of respondents not practising family planning or spacing methods. 42 6% of the respondents favour up to three children in a family and 7.3% of them favour only two children. Earlier the model number fixed for a family was three children, which has now been revised to two. In the light of this fact, it may be said that 50% of the Muslim women are in favour of the State policy with regard to the size of the family. On the whole the family welfare programme is quite popular among Muslim women of this urban setting and disfavour is only of the order of 17.4%. Thus it may be interpreted that urban women are no less conscious of the necessity of family planning and planned parenthood than their Hindu counterparts. They are well aware of the dangers of unplanned parenthood to the family as well as to the nation.

Economic Life

The economic life of Indian women in general and Muslim women in particular is tagged with their patriarchs. Till recently the women did not anticipate any role of the fairer sex beyond the family affairs. But under the influence of various currents of modernisation, urbanisation and industrialisation this class of Indian society has started thinking on the lines of family and national development, and for that working in fields to supplement the developmental needs of the present and the future generation. Women of the present age are feeling that a single earning head cannot meet the demands of fast moving society, and, hence, some of them have developed courage to come out and work shoulder to shoulder with their male counterparts. As would appear from the 'characteristics of the sample' given in the introductory chapter, 45 respondents (15.0%) are earning through outdoor services and are supplementing the income of their families. This number being too small, a systematic and elaborate study was not possible. Hence no separate chapter could be planned on this aspect of women's life. In this connection only much can be said that Indian Muslim women are not totally aloof from the economic field. There are women teachers at primary, secondary school levels, college levels and even university levels. Many of the Muslim women do cottage work like embroidery, sewing of ready-made clothes, bidi making and such other petty works. But it is a fact that Muslim women are far behind their Hindu and Christian counterparts in this field.

General

Muslims in India have their own place and problems. Being rulers for centuries over the country and having settled on this soil for generations past they cannot alienate themselves from the problems and the future of the nation and the Indian community, for the simple reason that their existence and future is tagged with the existence and progress of the nation as a whole. But in setting a professing democratic system one is bound to remain vigilant and alert to play his role both as an individual and as a responsible citizen of the country. This is a competitive age. One who will lag behind in the race of life, he will bear the brunt on himself and no other person is going to bother for him. Sooner they recognize the demand and call of the time, better he will live. Unfortunately, the division of the country brought many political, economic and social problems for Indian Muslims. Suspicions and stigma became their fate. These situations counted upon their future programme of life for decades which left them behind those who were fortunate to be born in the majority community. Their numerical supremacy made them the ruler of the country, whereas Muslims were left to defend the accusations made in public and the press media against them, for no fault of theirs. A section of the majority community is out to accuse and defame the Muslims of India. It was only after the fall of the then East Pakistan that propaganda has lessened its vehemence and the Indian Muslims have begun to concentrate to the problems of their life and future. Even those who were in lurking position decided once and for all to live as an Indian and to die as an Indian.

For the first time in the history of post-independence era the Muslims of India, as a community, showed their might and willingness to be a true Indian in 1979 J.P. Andolan and General Elections when the age-old rule of the Congress Party was completely befallen and Janata Party was erected on the throne. Since then the bogey of suspicion has further doomed down, and the Muslims are considered to be as good a citizen of the country as a Hindu. Coming to the practical field of life, Muslims were confronted with various currents and cross-currents of modernisation, secularisation, urbanisation, Indianisation and Islamisation. These new socion-political currents and cross-currents posed a new dimension of problems with the demand from this biggest minority to assimilate itself into the mainstream of the nation. The severity of this new demand posed a new problem before Muslims of India and they had to show their power of adaptation alongwith maintaining their own identity as an independent self-reliant culture. Having their own well-defined and sophisticated code of conduct, Muslims could not alienate themselves from it. But they had to make room for the national demands, if not to bow before unreasonable phobia of Hindukaran let loose in the name of Indianisation.

Social sciences being the theoretical part of human life, cannot be separated from political and economic aspects of human life. All currents, regardless of their nomenclature and nature, if they affect the living, thinking or behavioural pattern(s) of an individual or a society, form part of this science. Modernisation, urbanisation, secularisation, industrialisation, Indianisation and Islamisation are all factors influencing and bringing, or at least tending to bring, changes in the mode of living, pattern of thinking, and manner of reacting against them. It is this reactional or behavioural mode which makes the subject of social science, or sociology. Every aspect of human life follows exeeutive orders and reflects its own mode of reaction or adaptation. Every individual has its own belief and code of conduct, and he has to reconcile with the executive and social orders of the land where he resides. Every individual has thus to follow three types of laws and orders, e.g., (1) the religious orders, (2) the social orders, and (3) the executive orders. There is no problem so long as none of them tend to encroach upon the other. From the point any of these orders shows an encroaching tendency, a problem takes birth to invite the attention of social scientists. Take the instance of family planning regulations under the Emergency, which aroused such a vehement reaction against the rule of Indira Gandhi that the entire system had to go. Again came the problem of Shah Bano's case, under the pretext of which the Cong. (I) Government in the Centre tried to impose a burden, not sanctioned by Islam, on the Muslim men. It being a pretext of further encroachment upon the Islamic injunctions through legislation Muslim community of India as a whole stood against it and the government had to bow down before the pressure of huge masses. So is the case of other forces and currents of modernisation, urbanisation, etc. which make the subject-matter of research. It is this context which has prompted the present research on sociological lines.

Bibliography

Ahmad, Imtiaz, 'Family, Kinship and Marriage among Muslims in India', Manohar Book Service, New Delhi, 1976.

———, 'Caste and Social Stratification among the Muslims', Manohar Book Service, New Delhi, 1973.

———, 'Modernization and Social Change among Muslims in India', Manohar Publications, New Delhi, 1983.

Ahmad, Aqil, 'Mohammadan Law', Central Law Agency, Allahabad.

Ahmad, Saghir, 'Class and Power in a Punjabi Village', New York, Monthly Review Press, 1977.

Alankar, S. V., 'Patliputra ki Katha', Hindustan Academy, Allahabad, 1949.

Ali, S.A., 'The Spirit of Islam', S.K. Lahiri, Calcutta, 1902.

Ashraf, K.M., 'Life and Conditions of the People of Hindustan', Munshiram Manohar Lal, New Delhi, 1970.

Shad Azimabadi, 'Tarikh-e-Bihar' (Urdu), Subh-e-Sadique, Patna, 1893.

Brijbhushan, Jamila, 'Muslim Women in Purdah and Out of It', Vikas Publishing House, Pvt., Ltd., New Delhi, 1980.

Broom, Leonard and Seltznick Philip, 'Society', Paterson & Co., Evanston, Ill., 1955.

Buchanan, Francis H., 'An Introduction to the Districts of Bihar and Patna', Govt. Press, Bihar, Patna, Vol. I, 1812.

Das, S., 'The Status of Indian Women', Ess Ess Publications, New Delhi, 1979.

Dayal, P., 'Commercial Ribbons in Patna: Spatial Growth and Function Structure', National Geographical Journal of Ind., V. XXIII, Parts 3 and 4, 1976.

de Souza, Alfred (ed.), 'Women in Contemporary India and South Asia', Manohar Book Service, New Delhi, 1980.

Fairchild, Henry Pratt (ed.), 'Dictionary of Sociology', Adams & Co., Littlefield.

Ghosh, M., 'Patliputra', the Patna Law Press, 1919.

Hunter, W.W., 'A Statistical Account of Bengal', Vol. XI, Concept Publication Co., Delhi (Repr.), 1976.

Husain, S. Abid, 'The Destiny of Indian Muslims', Asia Pub. House, Bombay, 1965.

Imam, Zafar (ed.), 'Muslims in India', Orient Longman, New Delhi, 1975.

Karimi, S.M., 'Origin and Evolution of Towns in Ancient Bihar', Journal of the Bihar Research Society, Vol. LIX, 1-4.

Khan, Mazharul Haque, 'Pathology of the Muslim Society', Amar Prakashan, Delhi, 1978.

Kidwai, Sk. M.H., 'Women', Seema Publications, Delhi, 1976.

Kosambi, D.D , 'The Culture and Civilization of Ancient India in the Historical Outline', Vikas Publication, New Delhi, 1970.

Kumar, N., Bihar District Gazetteer, Patna, 1970.

Lari, S.M.R. Mujtaba, 'Western Civilization through Muslim Eyes', Biddles Ltd., Britain, 1977.

Levy, Renben, 'The Social Structure of Islam', Cambridge University Press, USA, 1962.

Madan T.N. (Ed.), 'Muslim Communities of South India', Vikas Publishing House Pvt. Ltd., New Delhi, 1976.

Mahjubah, A Monthly Magazine of the Islamic Republic of Iran, Tehran, 1983.

Menon, Indu, 'Status of Muslim Women in India', Uppal Publishing House, New Delhi, 1981.

Mishra, S.C., 'Muslim Communities in Gujrat', Asia Pub. House, Bombay, 1964.

Mujeeb, M., 'The Indian Muslims', George Allen & Unwin, London, 1967.

Nehru, Pt. J.L., 'A Glance at World Histoy', Vol. I.

Nooruddin, Saleema, 'Purdah No Bar to Progress', Muslim Review, 1933.

Ojha, Pt. G.S., 'History of Medieval Civilization', Journal of Aligarh Historical Research Institute, Aligarh, 1941.

Quasemi, Maulana Mujahidul Islam, 'An Interview', pub. in Mahjubah, a monthly magazine of the Islamic Republic of Iran, Tehran, June 1983.

Qutb, Mohammab, 'Islam, the Misunderstood Religion', the Board of Islamic Publications, Delhi, 1968.

Rashid, A., 'Society and Culture in Medieval India', Firma K.L. Mukhopadhayay, Calcutta, 1969.

Raza, S. Musi, 'Changing Patterns of Muslim Community in Bihar', an unpublished Ph. D. Thesis, Patna University, 1976.

Roy, Shibani, 'Status of Muslim Women in India', B.R. Publishing Corporation, Delhi, 1979.

Sarfarazuddin, 'Social Structure of a Muslim Village in Bihar', Unpublished Ph. D. Thesis, Patna University, 1983.

Shustery, A.M.A., 'Outlines of Islamic Culture', Bangalore Publishing Co., Bangalore, 1937.

Siddiqui, M.K.A., 'Muslims of Calcutta', Anthropological Survey of India, Calcutta, 1974.

Siddiqui, N.A., 'Population Geography of the Muslims of India', S. Chand, Delhi, 1976.

Towards Equality, 'Report of the Committee on the Status of Women in India', Department of Social Welfare, Govt. of India, New Delhi, 1974.

Index